POST-MODERNISM AND THE SOCIAL SCIENCES

POST-MODERNISM AND THE SOCIAL SCIENCES

INSIGHTS, INROADS, AND INTRUSIONS

Pauline Marie Rosenau

PRINCETON UNIVERSITY PRESS

PRINCETON, NEW JERSEY

LIBRARY OF CONGRESS CATALOGING-IN-PUBLICATION DATA

ROSENAU, PAULINE MARIE, 1943–

POST-MODERNISM AND THE SOCIAL SCIENCES : INSIGHTS, INROADS,

AND INTRUSIONS / PAULINE MARIE ROSENAU.

P.   CM.

INCLUDES BIBLIOGRAPHICAL REFERENCES AND INDEX.

ISBN 0-691-08619-2 — ISBN 0-691-02347-6 (PBK.)

1. POSTMODERNISM—SOCIAL ASPECTS. 2. SOCIAL SCIENCES—PHILOSOPHY.

3. SOCIAL MOVEMENTS. I. TITLE.

HM73.R59   1991   300'.1—DC20   91-19258   CIP

THIS BOOK HAS BEEN COMPOSED IN LINOTRON GALLIARD

PRINCETON UNIVERSITY PRESS BOOKS ARE PRINTED

ON ACID-FREE PAPER, AND MEET THE GUIDELINES FOR

PERMANENCE AND DURABILITY OF THE COMMITTEE ON

PRODUCTION GUIDELINES FOR BOOK LONGEVITY

OF THE COUNCIL ON LIBRARY RESOURCES

PRINTED IN THE UNITED STATES OF AMERICA

7   9   10   8   6

IN MEMORY OF

MY MOTHER AND FATHER,

BOTH FORCEFUL PARENTS, STRONG

MODERN SUBJECTS, WHO HAD NO CONFUSION

ABOUT THEIR IDENTITY OR THEIR VALUES

Marguerite Ione Rosenberg(er)
1911–1991

Earl William Hansen
1907–1982

CONTENTS

PREFACE

P AST EXPERIENCE tells me that detached efforts to evaluate post-modern modes of thought are quintessentially "no win" ventures. Those who subscribe to the basic tenets of post-modernism are likely to feel my assessment is unfair, or misguided, or an attempt to represent the unrepresentable. Those who reject the basic premises of post-modernism, however, are likely to be distressed that I have sought to be fair-minded about inquiries they regard as intellectually flawed, morally noxious, or otherwise objectionable. So I proceed with the full knowledge that what follows will never be considered adequate by all readers for every purpose.

At the same time my formulation of the key issues may be helpful for those whose confusion about post-modernism has been accompanied by a sense that it addresses important questions. Such is my purpose: the book will be successful if it communicates the essential themes (or alternative interpretations) of post-modernism and thus facilitates an understanding of what, on the face of it, appears confusing to many thoughtful people.

It is a measure of the nature of post-modernist thinking that it generates intense controversy. And little wonder! At stake are questions that pertain to the deepest dimensions of our being and humanity: how we know what we know, how we should think about individual endeavor and collective aspirations, whether progress is meaningful and how it should be sought. Post-modernism questions causality, determinism, egalitarianism, humanism, liberal democracy, necessity, objectivity, rationality, responsibility, and truth. It takes on issues that are profoundly fundamental for the future of social science.

Because of inherently controversial nature of these matters, I have tried to evaluate the various post-modernist perspectives not so much in terms of my own values as in terms of what the post-modernists themselves suggest they are about. But let me not dissimulate. It is my book. My values do underlie it through and through. Most notably, I believe that the social sciences have much to offer in the endless struggle to enhance the human condition; at the same time I am saddened that the full potential of the social sciences has so seldom been realized, but I also believe that the social sciences are always in the process of evolving. Therefore, it would be a grievous error not to explore how a post-modern perspective might contribute to the process.

No author is ever alone in writing a text, and my indebtedness goes beyond the footnotes and bibliography. It is with great pleasure that I begin by thanking my loving husband, James N. Rosenau, for his enthusiastic support and unwavering encouragement over the years that I spent writing this book. An author, a professor and now a playwright, he nourished my interest in post-modernism from the start. His words of encouragement sustained me through the difficult periods; he made the difference.

I also wish to acknowledge with much appreciation the many friends, colleagues, and students who have read and commented on particular portions of this book over the last several years, most particularly Richard Ashley, Harry and Maryliz Bredemeier, Robert Cox, Michael Dear, Isabelle Grunberg, Howard Kendler, and Barbara Rosecrance. The students at the University of Quebec who took my course, "Forces sociales et vie politique," those enrolled in my seminar on post-modernism at the University of California at Irvine where I was a visiting professor, Spring 1988, and those currently at the University of Southern California, all contributed to the ongoing discussion of the issues addressed in this book. I am grateful to Lisa Nowak Jerry, who competently, carefully, and expeditiously edited the manuscript. Finally, Stephen Schecter, Jean-Guy Vaillancourt, and Erica Verba assisted in proofing the final printed version. A special word of thanks in this respect goes to my daughter, Véronique Vaillancourt.

Inasmuch as I am a "modern" author I assume, of course, "responsibility" for this text and for whatever "errors" remain. I hope my readers will not be too frisky with their interpretations of my text. I want to specifically discourage efforts to "re-invent" this text through the "very act of reading."

NOTE: Pauline Marie Rosenau is Professor of Political Science at the University of Quebec–Montreal. She formerly wrote under the name Pauline Vaillancourt.

GLOSSARY OF POST-MODERN TERMS

agent or *agency* — someone assumed to have authority and power, causal force.

author — person who writes or creates a text, or one who is responsible for an outcome.

celebrate — approve of something, applaud a point of view.

chronophonism — the modern assumption that time is chronological or linear. Post-modernists are opposed to chronophonism (Derrida 1981).

countermemorializing analysis — an analysis that denies a referent reality, rejects foundations, and ignores origins (Ashley and Walker 1990b: 400).

de-centering — absence of anything at the center or any overriding truth. This means concentrating attention on the margins.

deconstruction — a post-modern method of analysis. Its goal is to undo all constructions. Deconstruction tears a text apart, reveals its contradictions and assumptions; its intent, however, is not to improve, revise, or offer a better version of the text.

differend — difference in the sense of dispute, conflict, or disagreement about the meaning of language (Lyotard 1988b: 193–94).

différance — a structuring principle that suggests definition rests not on the entity itself but in its positive and negative references to other texts. Meaning changes over time, and ultimately the attribution of meaning is put off, postponed, deferred, forever (Derrida 1972; 1981: 39–40).

discourse — all that is written and spoken and all that invites dialogue or conversation. Discourse "even promotes its own reformulation" (Agger 1990: 37).

evoking — acceptable post-modern alternative to re-presenting or representing. It is assumed to free one's analysis of objects, facts, descriptions, generalizations, experiments, and truth claims (Tyler 1986: 129–30).

foundationalism — an attempt to ground inquiry or thought on pre-given principles assumed true beyond "mere belief or unexamined practice" (Fish 1989: 342; Bernstein 1986: 8–12). Post-modernists are antifoundational. They contend that "questions of fact, truth, correctness, validity, and clarity can neither be posed nor answered" (Fish 1989: 344).

genealogy — history of the present that looks to the past for insight into today. It focuses on "local, discontinuous, disqualified, illegitimate knowledges." Genealogy dismisses the possibility of any view of history as a "unitary body of theory which would filter, hierarchise, and order

... in the name of some true knowledge and some arbitrary idea of what constitutes a science and its objects" (Foucault 1980: 83).

heroic — modern social scientists sometimes focus on one event or person; and in so doing, post-modernists argue, they create heroes, attach excessive importance to the capacities of a single individual to effect change or influence specific, dramatic events. Post-modernists, rejecting this approach (heroic analysis), neither focus on individuals nor construct heroes. Many post-modernists call for the end of the subject, the death of the author.

hyper-reality — reality has collapsed, and today it is exclusively image, illusion, or simulation. The model is more real than the reality it supposedly represents. The hyper-real is "that which is already reproduced" (Baudrillard 1983c: 146). It is a model "of a real without origin or reality" (Baudrillard 1983c: 2).

hyper-space — post-modern term referring to the fact that our modern concepts of space are meaningless. Space doesn't act according to modern assumptions. It has been annihilated, and spatial barriers have disappeared. Everything is in geographical flux, constantly and unpredictably shifting in space.

imploding, implosion — tendency for phenomena in a post-modern world to explode inwardly, thus destroying themselves and one's assumptions about them (Baudrillard 1983a). Meaning disappears altogether (Baudrillard 1983c: 57).

intertextual — infinitely complex interwoven interrelationships, "an endless conversation between the texts with no prospect of ever arriving at or being halted at an agreed point" (Bauman 1990: 427). Absolute intertextuality assumes that everything is related to everything else.

logocentric — an adjective used to describe systems of thought that claim legitimacy by reference to external, universally truthful propositions. Post-modernists are opposed to logocentric thought. They say such systems are really grounded in self-constituted logic. They consider them circular, self-referential, and self-satisfying. As post-modernists see it, no grounds exist for defensible external validation or substantiation (Derrida 1976: 49).

moment — indefinite point in time with undetermined duration or nonspecific geographical location or place. Post-modernists also use this term to refer to the stages or steps of social analysis.

move — as in chess, it is strategic. To "move" means to defend a position or take the discussion or analysis in a certain direction.

narrative — post-modern opinion of this concept varies, depending on the type of narrative under discussion. Post-modernists severely criticize meta-narratives, global world views, mastercodes. Meta-narratives are modern and assume the validity of their own truth claims, however, mini-narratives, micro-narratives, local narratives, traditional narratives are just stories that make no truth claims and are therefore more acceptable to post-modernists.

paralogism, paralogical — refers to the unknown, what is admittedly false knowledge. But for post-modernists it can also refer to those practices that "exploit the destabilization of the language games of Truth" in order to point to how little we really know, how much what we do know is pure linguistic convention of an arbitrary character (Smith 1988: xxiii; Lyotard 1984: 60).

pastiche — a free-floating, crazy-quilt, collage, hodgepodge patchwork of ideas or views. It includes elements of opposites such as old and new. It denies regularity, logic, or symmetry; it glories in contradiction and confusion.

performativity — modern criteria by which judgment is made on the basis of pragmatic performance or outcome ("capacity, efficiency, control," according to Benhabib 1984: 105). It is not acceptable to most post-modernists (Lyotard 1984) who understand it as an extension of modern faith in reason. Post-modernists argue that performativity discourages diversity and autonomy, flexibility and openness.

phonocentric — Derrida, a post-modernist, argues that modern analysis focuses on speaking and the oral text. He criticizes this tendency to attribute special status to the spoken word and labels it phonocentric. Derrida contends that the written word is superior to the spoken (Derrida 1981: 24). Post-modernists are antiphonologocentrist (Berman 1990: 14).

privileged — to give special attention or attribute priority to an argument, a person, an event, or a text. Post-modernists oppose privileging any specific perspective.

project — organized, formal, modern ventures or activities. It implies having a strategy, a game plan, a design, a self-justifying, often hidden goal. Modern political parties, for example, have "projects." For post-modernists this is a term of criticism.

le quotidien — daily life analysis or everyday life focus. Post-modernists see it as a positive alternative to global theory.

reader — observer. Post-modernism is reader-oriented and gives readers the power of interpreting a text that, in modern terms, belonged to the author. Post-modern readers are dramatically empowered.

readerly text, "lisible" (French term) — a modern text that is written with the intention of communicating a specific, precise message. It assumes a passive reader that merely takes in the message (Barthes 1970; 1979: 77). The writer's role is one of representation, that is, representing reality. Compare "writerly text."

reading — understanding, interpretation. In post-modern terms one speaks of "my reading," "your reading," or "a reading," without reflecting on the adequacy, the validity of said reading.

re-present — the underlying assumption of modern representation that it is possible to present something over again, to replace one object (concept, person, place, or time) with another, without loss of content or violation of intention. The post-modernists say this is impossible.

rhetoric — in the modern sense denotes "artificial eloquence" as opposed to serious, rigorous, scientific discourse. But for post-modernists it is taken in its more classical definition to mean oratory, the artful presentation of ideas that play with symbols and the construction of meaning in an open text that has no design or intention of imposing a hegemonic view or of insisting on its own superiority.

simulacrum — a copy of a copy for which there is no original (Baudrillard 1983c; Elgin 1984: 877–79.) No distinction can remain between the real and the model.

site or *space* — not merely geographic location; places that cannot be definitely determined. It may also refer to opportunities. Sometimes it alludes to the topic or problem being studied.

story, storytelling — see narrative; an explanation that makes no truth claims but admits to being the teller's point of view based only on his or her experience. Traditional, local narratives are stories.

subjectivity — post-modernists use this term to refer to an emphasis on the subject as a focus of social analysis. The post-modernists criticize subjectivity. Post-modernists do not employ this word in its modern sense of philosophical relativism or tentativeness or the opposite of objectivity.

text — all phenomenon, all events. Post-modernists consider everything a text.

totalizing — assumes a totality, a total view. By extension this rejects other perspectives. Post-modernists criticize totalizing theories.

voice — the modern conception of the author's perspective. Post-modernists question the attribution of privilege or special status to any voice, authors, or a specific person or perspectives. The "public" voice, however, is more acceptable to post-modernists because it democratizes rhetoric, makes discourse broadly understandable, and at the same time subverts "its own expert culture" (Agger 1990: 214).

writerly text, "scriptible" (French term) — a post-modern text that is written to be rewritten by the reader with every reading. This open text invites interpretation and re-interpretation (Barthes 1970; 1979: 77; Jefferson 1982: 100–101). The reader's role is that of production, construction. Compare "readerly text."

POST-MODERNISM AND THE SOCIAL SCIENCES

1

INTO THE FRAY: CRISIS, CONTINUITY,

AND DIVERSITY

POST-MODERNISM haunts social science today. In a number of respects, some plausible and some preposterous, post-modern approaches dispute the underlying assumptions of mainstream social science and its research product over the last three decades. The challenges post-modernism poses seem endless. It rejects epistemological assumptions, refutes methodological conventions, resists knowledge claims, obscures all versions of truth, and dismisses policy recommendations.[1]

If social scientists are to meet this challenge and take advantage of what post-modernism has to offer without becoming casualties of its excesses, then an adequate understanding of the challenge is essential. This book seeks to fill the need for an evaluation of the relevance of post-modernism in the social sciences, its essential elements, its central foci and organizing premises, its strengths and weaknesses, its appeals and pitfalls. If, as seems likely, intense controversy over the merits of the challenge lies ahead, then clarity about its bases and implications can facilitate constructive dialogue and help us make "sense of the post-modern-induced anarchy" in the social sciences (Dear 1988: 5). To initiate such a dialogue, the chapters that follow are grounded on four main purposes: first, to explore the range and complexity of post-modern approaches with special attention to their ori-

[1] Most of what is written here with reference to post-modernism also applies to post-structuralism. Although the two are not identical, they overlap considerably and are sometimes considered synonymous. Few efforts have been made to distinguish between the two, probably because the differences appear to be of little consequence. (See the following for references to these two terms: Callinicos 1985: 86; Hohendahl 1986: 49; Honneth 1985: 147–57; Huyssen 1984: 37–45; Sarup 1989: 131; Walker 1988a: 86. Huyssen argues for the "fundamental non-identity of the two," but most of the others see them as similar). As I see it the major difference is one of emphasis more than substance: Post-modernists are more oriented toward cultural critique while the post-structuralists emphasize method and epistemological matters. For example, post-structuralists concentrate on deconstruction, language, discourse, meaning, and symbols while post-modernists cast a broader net. There also seems to be an emerging difference concerning the status of the subject and object (discussed in Chapter 3). The post-structuralists remain uncompromisingly anti-empirical whereas the post-modernists focus on the concrete in the form of "le quotidien," daily life, as an alternative to theory. Those post-modernists who hark back to the pre-modern are classical empiricists, privileging sense experience, a highly personal individual, nongeneralized, emotional form of knowledge (Vaillancourt 1986a: 31–36).

gins in the humanities; second, to explain and illustrate their applications to the social sciences; third, to examine some consequences of their adoption in the social sciences; and fourth, to provide the beginnings of a general assessment.

All signs point to a veritable explosion of interest in post-modern approaches to the social sciences: courses and textbooks devoted to these approaches are offered, departments are gaining reputations for their post-modernist emphasis, particular scholars have emerged as recognized leaders of the movement, and established journals have published post-modern proponents along with their angry responses.[2] The post-modern impact in the fields of anthropology, law, women's studies, planning, urban studies, geography, sociology, international relations, and political science has been greater than in the case of economics and psychology, where its development has been slower.[3]

The appearance of post-modernism in the humanities and the social sciences signals more than another novel academic paradigm. Rather, a radically new and different cultural movement is coalescing in a broad-gauged re-conceptualization of how we experience and explain the world around us. In its most *extreme* formulations, post-modernism is revolutionary; it goes to the very core of what constitutes social science and radically dismisses it. In its more *moderate* proclamations, post-modernism encourages substantive re-definition and innovation. Post-modernism proposes to set

[2] See, for example, the following symposia: *Theory, Culture and Society* 5 (June 1988); *International Organization* 38 (1984): 225–328; *Alternatives* 13 (1988): 77–102; *Millennium, Journal of International Studies* 17 (1988), especially the articles by Der Derian, Ashley, Kratochwil, and Brown; *Texas Law Review* 60 (March 1982); *Cultural Critique*, no. 5 (Winter 1986–87); *Telos*, no. 62 (Winter 1984–85) (Special Issue on Debates in Contemporary Culture); *Southern California Law Review* 58 (January 1985), "Interpretation Symposium"; *New German Critique*, no. 33 (Fall 1984); *Political Theory* 16 (May 1988); *International Studies Quarterly* 33 (1989), especially the articles by Yosef Lapid, K. J. Holsti, and Thomas Biersteker. *International Studies Quarterly* 34 (1990) is a special number entitled, "Speaking the Language of Exile: Dissidence in International Studies" and most of the articles are post-modern critiques. *History and Theory* 28 (1989) and 29 (1990) offers an exchange between Ankersmit and Zagorin on the merits of post-modern history.

[3] Even in psychology and economics post-modernism is making enormous gains that will be reflected in publications appearing throughout the next few years. Articles are also beginning to appear on post-modernism in unexpected places, from commercial bulletins and applied social science journals to scholarly publications in the natural sciences. For example post-modernism has made its debut in forestry (Wikstrom 1987a; 1987b), engineering (Platten 1986), management (Carter and Jackson 1987), industrial organization (Swyngedouw 1986), property development (Seidl 1988), business (Anonymous 1982), systems analysis (Nodoushani 1987), organizational analysis (Cooper and Burrell 1988), accounting (Arrington and Francis 1989), public relations (Wolter and Miles 1983), public administration (Caldwell 1975), and corporate design (Crooks 1984). The message evident throughout these applications is that post-modernism is "good business." It is economically viable and compatible with a public relations point of view.

itself up outside the modern paradigm, not to judge modernity by its own criteria but rather to contemplate and deconstruct it. Ironically, on occasion this flamboyant approach arrives at conclusions that merely reinforce those already evident in the social sciences. Threads of post-modern arguments weave in and out of those advanced by more conventional critics of modern social science, and so post-modernism is not always as entirely original as it first appears. Nevertheless, taken together, both the extreme and moderate approaches constitute one of the greatest intellectual challenges to established knowledge of the twentieth century (Wisdom 1987: 159).

Modernity entered history as a progressive force promising to liberate humankind from ignorance and irrationality,[4] but one can readily wonder whether that promise has been sustained.[5] As we in the West approach the end of the twentieth century, the "modern" record—world wars, the rise of Nazism, concentration camps (in both East and West), genocide, worldwide depression, Hiroshima, Vietnam, Cambodia, the Persian Gulf, and a widening gap between rich and poor (Kamper and Wulf 1989)—makes any belief in the idea of progress or faith in the future seem questionable. Post-modernists criticize all that modernity has engendered: the accumulated experience of Western civilization, industrialization, urbanization, advanced technology, the nation state, life in the "fast lane." They challenge modern priorities: career, office, individual responsibility, bureaucracy, liberal democracy, tolerance, humanism, egalitarianism, detached experiment, evaluative criteria, neutral procedures, impersonal rules, and

[4] Some maintain that the modern age ranged from the fifteenth to the nineteenth centuries and that post-modernism has been evolving for the last 150 years (Nelson 1987: 4). Others contend that post-modernity originated in the late 1960s and early 1970s (Ferry and Renaut 1985; 1987; Heller 1987; Huyssen 1984). They also disagree about whether the modern and the post-modern overlap or are distinct, whether post-modernism signals a genuine break with modernity or is merely its logical continuation (Hassan 1985; Graff 1979; Calhoun 1990).

[5] Modernity itself is a complex and heterogeneous phenomenon, and I do not plumb its depths or explore its various currents here. Several books of interest that address the question of modernity itself include Toulmin's *Cosmopolis: The Hidden Agenda of Modernity* (1990), Kolakowski's *Modernity on Endless Trial* (1990), Giddens's *The Consequences of Modernity* (1990), and Heller's *Can Modernity Survive?* (1990).

In this book I go along, for the purposes of argument, with the post-modern equation of the modern with one of its major currents, that which incorporates the Enlightenment heritage and urges the social sciences in a positivist direction. This, of course, leaves out those elements of the modern, such as the hermeneutic tradition or historicism, which are less vulnerable to many post-modern criticisms. As R. W. Cox points out, "The hermeneutic tradition—Vico, through German historicism, to Sorel, Croce, Weber and Gramsci—can be traced as coexisting with Enlightenment thinking and positivism but is quite distinct from it. It is alive and flourishing in those who have taken inspiration from the *Annales* historians and Braudel in particular" (personal correspondence, December 13, 1990).

rationality (Jacquard 1978; Vattimo 1988). The post-modernists conclude there is reason to distrust modernity's moral claims, traditional institutions, and "deep interpretations" (Ashley 1987: 411). They argue that modernity is no longer a force for liberation; it is rather a source of subjugation, oppression, and repression (Touraine 1990).

Post-modernism challenges global, all-encompassing world views, be they political, religious, or social. It reduces Marxism, Christianity, Fascism, Stalinism, capitalism, liberal democracy, secular humanism, feminism, Islam, and modern science to the same order and dismisses them all as logocentric, transcendental totalizing meta-narratives that anticipate all questions and provide predetermined answers.[6] All such systems of thought rest on assumptions no more or no less certain than those of witchcraft, astrology, or primitive cults (Shweder 1986: 11). The post-modern goal is not to formulate an alternative set of assumptions but to register the impossibility of establishing any such underpinning for knowledge (Ashley and Walker 1990a: 264; Culler 1982: 155; Norris 1982: 31–33), to "delegitimate all mastercodes" (Hassan 1987: 169). The most extreme post-modernists urge us to be comfortable in the absence of certainty, learn to live without explanation, accept the new philosophical relativism (Bauman 1987: 3–4).

Post-modernists question the superiority of the present over the past, the modern over the pre-modern (Vattimo 1988). They reject any preference for the complex, urban life-style of the intellectual over the rural routine of the peasantry in the countryside (Karnoouh 1986). Therefore, they attribute renewed relevance to the traditional, the sacred, the particular, and the irrational (Touraine 1990). All that modernity has set aside, including emotions, feelings, intuition, reflection, speculation, personal experience, custom, violence, metaphysics, tradition, cosmology, magic, myth, religious sentiment, and mystical experience (Graff 1979: 32–33) takes on renewed importance. Some post-modernists look with nostalgia on the past and particularly on the "self-managing, self-reproducing" popular culture of pre-modern times (Bauman 1987: 67); a few even romanticize the period when people lived in caves (Gebauer 1989). The post-modern "remembers, recollects" and asserts that there is no special value for the new (Vattimo 1988: 101).

Post-modernists question any possibility of rigid disciplinary boundaries between the natural sciences, humanities, social sciences, art and literature, between culture and life, fiction and theory, image and reality in nearly every field of human endeavor (Gregory 1989: 68; Lash and Urry 1987:

---

[6] See glossary for a definition of these and other unfamilar post-modern terms that follow.

287; Lyotard and Thébaud 1985; Vattimo 1988).[7] They consider conventional tight definitions and categorizations of academic disciplines in the university context simply to be remnants of modernity. No surprise, then, that post-modern trends, breaking through these boundaries, are apparent in architecture, art, dance, film, journalism, linguistics, literary criticism, literature, music, philosophy, photography, religion, sculpture, theater, and video, as well as in the social sciences and, increasingly, the natural sciences.

An example illustrates post-modernism's radically interdisciplinary character. The post-modern challenges to modern rational organization radiates across fields. Post-modern art, therefore, emphasizes the aesthetic over the functional. In architecture this means abandoning a modernist, efficient, pragmatic layout of mass and space and, instead, "giving people buildings that look the way they feel," that is, that reflect alienation, anxiety, chaos (Seabrook 1991: 126). Appearance and image have priority over the technical, practical, and efficient (Hutcheon 1986–87). In literature challenging rationality leads post-modern novelists to suspend strict linearity of plot: any organized story elements or design must be provided, invented by each reader. In psychology it questions the conscious, logical, coherent subject (Henriques et al. 1984). In the fields of administration and public planning, suspicion of rational organization encourages a retreat from central planning, a withdrawal of confidence from specialists and experts. In political science it questions the authority of hierarchical, bureaucratic decision-making structures that function in carefully defined, nonoverlapping spheres. In anthropology it inspires the protection of local, primitive cultures and opposition to "well-intentioned" First World planned intervention that seeks to modify (reorganize) these cultures. In philosophy this translates into a renewed respect for the subjective and increased suspicion of reason and objectivity.

Post-modernists in all disciplines reject conventional, academic styles of discourse; they prefer audacious and provocative forms of delivery, vital and intriguing elements of genre or style and presentation. The distinctness and specificity of post-modernism itself is certainly, in part, a function of these characteristics. Such forms of presentation shock, startle, and unsettle the complacent social science reader. They are explicitly designed to instigate the new and unaccustomed activity of a post-modern reading. Post-modern delivery is more literary in character while modern discourse aims to be exact, precise, pragmatic, and rigorous in style. But the post-

[7] Michel Foucault is an example of the cross-disciplinary character of post-modernism. He was at once a philosopher, historian, social theorist, and political scientist. Jacques Derrida, is another example; he is, among other things, a philosopher, art critic, and architectural consultant (Giovannini 1988; Seabrook 1991: 74).

modern emphasis on style and presentation does not signify an absence of concern with content.

Post-modern social science focuses on alternative discourses and meaning rather than on goals, choices, behavior, attitudes (Potter and Wetherell 1987), and personality. Post-modern social scientists support a re-focusing on what has been taken for granted, what has been neglected, regions of resistance, the forgotten, the irrational, the insignificant, the repressed, the borderline, the classical, the sacred, the traditional, the eccentric, the sublimated, the subjugated, the rejected, the nonessential, the marginal, the peripheral, the excluded, the tenuous, the silenced, the accidental, the dispersed, the disqualified, the deferred, the disjointed—all that which "the modern age has never cared to understand in any particular detail, with any sort of specificity" (Nelson 1987: 217; Pfeil 1988). Post-modernists, defining everything as a text, seek to "locate" meaning rather than to "discover" it. They avoid judgment, and the most sophisticated among them never "advocate" or "reject," but speak rather of being "concerned with" a topic or "interested in" something. They offer "readings" not "observations," "interpretations" not "findings"; they "muse" about one thing or another. They never test because testing requires "evidence," a meaningless concept within a post-modern frame of reference.

A warning is in order for readers unfamiliar with post-modern perspectives. Such readers ought not conclude that the juxtaposed concepts in the previous paragraph imply subtle reorientations, mere jargon, or intellectual niceties. These different terminologies incorporate adversarial views of the world. Learning these words and understanding their usage involve more than new ways of communicating; such intellectual activity requires re-setting the codes one normally employs in social science analysis, turning around one's thought processes.

Post-modernists rearrange the whole social science enterprise. Those of a modern conviction seek to isolate elements, specify relationships, and formulate a synthesis; post-modernists do the opposite. They offer indeterminacy rather than determinism, diversity rather than unity, difference rather than synthesis, complexity rather than simplification. They look to the unique rather than to the general, to intertextual relations rather than causality, and to the unrepeatable rather than the re-occurring, the habitual, or the routine. Within a post-modern perspective social science becomes a more subjective and humble enterprise as truth gives way to tentativeness. Confidence in emotion replaces efforts at impartial observation. Relativism is preferred to objectivity, fragmentation to totalization. Attempts to apply the model of natural science inquiry in the social sciences are rejected because post-modernists consider such methods to be part of the larger techno-scientific corrupting cultural imperative, originating in the West but spreading out to encompass the planet (Lyotard 1984). Post-modernists search out the intellectual weaknesses, excesses, and abuses of modernity. They speak to "puzzles" and strive to "illuminate" general issues, not an easy task if at the same time an effort must be made to avoid offering an alternative point of view.

Timing alone assures that the post-modern challenge to the social sciences was no accident. Its arrival, concurrent with—and perhaps in response to—societal upheaval, cultural transformation, political change, deep philosophical debate over core values, and disciplinary crises, permits a receptive welcome, one that might not be possible in other recent junctures (Featherstone 1988: 207–8). Most important, its complaints and its preferred themes resonate with meaning attuned to the exact nature of these disturbances.

The emergence of post-modernism may simply reflect intellectual currents in the larger society, but in the social sciences it also reacts to uncritical confidence in modern science and smugness about objective knowledge. Historically, science attacked the arbitrary authority of church and monarch, both of which based their legitimacy on theology. Modern science established its reputation on objectivity, rigorous procedures of inquiry, the material rather than the metaphysical. Science, in turn, came to claim its own monopoly of truth. Its authority expanded and superseded that held by its more irrational and arbitrary antecedents (Levine 1987: 39). Post-modernists are uneasy with their more conventional colleague's uncritical acceptance of philosophical foundationalism, the Enlightenment heritage, and the methodological suppositions of modern science.

The post-modernism challenge to modern social science can be compared with earlier efforts, marked by years of conflict and debate, to apply the model of the natural sciences to the study of society. The underlying assumptions and methods of the social sciences were, in many cases, transformed as social scientists, adhering to a positivist and determinist view of modern science, sought to emulate their colleagues in the natural sciences. Just as conventional social science approaches were faced with behavioral perspectives and methodologies borrowed from the hard sciences in the 1950s and 1960s, so recent years have witnessed the appearance of another paradigmatic crisis of equally substantial proportions, this time based on post-modern intrusions from the humanities. But there is a difference. Those applying the post-modernism of the humanities to the social sciences do not seek to "improve and perfect" the social sciences so much as to make their underlying assumptions explicit and undermine their foundational claims.

The positivist, empiricist, rational-logical model of modern science remained central to the social sciences as long as the consensus about the success of this paradigm held firm. But that consensus was vulnerable, and the post-modern opening arrived just as apparent inadequacies made qualifications to modern science seem reasonable. First, impatience with the failure to produce the dramatic results promised by modern science's most enthusiastic supporters increased and fostered cynicism, in both the social sciences (Birch 1988a; Shweder and Fiske 1986: 4–6) and the hard sciences (Widgery 1989: 897).[8] Cumulation of research results was very slow, and exasperation marked efforts to improve predictive capacity. If modern science was a self-correcting process in the long term, then its short-term errors, passed off as truth, were tragic in some cases (for example, the Thalidomide case). Expectations were said to have been inflated and promises unfilled. Second, attention began to focus on the abuse and misuse of modern science. It became clear that in some cases modern science legitimated the preferences of the powerful, justified normative positions that were mere preferences rather than "scientific facts." "Scientific" research results were employed in an ad hoc fashion to "prove" the value of subjective political policy preferences. Modern science was accused of covering up government abuses in democratic societies and working to sustain totalitarian states (Krippner 1988: 131). Third, a discrepancy was apparent between the way modern science was supposed to function in theory and how it actually worked (Kuhn 1970; Toulmin 1985: 28–29). Modern science was seen as not living up to its own formal standards (Feyerabend 1975). Fourth, the ill-founded belief that science could solve all problems confronted the obvious incapacity of modern science to remedy the major problems of the twentieth century. What could science do about "the threat of nuclear weapons and toxic chemical concentrations"? What does it have to say about "hunger, poverty, environmental deterioration, or insults to the Earth's life-support systems" (Harman 1988: 122; Capra 1982: 22–25)? Fifth, modern science took little notice of the mystical and the metaphysical dimensions of human existence; rather, it made such matters appear trivial and unworthy of attention. Lastly, it had little to say about the normative and the ethical, the purposes to which knowledge, scientific or otherwise, should and would be put. "Experienced reality does not conform to the 'reality' they taught us in science class; the 'scientific worldview' is not an adequate guide for living life or for managing a society" (Harman 1988: 122). Modern science made everything too concrete; it forgot the poetics (Lyotard 1982: 65). In short, post-modernism in the social sciences is, at least in part, a response to the perceived inadequacies of scientific social science.

---

[8] This gave rise to a whole range of post-positivist protests, not all of them post-modern by any means. See Shweder and Fiske 1986 as an example.

Post-modernism's appeal is broad and varied, difficult to identify. Part of its magic is that its open-endedness and lack of specific definition is at once attractive to the affluent, the desperate, and the disillusioned of this world. Post-modernism may be, in part, the luxury of a generation for whom scarcity seems remote, a generation preoccupied with liberty rather than necessity, with the individual rather than the collective. This may account for the scant attention it has received in Eastern Europe, China, or the USSR where the attraction of modernity is still new and the consumer society associated with it yet to be fully experienced. Does this mean that post-modernism flourishes only when people become accustomed to modernity and take it for granted?

Post-modernism is also the product of desperation. For example, the enthusiastic reception post-modernism has received in some sections of the humanities and social sciences may well reflect a broad change in the position of intellectuals in the West. Economic privation leaves scholars responsive to nostalgia and resentment (Stauth and Turner 1988); academicians in the 1970s and 1980s faced a very poor job market, and many were unemployed (Habermas 1986: 150). Ineffectiveness and loss of credibility result in their no longer being capable of supplying the "proof that what is being done is universally correct and absolutely true, moral and beautiful" (Bauman 1988: 221).

Post-modernism's appeal may also reflect disillusioned optimism. As I discuss in Chapter 8, the strain of seeing one's hopes and dreams come to nought may lead some to recoil in frustration from the impediments encountered to their projects (Sorel 1987: 193) and to embrace post-modernism. If this is the case, then post-modernism can be employed to legitimate political and social inaction, "our unjustifiable and unhappy complacency, even [a denial of] our own responsibility for our own lives" (Shusterman 1988: 353).

Those attracted to post-modernism are not evenly distributed throughout the disciplinary ranks in the social sciences. It holds more interest for graduate students and junior faculty than for those further along in their careers. Does post-modernism's selective base of attraction merely indicate that newness threatens those who have invested so heavily in other paradigms? Or does post-modernism simply reflect adolescent rebellion, midlife professional crisis, opposition to the "establishment" by those who feel deprived of power? Could it be that the very content of post-modernism, with its emphasis on the marginal, the ignored, the decentered, those deprived of power, explains this differential attraction within disciplines? These questions are not trivial, and the answers are elusive, as evidenced throughout the ensuing chapters.

1. Post-Modern Lineage: Some Intellectual Precursors

The post-modern turn is not native to North America; rather it is an adopted child of continental Europe, predominantly of French and German descent. As one important French intellectual smugly points out, post-modernism and post-structuralism sell as well in the North American intellectual market as Beaujolais Nouveau (Morin 1986: 82).[9] The irony is that, although the French get most of the credit for developing post-modernism, German philosophers, mainly Nietzsche and Heidegger, inspired it. Despite this intellectual debt, contemporary German philosophers, especially Jürgen Habermas (1981, 1983, 1986), are among post-modernism's most severe critics. But post-modernism is not always received so sympathetically in France either. Important French post-modernists, particularly Jacques Derrida, have of late lost credibility in their own country (Ferry and Renaut 1985). Nevertheless the appeal of post-modernism continues to grow outside France.

Does the apparent decline of post-modernism in France and other continental European countries indicate that it is on the wane (Bonnefoy 1984)? Not necessarily. A closer look reveals other dynamics. Rather than disappearing, post-modernism has become synonymous with inquiry itself in many areas of the humanities, so much so that its nomenclature need not be made explicit. Literary criticism at many universities, for example, implies a post-modern, deconstructive orientation. In addition, much discussion in the social sciences today takes place within the post-modern agenda, assuming its terminology and its intellectual orientation without question. Conceptual approaches, including post-positivism, neo-structuralism, post-contemporarism, post-structuralism, and post-Marxism, overlap with post-modernism substantially and monopolize an enormous amount of intellectual energy. Finally, certain themes, central to post-modernism, preoccupy attention in countries where post-modernism is said to be *"dépassé"*: the death and return of the subject (Frank 1988; Vattimo 1988), individualism (Lipovetsky 1983), the identity of the individual (Ferry and Renaut 1987; Renaut 1989), antihumanism (Ferry and Renaut 1985; Soper 1986), cynicism (Sloterdijk 1987), the philosophy of Heidegger and Nietzsche (Farias 1989; Fedier 1988; Ferry and Renaut 1988;

[9] Beaujolais Nouveau is what the French used to call a "junk" wine. It is the freshly pressed grapes of the autumn harvest and used to be drunk only by those who could not afford to purchase the more expensive aged wines. Thanks to French public relations efforts, the international wine market has been convinced that this "highly desirable" wine is in such short supply that the French government must regulate how much is to be sold to each country and the exact hour and day of the year on which it is to be released. In some countries people stand in line overnight to be among those "lucky" enough to purchase a few bottles.

Le Débat, January, 1988), nihilism (Vattimo 1988), and the Paris May 1968 tradition (Ferry and Renaut 1985).

As is so often the case with what seems dramatically innovative, post-modernism is not entirely original. Its precursors can be traced and credited (Strathern 1987): post-modernism represents the coming together of elements from a number of different, often conflicting orientations. It appropriates, transforms, and transcends French structuralism, romanticism, phenomenology, nihilism, populism, existentialism, hermeneutics, Western Marxism, Critical Theory, and anarchism. Although post-modernism shares elements with each, it has important quarrels with every approach.

Some examples illustrate the specifics of the post-modern genealogy. Post-modernists agree with Western Marxists that modern science is myth and Enlightenment heritage is totalitarian and dominating (Horkheimer and Adorno 1972; Marcuse 1956, 1969). Critical Theory urges a suspicion of instrumental reason, modern technology, and the role of the media in a modern consumer society (Kellner 1989a), and post-modernism also adopts these views. French structuralism contributes a suspicion about humanism, the subject, and the author. In common with Nietzsche and Heidegger, post-modernists share a skepticism about the possibility of truth, reason, and moral universals, a conviction that terms like good and bad are inappropriate, and an insistence that subjective and conflicting interpretations are the closest humans can come to "understanding" (Granier 1977; Deleuze 1983; Miller 1981; Vattimo 1988). Nihilism and some forms of post-modernism are equally pessimistic about life; they stress the uncertainty of understanding the human condition and underline the ultimate realization that knowledge is a contradiction. From ethnomethodology (Garfinkel 1967) comes the view that "meaning is free to vary across divergent contexts" (Gergen 1986: 140). Symbolic interaction provides the notion that the meaning we attach to social relations is a human construction, not an objective reality (Goffman 1959; Berger and Luckmann 1966). Edmund Husserl and phenomenology (Schutz 1962–66) encourage a reconsideration of personal knowledge, a rejection of logocentric world views, and a suspicion of "lessons" that come to us from the past, from history (Husserl 1960); post-modernism takes up these themes. With populism, post-modernism shares spontaneity and a certain anti-intellectualism, a tendency to idealize the masses and their personal and private resistance (Featherstone 1988: 212–13; Stauth and Turner 1988: 524; Benhabib 1984: 125; Baudrillard 1983a: 40–48). Paralleling anarchism, the post-modernists question authority and the arbitrary imposition of any singular, systemic, point of view; both tolerate different, even contradictory perspectives. From existentialism as formulated by Sartre, they acquire antihumanism. Hermeneutics contributes to post-modernism's critique of empiricism, rationality, universalistic science, and direct, mechanical causality. From romanticism the post-modernists inherit a critical stand vis-à-vis the objective, all that is supposedly permanent, and the unity of time and place. The romantics may well have inspired the post-modern focus on fantasy, feelings, emotions, the metaphysical, the sacred, the exotic, the deviant, the primitive, and the unusual. The romantics question dominant aesthetic values by arguing that there are no truly universal criteria of beauty, goodness, and truth. The post-modernists, much like the romantics, feel they live in "in a twilight world of transition between an unsatisfactory present and an unworkable past . . . a world in which conventional social maps" are no longer effective, but at a point in time when new ones have yet to be constructed (Gouldner, 1973: 327–33).

At the same time post-modernists of one persuasion or another would take issue with some points in all these views. They do not agree with hermeneutics if, in its search for explanation, it assumes that one interpretation is better than others, if its goal is to recover a singular meaning for any political or social act (Bauman 1990: 425–26). They question structuralism's commitment to science, rationality, reason, and logic (Morris 1988: 345) and Critical Theory's emphasis on extratextual explanations of social phenomenon. They see the Western Marxist project of "emancipation" as logocentric and humanist, criticize its emphasis on the societal totality at the expense of *le quotidien* (the local or daily life), and consider the critical theorist's search for truth to be naive (Ricci 1984: chap. 5). Some dismiss the concerns of those anarchists, such as Murray Bookchin (1989–90: 50), who call for grass-roots democracy, confederalism, and a rational society.

This cut-and-paste character of post-modernism, its absence of unity, is both a strength and a weakness. Everyone can find something about it with which to agree. But, because it is not an "invisible college" (Crane 1972), an infinite combination of alternatives allow different and varying ways to put together the elements that constitute post-modernism. No wonder its harmony is disrupted by argument; no wonder it is characterized not by orthodoxy so much as by diversity, competing currents, and continual schism (Hassan 1987: 167). Whether one reads post-modernism as skeptical and cynical or as affirmative and optimistic, or as something else entirely, depends in part on which authors and traditions inspire one's understanding of it. Post-modernism is stimulating and fascinating; and at the same time it is always on the brink of collapsing into confusion.

2. Affirmative and Skeptical Post-Modernism

The divergent, even contradictory expositions of post-modernism underline the need to distinguish among its various orientations if we are ever to be able to talk about it at all. There are probably as many forms of post-modernism as there are post-modernists (Featherstone 1988: 207). If it were not so clumsy, we could speak of post-modernisms. But within this diversity of post-modern pronouncements, as far as the social sciences are concerned, two broad, general orientations, the *skeptical* post-modernists and the *affirmative* post-modernists, can be delineated.

The skeptical post-modernism (or merely skeptics), offering a pessimistic,[10] negative, gloomy assessment, argue that the post-modern age is one of fragmentation, disintegration, malaise, meaninglessness, a vagueness or even absence of moral parameters and societal chaos (Baudrillard 1983b; Scherpe 1986–87: 101). Inspired by Continental European philosophies, especially Heidegger and Nietzsche, this is the dark side of post-modernism, the post-modernism of despair, the post-modernism that speaks of the immediacy of death, the demise of the subject, the end of the author, the impossibility of truth, and the abrogation of the Order of Representation. Post-modernists of this orientation adopt a blasé attitude, as if "they have seen it all" and concluded that nothing really new is possible (Gitlin 1989: 103). They argue that the destructive character of modernity makes the post-modern age one of "radical, unsurpassable uncertainty" (Calinescu 1987: 305), characterized by all that is grim, cruel, alienating, hopeless, tired, and ambiguous. In this period no social or political "project" is worthy of commitment. Ahead lies overpopulation, genocide, atomic destruction, the apocalypse, environmental devastation, the explosion of the sun and the end of the solar system in 4.5 billion years, the death of the universe through entropy. Even where there is room for happiness, farce, parody, pleasure, "joyous affirmation" (Derrida 1978: 292), these are only temporary, empty meaningless forms of gaiety that merely mark a period of waiting for catastrophe (Scherpe 1986–87). If, as the skeptics claim, there is no truth, then all that is left is play, the play of words and meaning.

Although the affirmative post-modernists, also referred to as simply the affirmatives, agree with the skeptical post-modernists' critique of modernity; they have a more hopeful, optimistic view of the post-modern age. More indigenous to Anglo-North American culture than to the Continent, the generally optimistic affirmatives are oriented toward process. They are either open to positive political action (struggle and resistance) or content with the recognition of visionary, celebratory personal nondogmatic proj-

---

[10] When I characterize the skeptical post-modernists as pessimistic I mean they are distrusting. They emphasize the negative and lack confidence or hope in anything. They are inclined to anticipate the worse possible outcome. I am not using the word pessimism as Sorel employs it (1987: 192–95); Sorel suggests that pessimists are pragmatic realists, in touch with the constraints and limitations imposed by the human condition. Pessimists, he argues, adjust to this, and they value efficacy over any naive pursuit of Truth. This is not the case with the skeptical post-modernists.

ects that range from New Age religion to New Wave life-styles and include a whole spectrum of post-modern social movements. Most affirmatives seek a philosophical and ontological intellectual practice that is nondogmatic, tentative, and nonideological. These post-modernists do not, however, shy away from affirming an ethic, making normative choices, and striving to build issue-specific political coalitions. Many affirmatives argue that certain value choices are superior to others, a line of reasoning that would incur the disapproval of the skeptical post-modernists (Bordewich 1988; Frank 1983: 405; Levin and Kroker 1984: 15–16).

There is a range of extreme to moderate versions of both affirmative and skeptical post-modernism, and the two dimensions cross-cut one another. In the case of both the affirmatives and the skeptics, the extremists are distinguished from the moderates primarily by the intensity of their opinion and their willingness to carry their post-modern conviction to its most extravagant, excessive conclusion—no matter what the outcome or consequences. On balance our concern focuses on the skeptics and affirmatives with only an occasional reference to extreme and moderate post-modernism.

There are both advantages and disadvantages to the categories of skeptical post-modern and affirmative post-modern. They overlap at the edges and do not constitute the neat "mutually exclusive, jointly exhaustive" groupings so clearly desired by modern social science.[11] But these categories are useful, and I refer to them in the chapters that follow because they not only group together individuals with similar views but also facilitate an understanding of apparent contradictions within post-modernism. Dif-

---

[11] Ben Agger (1990) proposes a distinction between establishment post-modernists (who support the End-of-Ideology philosophy) and radical, critical post-modernists. His distinction overlaps my own with one important terminological, not substantive, difference. Although he calls the establishment post-modernists "affirmative," I reserve this term for those post-modernists who assert a positive political or societal project, many of whom Agger would classify as radical and critical. Todd Gitlin (1989) develops the categories "cool" and "hot" post-modernism, which are of more interest to the arts and humanities or perhaps the sociology of culture than social sciences in general. There is some overlap between his "cool" category and what are called skeptics here and his "hot" post-modernists and the affirmatives. David Griffin (1988a: x–xi) distinguishes between "deconstructive or eliminative" post-modernism and "constructive or revisionary" post-modernism and locates his own attempt at establishing a post-modern science in the latter category. In a similar emotion-laden effort G. Graff (1979: 55–60) contrasts "apocalyptic, desperate" post-modernism with "visionary, and celebratory" post-modernism. Hal Foster discusses the difference between post-modernism of reaction and post-modernism of resistance (1983: xi–xii); the former celebrates the status quo while the latter resists it. In another context Foster distinguishes (1984) between "neo-conservative" post-modernists who are close to the affirmatives (retain the tradition of narrative, conventional history, subject, representation and humanism) and "post-structural" post-modernism that resembles the skeptics (anti-subject, anti-representation, anti-history, and anti-humanist).

ferentiating between the two allows us to explain how post-modernism can have such diverse implications in the social sciences. These categories also highlight the possibility of different scenarios for the future of post-modernism in the social sciences.

No single author cited in this book and no specific illustration of a skeptical or affirmative post-modern approach can be regarded as completely authentic or absolutely adequate. No example offers perfect congruence with every descriptive element attributed here to post-modernism. This should be no surprise because post-modernism itself is not static and unchanging; rather, it is endlessly dynamic, always in transition.

Because the very term post-modernism has come to represent controversy and criticism, many post-modernists avoid the label. Some argue that the word post-modern promotes a singular view of reality, encourages closure, and denies complexity. So they retreat from it to avoid its pejorative associations as something bizarre and frivolous. They refer to themselves in less contested terms, such as post-contemporary. Or they might suggest their work is merely "interpretative."

3. Conventions

Based on the foregoing it should be clear that the term post-modern is employed so broadly that it seems to apply to everything and nothing all at once. Sometimes it is employed as a synonym for the future (Barilleaux 1988 and Rose 1988 are examples). But in this book it is used in a more rigorous sense; I refer to a specific philosophical perspective replete with epistemological assumptions, methodological preferences, and substantive foci even if the exact character of each of these may be a matter of debate.

Much the same can be said about the term, "social sciences." Although there may be a general consensus on the broadest level within the academic community as to what it embraces in terms of academic field divisions and a general concern with human society, agreement breaks down over specific content, epistemology, and methodology. These latter quarrels are not the major interest here. Narrow, exclusionary definitions of the social sciences are avoided, and examples are drawn from a wide range of fields even if they are not always and everywhere housed under the rubric of "social sciences" in every university directory. It is, of course, true that on some occasions and in certain places, specific disciplines may have a special status, but I propose that these instances should not preclude considering them here. Finally, while I refer to the social sciences as if they were analytically separable from the natural sciences and the humanities, this is an admitted simplification. All three intermingle at the edges, and the boundaries between them are a source of debate.

The ensuing chapters are neither hostile to post-modernism, nor should they be construed as sympathetic or apologetic. No effort is made to adhere to post-modern guidelines for inquiry. On the contrary, it is likely that these will be violated, though not through disrespect or malice. Rather, any violation can be construed as an inevitable consequence of seeking to cut through the intentional stylistic ambiguity, some would say obscurantism, that characterizes post-modernist writing and to communicate to an audience broader than the post-modern community itself.

Because the reader is not expected to possess, in advance, a knowledge of post-modernism's special terminology or jargon a glossary of common post-modern terms is included at the beginning of this volume. Jargon and the use of language is a special problem because post-modernists are notorious for inventing and discarding terms. "Their creation of jargons and specialized, neologistic vocabularies is authorized precisely by subsequent rejection and replacement by other jargons and vocabularies; the perils of language require that it be treated as scaffolding, always waiting to be taken down" (Kellner 1987: 9). Such a view is not new to the social sciences. Academics often defend jargon by arguing that the function of such specialized vocabulary is to facilitate communication. Traditionally, critics complain that jargon excludes the uninitiated and limits understanding to those who have invested considerable energy in acquiring the information necessary to comprehend it. But post-modernists reject both these views. The skeptics are dubious about the possibility of communicating altogether. They assume that "words are not determined on a one-to-one basis by the idea or thing which they supposedly represent" (Jefferson 1982: 108–9), and so they see little reason to make especially strenuous efforts to communicate exactly what they mean in any case. They argue that jargon, defined as playing with words, is interesting in and of itself. The generally relaxed post-modern linguistic temper makes for flexibility, but at the same time it contributes substantially to confusion and ambiguity. The glossary then is also an effort to break through potential terminological disarray.

Fairness about a topic as controversial as post-modernism is difficult to achieve if only because linguistic convention, at the moment, discourages neutrality. Even how one writes the word—"postmodern" or "post-modern"—signals a position, a bias. The absence of the hyphen has come to imply a certain sympathy with post-modernism and a recognition of its legitimacy, whereas the hyphen indicates a critical posture.[12] It has been suggested that conservative opponents of post-modernism employ the hy-

---

[12] Exceptions to this rule occur with increasing frequency. For example, Dumm (1988: 224) is highly favorable to post-modernism but employs the hyphen because it reminds of "aporias of modernity."

phen and radical supporters omit it (Hassan 1985: 125), but this is an oversimplification because opinion about post-modernism cross-cuts the left-right continuum (see Chapter 8, section 3). Whatever the case, the use of the hyphen here reflects the grammatical conviction that this is the most appropriate usage and should not be interpreted as a statement of normative judgment or pejorative innuendo.

In addition, my attempt to be self-conscious about post-modernism, to explain it or theorize about it, may be inherently objectionable to those post-modernists who view such endeavors as necessarily misguided, as flawed attempts at systemization (Ashley and Walker, 1990a: 265–66; Featherstone 1988: 204; Lyotard 1988b: xi). I have already offended by looking for origins, foundations, past traces of post-modern views, by indicating precedent and precursors in the social sciences, by striving to make the "unthought" as "accessible" or as transparent as possible (Hoy 1989: 450), by categorizing and classifying to facilitate understanding. But here we really have no other option but to transgress by the very act of inquiry. This project necessarily requires a modern emphasis on synthesis and unity, rather than the post-modern preference for preserving difference and complexity. If those outside its inner circle are to achieve an understanding of post-modernism, then comparisons with modern views seem essential; this goal urges us on to generalization and simplification. To consider everything a unique occurrence leaves one unable to go beyond description.

Attention here is on post-modernism's contribution, developed in literature, linguistics, literary criticism, and philosophy, to the social sciences. Post-modernism is equally important in art, photography, architecture, the visual and performing arts, but post-modernism in literature and philosophy serves as a more frequent and recurring reference point for social science. In addition, similarities of form and content suggest that the close, neighboring disciplines are more proximate to the issues faced by the social sciences. Even with this limitation only a sampling of post-modernism's methodological core and its specific substantive counsel can be discussed. Those theoretical and methodological dimensions most likely to be pertinent for social scientists reviewed here include author, text, reading, subject, history, time, geography or space, truth, theory, representation, deconstruction, interpretation, science, and politics. Although the implications for the social sciences may not be self-evident, the following discussion confirms that they are substantial.

While exposition is the main focus of this study, critique also has a place. In the best sense responsible examination requires an assessment of limits. As with all criticism the most forcefully stated and unqualified expositions are the most frequently targeted, and so throughout this book I attach less credibility to extreme post-modern forms than to more moderate presentations. Examples are available for every criticism presented here, but none applies universally.[13]

In many respects the ensuing assessments of post-modernism are modern in tone and character. Admittedly, modern assessments of both the substantive and methodological contributions of post-modern social science are unfair because they employ criteria alien to the object being judged: they frame criticism according to modern criteria rather than in conformity with post-modern guidelines. But one is left without a choice, especially as concerns the skeptics, because the post-modernists themselves fail to make explicit how one is to evaluate divergent texts or choose between incompatible interpretations. Within a post-modern world truth is absent, and this renders evaluation and judgment relatively meaningless. In the absence of any alternative criteria for evaluation, what option remains except to measure post-modernism with a modern gauge?

Yet, this should not be taken as an uncritical, blind acceptance of modernism. It signifies exasperation and a recognition that an imperfect paradigm is preferable to a post-modern prison house of silence where, as extreme post-modernists put it, no words are acceptable or adequate and none can legitimately be uttered because authentic, accurate, communication is impossible. Nevertheless, an effort to assess the contribution of post-modern social science on its own terms is made wherever possible, even as it is also evaluated according to modern criteria because it exists in a world that stubbornly remains very modern in many respects. And is this really so unfair, given that many post-modernists do much the same thing when they employ a post-modern perspective to judge modern social science?

4. An Overview

Having offered a general introduction to post-modernism, to its intellectual precursors, and to the distinction between skeptical and affirmative post-modernisms in this chapter, I find it useful to present an overview to the chapters that follow. In so doing I hope to allow the reader some feel for the coherence inherent in this arena of inquiry that prides itself on a readiness to be incoherent.

Chapter 2 explores how post-modernism revises the generally accepted relationship of author, text, and reader. The conventional view of each term is compared with its post-modern variation. The importance of the

---

[13] Readers should note that my parenthetical text references are multipurpose. Some indicate the source of a quote or an idea. Others refer to a work that supports the point of view I am arguing. In some cases they indicate an example of what I am talking about. Finally, on occasion they refer the reader to a more comprehensive discussion of a topic.

author, as both individual and accountable agent, is diminished within a post-modern optic. The hypothesized demise of the author symbolizes a decline of responsibility and a protest against author(ity). Post-modernism privileges the text and elevates the reader. The post-modern text is open and has no objective content. Readers are given extraordinary power to define and create textual meaning. Everything is defined as a "text"; thus, the relevance of post-modernism expands. Examples are drawn from constitutional law, international relations, journalism, political science, and anthropology.

In Chapter 3 we see that while post-modernists in the humanities call for the death of the subject, a subjectless post-modern social science is severely constrained.[14] The skeptical post-modernists "resist" the unified, coherent subject as a human being or a concrete reference point. They dispute the subject's stable identity, the assumptions ensuring its free will, and the philosophical humanism the subject's existence implies. Some skeptics propose the post-modern individual as a substitute for the modern subject. The affirmatives are, in general, more sympathetic to the subject. They call for a return of the subject, its repositioning in the social sciences. In the end it is not the death of the subject that is of greatest interest in the social sciences so much as the birth of the post-modern individual and the "return of the new subject." Examples are offered from psychology, sociology, anthropology, political science, and women's studies.

In Chapter 4 post-modern arguments against conventional history, linear time, and predictable geography or space are outlined. All post-modernists agree that conventional versions of these variables constrain thought and limit understanding. History has a much diminished status within a post-modern approach. They are suspicious of inquiries concerned with knowing and representing the past. The skeptics collapse history into the instantaneous second between yesterday and tomorrow; time becomes disparate, crisscrossed, layered, and misaligned rather than homogeneous, evolutionary, purposive, and regular. Post-modern hyperspace can be created and made to disappear. Be they political, economic, cultural, or social, time and geography refuse to behave as expected or to intersect neatly at the corners. Post-modern planning, international relations, political sociology, urban politics, political theory and geography provide examples.

The revisions of history, time, and space proposed by the skeptical post-modernists present substantial challenges to social science. If their conceptions of time and space as uncontrollable and unpredictable are acknowl-

---

[14] Doing away with the subject logically coincides with the death of the author. These two post-modern concepts overlap as categories (Edelman 1988: 9), but I consider them separately here. The author is a subtype of subject, but not all subjects are authors.

edged, then confusion, what the post-modernists call pastiche, reigns. The skeptics speak of post-history, and their argument parallels that of the End-of-History movement. As time and space dissolve, nothing can be assumed entirely present or absent. The unexplained is the order of the day. But not all interpretations of post-modern time, space, and history are so radical. Some of these ideas were anticipated by others in the social sciences, and they can be accommodated without major disruption. Affirmative post-modernists agree with the need to transform what they view as the more repressive qualities of time, space, and history. They look to New History for inspiration and propose micro-narratives and genealogy to replace conventional modern forms of history. They give priority to local and regional spaces. They are not so set on repudiating conventional space and time so much as relativizing them. None of the affirmatives' proposals concerning time, space, and history go so far as to prohibit social science.

Chapter 5 focuses on the concepts of theory and truth. In a post-modern world theory is no longer "innocent" in the sense of being detached; truth ceases to be naive in the sense of neutrality and objectivity. For the skeptical post-modernists this means abandoning truth and theory and embracing a philosophical relativism in their place. Language, they argue, transforms truth and theory into largely linguistic conventions, and for the skeptics this means that it is impossible to say anything with confidence. A pluralism of more or less equal views exists, in which the skeptics consider all to be interesting and worthy of attention.

The absence of truth for the affirmatives yields intellectual humility and tolerance. They see truth as personal and community-specific: although it may be relative, it is not arbitrary. For these post-modernists theory is reduced in stature, but they neither reject it altogether nor call for an absolute equality of all theories. For the affirmatives theory is unsystematic, decentered, heterological, and makes no claim to a privileged voice. Some of them substitute a substantive focus on the local, on daily life, and on traditional narrative for the hegemonic theory of mainstream social science. This chapter illustrates the problems post-modern views of truth and theory present to the social sciences in the fields of women's studies, public administration, sociology, anthropology, political science, and psychology.

Chapter 6 examines post-modern conceptions of representation. Post-modernists generally reject modern representation. Skeptical post-modernists argue that representation is epistemologically, methodologically, and substantively fraudulent. What is of greatest importance can never be re-presented: the superb, the non-general, the unique, the idiosyncratic, the "sublime" (Lyotard 1982: 68), the eccentric. They call for an end to the "Order of Representation" because representation denies difference and brings closure. Without representation, however, modern social science is problematic, and comparative analysis is impossible. The affirmatives dispute modern representation, but they retain the possibility of epistemological representation because they see no way to do without it. Responses to the crisis of representation in anthropology, sociology, and political science are reviewed and evaluated.

There is a tension within post-modernism concerning democracy and representation. When the skeptical post-modernists repudiate representation, many simultaneously dismiss democracy. For the affirmatives, rejecting modern representation leads to demands for more authentic representation or a call for more and better democracy even to the point of each citizen "representing" himself or herself. Public-sphere theory appeals to many of these post-modernists because it attaches little importance to representation. Skeptical post-modernists, however, fault the public-sphere theorists for their emphasis on reason and their assumption of rational communication.

Chapter 7 considers post-modern views of epistemology and methodology and describes the post-modern methods of deconstruction and intuitive interpretation. The skeptics and affirmatives challenge those versions of modern social science that claim objectivity, causality, a materialist reality, and universal rules of inquiry. Skeptical post-modernists argue that reality is pure illusion: everything is intertextual, not causal or predictive. Their preferred methods include anti-objective, introspective interpretation and deconstruction. Relativism and uncertainty characterize their views. They doubt the value of reason and contend it is impossible to establish standard criteria for judging intellectual production.

Affirmative post-modernists also indict modern social science. Their own understanding of reality is constructivist or contextualist. Explanation is not only weakly intertextual but also teleological. Positive value orientations and specific normative goals openly guide the affirmatives' version of social science. Methodology depends on emotion, intuition, and imagination. Although ambivalent about reason, few affirmatives are willing to abandon it altogether. They sometimes evaluate knowledge claims on the basis of normative preferences or community standards.

Chapter 8 considers the political orientations of skeptical and affirmative post-modernists and the consequences of these for their expectations about social science. The skeptics are political agnostics, proposing that all political views are mere constructions and generally avoiding advocacy of any type. Some are pessimistic about the possibility of changing society. Hence they argue for nonparticipation as the most revolutionary position in the post-modern age. Others consider play and euphoria the best alternatives to traditional, modern political action. In some cases they employ these as substitutes for social science. In the extreme, some skeptics talk of terror, suicide, and violence as the only truly authentic political gestures that remain open.

Affirmative post-modernists are more politically optimistic. They support a wide range of new political and social movements and advocate pluralism and tolerance rather than partisan and dogmatic postures; but not all of them live up to these values. Although some support issue-specific political movements (alliances around peace, ecology, and the environment), others, such as the New Age affirmative post-modernists, are more spiritually inclined. The expression of affirmative post-modern politics in the Third World takes the form of populist, fundamentalist, nationalist, post-modern social movements. These organizations call for returning to the primitive, sacred, and traditional society as well as rejecting First World ideologies, technologies and economics.

Chapter 8 addresses the question of whether a post-modern social science would be inherently left-wing or right-wing. A broad range of opinion on the intrinsic left or right political character of post-modernism is examined including the views of Marxists, neo-Marxists, and post-Marxists. No consensus is found to exist. I conclude that post-modernism is so open, or so vague, that it can be incorporated by those of almost any political persuasion.

Chapter 9 offers a readerly conclusion. The precise form and character of a post-modern social science is sketched out; as a summary it refers to what was covered in previous chapters. I explain the affirmative post-modernists' difficult choice between intellectual consistency and relevance and mark out areas of critique not discussed elsewhere. Finally, I assess the future of a post-modern approach to the social sciences.

2

ABANDONING THE AUTHOR, TRANSFORMING
THE TEXT, AND RE-ORIENTING THE READER

We have always talked of talented or gifted writers; we should
talk of gifted and talented readers.
(Milorad Pavic quoted in Bruckner 1988: 15)

The author should die once he has finished writing, so as not
to trouble the path of the text.
(Eco 1983b: 7)

POST-MODERNISTS dramatically revise the conventional roles of author, text, and reader. They diminish the importance of the author and amplify the significance of the text and the reader. It is almost as if author, text, and reader have been competing for the spotlight. When the post-modernists abandoned the author a space was created; the text and reader filled the void. "The birth of the reader must be at the cost of the death of the Author" (Barthes 1977: 148).

The post-modern reader enters at center stage and assumes an unprecedented autonomy. No longer is the reader a passive subject to be entertained, instructed, or amused. S/he is given the freedom to attribute meaning to the text without consequence or responsibility. But post-modernists do not seek to constitute the reader as a new center of author(ity). Nor is the reader permitted to set up a meta-narrative or establish a new foundation for knowledge because post-modern readers are equal in the sense that none can claim special expertise or insight. In the extreme, all readings are equivalent.

The post-modern text also takes on a life of its own, independent of the author and without any pretense of an objective status. Everything comes to be defined as a text in a post-modern context, and yet the text is marked by an absence of any concrete and tangible content.

The reader and text are inter-referential. They easily "switch places . . . ; the story of the reader structuring a text flips over into a story of the text manipulating the reader " (Culler 1983: 118–19). Meaning does not inhere in a text; it resides in the interaction between the text and reader. Although the two may appear to share the limelight, the arrangement is not always peaceful. The reader may construct the text, but the text in turn controls the encounter. The outcome of every interaction, each confrontation between reader and text, is different and unique, temporary and never final. On occasion post-modernists have even advanced the counter-intuitive view that the reader is created by the text at the same time the text is written by the reader.

In a post-modern situation one reads and writes not in pursuit of truth or knowledge as envisioned by the Enlightenment project of modern science. Rather one reads for the pleasure of the experience. One can begin a book at the end, skip to the middle, return to the end, and conclude the reading by referring to the introduction (Barthes 1975). Any authorial "rationale" for order is erased. There is no singular content to worry about, no solitary, distinctive "reasoned" reading to be considered more warranted than another. What is actually going on can never be stated definitively, and it matters little in any case because there is no single meaning for any text.

Although the revised versions of author, text, and reader may not immediately seem especially relevant for the construction of a post-modern social science, they do set the stage for serious reconstructions of social analysis. Each term, author, text, and reader has its counterpart in the social sciences. Besides the most obvious equivalent, the author may be, among other things, an agent. The text can be understood as, for example, any event. A reader is an actor-receiver, a participant observer, and an observing participant all at once. By redistributing emphasis (power) away from the author and toward the reader and text in an almost zero-sum fashion, post-modernists argue, new and more interesting insights result.

This chapter presents the conventional view of the modern author and the post-modern repudiation of it. The origins and evolution of post-modern revisions are briefly sketched, and post-modern conceptions of the author are explored. The implications of the death of the author and re-definition of text and reader for the social sciences are explained. Traditional views of the text and reader relationship are compared to the post-modern transformation wherein reading becomes a personal confrontation in textual construction rather than a process of knowledge acquisition. We begin with the author.

1. The Author

a. The Conventional Authorial Role

In a modern context there is a general consensus about the definition of an author and his or her role. It seems reasonable to assume that the modern author has an advantage in determining what s/he meant. Most social scientists think of the author as an individual who produces books, articles, and pamphlets. If the resulting text is regarded "as the product of genius," and if it is "approached with reverence and an expectation of revelation" (Fowler 1987), then the prestige of the author is enhanced. But even in cases where the author is viewed in a less positive light, s/he is still assumed to be the privileged, if not final, "arbiter of meaning" (Skinner 1969). If this is the case, the meaning of a text is a simple function of the author's intentions, conscious or unconscious, and the reader need only discover these to understand what the text is all about (Hirsch 1973: 3; Skinner 1969).

Because of his/her assumed superior position, the modern author's role is to educate, instill moral values, or enlighten the reader (who is not held in such high regard). Equipped with this conception of the author, it often makes sense to examine the author's biography and socioeconomic background if we wish adequately to understand a text and assess what was written. An author's intentions, motivations, opinions, and the historical, political, and social context in which s/he lived are all assumed to influence what s/he wrote.

The modern author may be defined more broadly than just a person who produces a piece of writing. An expanded view transforms the author into an agent, someone who either creates a situation or is responsible for a larger play of events and a specific social outcome. This modern author in society is a "legislator," defined as a specialist, a manager, a professional, an intellectual, or an educator. Just as with the modern literary author, all these individuals assume privileged access to truth, reason, and scientific knowledge; they "know" and "decide things" by weighing the positive and negative and determining what is "true." These modern author-legislators arbitrate in the sense of choosing between opposing points of view in controversy. What they select becomes "correct and binding" (Bauman 1987). The modern author, defined broadly, may be singular or plural, an individual or collective agent; the act of authoring may have direct or indirect effects, intended or unintended consequences.

Post-modernism is attentive to the contemporary, pervasive disenchantment with the modern author in all its various forms (Bauman 1987: 4, 122–24). The death of the author in the humanities parallels the decline of the legislator in society. Post-modernists challenge the power and authority of the author in the social sciences by arguing that s/he has not produced the "best societal order." No post-modernist really believes the legislator has the "right answers" for a post-modern world. For example, in anthropology the ethnographer, the author-writer, has been accused of holding a monopoly of authority and deliberately distancing himself/herself from the reader (Strathern 1987: 258; Hatch 1987: 272). Some post-modern ethnographers propose to correct this situation by sharing the power of the author, authorial responsibility, with those being studied

(Clifford 1988: 51–53) and at the same time leaving everything open to a more active reading.

Post-modernists offer a number of reasons for revising the role of the author and removing his/her authority. They begin by arguing it is a mistake to give a modern author the final word as to the meaning of his or her text. Authorship is a confusing and ambiguous business. How, they ask, can we distinguish between a personal authorial statement and an attempt by the author to create a frame of mind, an effect. When the text is written in first person, a plurality of subjects results (the author and the first person). The situation is under-determined because it is impossible to know the relationship of the author to the text (Barthes, 1977: 142). It can also be difficult to distinguish between an author's intentions *for* a work and his or her beliefs *about* it. In addition, authors are not always conscious of the implications of what they are saying. For example, a judge writes a decision with a certain clear intention, but upon a second reading finds it has a sense s/he never anticipated (Dworkin 1983b: 259). Consider the example of all voters being eligible for jury service long before women obtained the right to vote. It was not the conscious and explicit intention of those who author(iz)ed extending the franchise to women to also attribute to them the obligation of jury duty, and yet that is precisely what occurred (White 1982: 438–39). Finally, deferring to the author's intentions when interpreting a text may serve as a pretense for imposing one's own view (Dworkin 1983b: 251, 258), and this makes the modern author a mere instrument of power.

b. The Rise and Demise of the Modern Author

Post-modernists argue that the concept of author is not a natural idea, that it only appeared in certain fields at particular points in history (Barthes 1977; Foucault 1979). Michel Foucault examines the ancestry of the author and contends that among primitive people there was no author. Primitive narratives were exclusively oral and collective in character. He conceives of authorship as a concoction of the modern bourgeoisie seeking to assign responsibility for controlling or policing what was written. Without an author, how could punishment be administered, or legal responsibility attributed, when troublesome texts appeared? Foucault continues that authorship first emerged not in literature but in the sciences during the Middle Ages. An author's prestige was required for authenticity, and the authority of scientific statements rested upon it. Only later, in the seventeenth and eighteenth centuries, did scientific texts come to be backed up, guaranteed, by the scientific community, rather than by specific individuals; the need for individual authorship then faded (Foucault 1979: 148–49). The literary author, however, did not become important until the modern epoch. S/he emerged about the same time as English empiricism, French rationalism, and faith in the Reformation—all of which emphasized the importance of the individual (Foucault 1979: 143).

More recently, structuralist precursors of post-modernism in the social sciences anticipated the post-modern revision of the author, and their perspective served as a transition between conventional, modern views of the author and the post-modern redefinition (Jefferson 1982: 99). For the structuralists, the author launches a text, shepherds its publication, and then withdraws; the author allows it to live an independent life of its own and retains no special right to define it. The structuralists reject the author as "the specific creator of a work" because creative works are said to "arise from their context (culture and knowledge . . .)" (Kurzweil 1980: 152, 210). What the author *intends* to write, what the speaker intends to say, is not very important because from the structuralist viewpoint meaning is not imparted by "the subjective intentions and wishes of its speakers," but rather results from the "linguistic system as a whole which produces it" (Jefferson 1982: 87). For example, structuralists suggest that in the case of authors (professors) who receive institutional support, the institutions actually "author" the texts produced because these organizations set and control the circumstances of authorship (Said 1976: 40). These structuralists deny much authority to authors; the text must stand on its own.

Just as post-modernists deem the author a relatively recent historical development, so do they argue that in the near future the author may, again, disappear entirely, a trend they regard as appropriate in a post-modern era. They treat nothing as ever being really original in the sense of being the exclusive work of a particular author; everything is a copy, a simulacrum (Baudrillard 1983c).[1] There is no author in the modern sense for commercial ads, televisions scripts, radio dialogue, or the speeches delivered by political candidates or elected presidents. In each case the author (ghost speech writer, advertising agency, screenwriter, or producer) may generate a text, but s/he has little control over it and is seldom given much recognition. Collective author(ity) is also in decline as bureaucracies function according to impersonal rules and no one acknowledges agency or responsibility.

c. Post-Modern Challenges to the Modern Author

The post-modern challenge to the "classical authorial function" (Wood 1979: 23), what some post-modernists provocatively call the "death of the author" (Barthes 1977: 148; Foucault 1979), is understood somewhat dif-

---

[1] As my students delight in pointing out, plagiarism is a "modern" concept and has no place in a post-modern world where the author's role is so diminished.

ferently by the skeptical and affirmative post-modernists. For the skeptical post-modernists this translates into the author's relinquishing of special authority to attribute a single, "correct" meaning to his/her text.[2] These post-modernists affirm that knowledge about an individual author's conscious intention or motivation in the production (writing) of a text is of little assistance in comprehending it. They contend that it is equally futile to search an author's life context or examine his/her personality for insight into a text. Because the text itself is elevated over the individual author, what the author intends is pretty much irrelevant. The reading of a text has "nothing to do with the author as a real person." What an author writes is generally not what s/he means anyway (Derrida 1976: 158).

The most extreme skeptical post-modernists presume the author inherently objectionable. The author connotes an ideological status that is at once political, inadmissible, and alien to post-modern social science. At best, they say, the modern author seeks to define and confine, to impose control and censure, by employing the analytical assumptions of the modernist framework. S/he puts the reader at the mercy of the author. A focus on the author implies ownership and a special status (Foucault 1979: 159). It assumes rationalism, individual motive, creation, and design. The modern author is not just an individual. S/he is a "dimension," a mood, a functional principle, a source of information, a model, the vehicle for a logocentric view, power, and (author)ity. Finally, the "author's voice" gives rise to "experts" who claim to have special access to what the author "really meant" (be it Lenin on Marx; Matthew, Mark, Luke, or John on Jesus; or whoever on whomever). Skeptical post-modernists protest against all such assumed, privileged interpretations.

The skeptical post-modernists contend that the *implicit* author as well as the explicit author must be erased from social science. The concept of hegemony in international relations is a good example. Hegemony is "an ensemble of normalized knowledgeable practices, identified with a particular state and domestic society . . . that is regarded as a practical paradigm of sovereign political subjectivity and conduct." Its functions are to set the standards, designate by opposition what is anormal, fashion the political agenda, establish the "ritual practices of enframing," without ever manifestly accomplishing any of these (Ashley 1989b). Structuralists are quite satisfied with the concept of hegemony, even though it involves a sort of explicit assumption of an author, because it does not refer to individuals as authors. But post-modern international relations experts consider hege-

---

[2] It has been suggested by some that the decline of the author is an invention of literary critics in the humanities who sought to curtail the supremacy of the author's interpretation in order to lend greater legitimacy to their own. In my view this cynical interpretation is mistaken because the death of the author fits so comfortably and consistently with all the other elements of post-modernist analysis, none of which particularly favor literary critics.

mony suspect because it *implies* an impersonal form of author or agency, effective inasmuch as it succeeds in never appearing organized, deliberate, or intentional. Post-modernists argue that the power relations inherent in hegemony as a concept are not obvious. It is not a question of consciously working toward a specific end. Hegemony's mastery is disguised, dependent on "its capacity to inhabit a domain . . . , to competently perform the rituals of power naturalized therein," and, in the end, to secretly and "silently affirm global practices and effect international purpose" (Ashley 1989b: 269). This makes hegemony no more welcome to post-modernists than when it appears in its more unmistakable, obvious authorial forms.

Affirmative post-modernists understand the decline of the author in somewhat less dramatic terms. Rather than abandoning the author altogether, they simply deny that authorial intention "wholly accounts" for meaning. They seek merely to *reduce* the author's authority (Norris 1988: 131). The author may live on, but in a much revised and diminished form.

When the affirmative post-modernists assert that in the social sciences the "death of the author" gives rise to the post-modern interpreter, they resurrect the author in a more modest role. The interpreter, unlike the legislator, makes no universal truth claims, has no prescriptions to offer. S/he only sketches out the various options and takes part as an equal in the "public debate" (Bauman 1987: 5–8).[3] The interpreter's view is valuable only if it is personally meaningful (Rorty 1979, 1982). Any particular truth is relevant or valid only to the members of the group or community within which it is formulated. Knowledge, then, is relative to the community, true in terms of the beliefs of one community but not for other communities; any rules of knowledge apply only inside the community (Fish 1989).

The interpreter plays an additional role in the social sciences, one without parallel in the humanities. The interpreter, mediating between the partial and various versions of truth that exist within distinct communities, explains and "interprets" them for those who live in other communities with different truths (Bauman 1987: 191). S/he is "concerned with preventing distortion of meaning in the process of communication" (Bauman 1987: 5), but not with asserting the superiority of one interpretation over another.[4]

d. Implications for the Social Sciences

In the social sciences the "death of the author" closes off the study of some topics, reinforces others, and opens up still others. First and most obvious,

---

[3] This concept is discussed in Chapter 6, section 4, concerning the public sphere.

[4] The skeptical post-modernists would question the affirmatives' suggestion that the interpreter's goal should be to perfect communication.

post-modernists diminish the importance of the author as a writer of texts. Post-modern social science then, spends little energy on discovering what the "author really meant." Second, the repercussions are even greater when the author is conceived of broadly, as an actor with political, economic, and social roles because in this case "the death of the author" has implications for agency, authority, accountability, causality, and responsibility. Some examples help illustrate these consequences for the social sciences.

On the most obvious level the post-modern "death of the author" largely eliminates one form of academic inquiry. The absence of the author erodes the legitimacy of historians, sociologists, psychologists, and other social scientists who seek to analyze the life experiences of a single individual, be it Aristotle, Keynes, Freud, Marx, or Mother Teresa. Political biography, as such, is an outmoded enterprise of the past. Post-modernists might rather propose to analyze or "deconstruct" the "texts" of these lives, but not for insight into the intentions or motives of the author.

The post-modern "death of the author" renders the "intent" of historical authors (those who wrote long ago, those whose writings still have special importance for us today) largely superfluous, and this is relevant for a range of topics in the social sciences. For example, if the status of author is diminished, the "exact" intentions of those who composed a text, such as a treaty, need not concern government or legal experts attempting to apply it. In the post-modern context the SALT II treaty can be interpreted independently of its authors' wishes because the text is granted independence and stands on its own. Post-modernists also question the concept of legal precedent or jurisprudence (understood to be the intentions of authors of previous, related decisions) within a legal system.[5] Each decision needs to be re-considered anew with potentially chaotic results for the legal system (Posner 1988). No claim can be made that the exact intentions of the founding fathers who drafted the United States constitution need be considered or respected. In a similar fashion, although some judges argue in the case of a will or testament "recovering" the author's meaning is what counts, post-modernists would look to "verbal meaning" or "plain meaning" (Hancher 1982: 510–11).

Post-modernists would not agree with the conventional social science view that the author represents causal agency or that authorship implies social responsibility. Either they deny the existence of agency and causality altogether, or they reverse it completely. Attributing causality within the terms of post-modernism is "tyranny" (Zeldin 1976: 242–43). Sometimes causality is redefined as so complex and interactive as to defy disentangle-

[5] For a summary of the law as literature and related questions, see Minow 1987: 86–89. Posner (1988) provides an interesting response to the post-modern—he argues that literary and legal texts are not the same.

ment and inhibit estimating probable future outcomes. It is, then, impossible to establish any specific causal links. This is called post-modern intertextuality, and it implies, in the extreme, that everything is related to everything else.[6] For the post-modern social sciences, then, the search for causes in terms of sources or origins of phenomena must be discontinued in an authorless, totally intertextual world where the agent is omitted.[7] The absence of causality results in a skepticism about the possibility of positivist or quantitative social science.

The demise of the author and of causality permits post-modernists also to hail an end to the burden of moral agency, be it attributable to an individual (such as an elected official or a company president) or a collective (decision-making bodies such as a cabinet or a board of directors). Because no single human being can be held accountable for a situation in the sense of having causal input, no one "authors" a text-event as such. For the social sciences the death of the author results in removing responsibility from human subjects (Pinter 1987: 147).[8] I am not responsible for how my children turn out; I did not author their lives, author(ize) their efforts, have author(ity) over their choices. Policy makers do not author decisions, so they cannot be held accountable in any specific sense for policy outcomes (texts). Similarly, if U.S. policy in Central America (a text) is independent of its author's intentions, then the Carter (Bush or Reagan) administration would not be viewed as the author (the responsible agent), answerable for the outcome. A condition of normative ambivalence, a moral vacuum, an absence of obligation or freedom from accountability may result; it depends on how one wishes to look at it.

Skeptical post-modernists reverse cause and effect in the political arena. In a modern world political accountability means that elected leaders are rewarded (reelected) for positive performance and punished (voted out of office) if they have been obviously negligent in carrying out the duties of office. In a post-modern world this relationship is reversed, and leaders are neither permitted to take credit nor held responsible for catastrophes that occur while they are in office. Leaders are "minor elements of a complex transaction." They "cannot provide security or bring about change" (Edelman 1988: chap. 3).

---

[6] Intertextuality is defined in the glossary and discussed further in Chapter 7, section 1.

[7] The methodological implications of the omitted author await additional consideration in Chapter 7.

[8] The skeptical post-modernists' linguistic relativism (discussed in Chapter 5) also permits the author to escape responsibility. "If we always say something other than what we mean, obviously, we cannot be blamed for what we say" (Schwartz 1990: 36). At the same time it attributes enormous power to the individual: s/he as a post-modern reader can "make anyone else's speech mean anything we choose to make it" (Schwartz: 1990: 30). Critics are quick to point out the dangers of attributing power without responsibility.

Although post-modern authoring does not always and inevitably require a total repudiation of what has gone before in the social sciences, it still constitutes a point of serious difference with modern outlooks. Post-modern authoring (writing) and a post-modern attitude to textual production are foreign to conventional social scientists who are masters of the closely written text. Post-modernists reject the obvious definition of a tangible author (as professor, writer, scholar), who does research and writes a text (a material message in the form of a book or article) to transmit information or knowledge to an audience (a physical reader), be they students, colleagues, or the general public.

The post-modern author assumes a novel role in an unexplored post-modern world. S/he strives to write an open text and seeks to compose it so ambiguously, with such an equivocal and enigmatic style, as to encourage an infinity of post-modern interpretations. S/he is dedicated to expanding and enlarging the space available to the reader, to encouraging a plurality of meanings, and to inventing a text that is exposed, unsettled, undefined—a text that embraces and encourages many interpretations. In the post-modern period one writes or authors, not in the pursuit of truth or knowledge as envisioned by the Enlightenment project, but for the pleasure of the experience alone.

Conventional social scientists generally take a very different tack; they intend to restrict interpretation, assign responsibility, clarify authority relations. They aim to "arrest ambiguity and control the proliferation of meaning" (Ashley 1989a). In the social sciences an author endeavors to communicate a precise message to a reader without loss of content or distortion of meaning. The intent is to write so tightly, reason so logically, that one's audience (students, colleagues, and anonymous reviews) is compelled to agree with the argument. To better understand this confrontation between the modern and the post-modern author we now turn to the text and reader.

2. The Text and the Reader

a. Privileging the Text

A modern text is traditionally viewed as written communication. It is an attempt to convey a precise message to a specific set of identifiable readers. Enmeshed in a situation, a historical period, a culture, it must be understood in its social, psychological, economic, and political environment. Modern readers politely "listen" to a text as it speaks to them. The text has a knowable content, determined by the author, who has his/her personal and identifiable motivations and intentions for writing it.

The structuralist precursors of post-modernism anticipated the evolu-

tion of the post-modern text by reinventing it according to their own notions. They rejected an understanding of a text as a simple effort at communication between author and reader. For the structuralist the text is
rather a "series of forms produced by the institution of literature and the
discursive codes of a culture" (Culler 1983: 82). It has a certain objective,
though hidden, content. Once written, the text is considered independent
in the sense that it is fruitless to search for meaning and explanations in the
origins of the text, its author's voice, or its context (Barthes 1979: 77).

Post-modernists go further than the structuralists; the post-modernists
undo formal structures and warrant that no two texts are ever alike and no
two readings of the same text are ever identical. The skeptical post-modernists regard the text as free of constraint, relieved of any objective content. They do not assume that any solitary, distinctive, reasoned reading of
a text is superior to any other. They privilege the text, but only in their
assumption that it has an importance in and of itself. "The text is all and
nothing exists outside it" (Derrida 1976: 158).[9] The post-modern text is,
then, for the skeptics, a collection of "relatively unconnected fragments,
which challenge the literary code that predisposes the reader to look for
coherence" (Fokkema 1984: 44). The affirmatives seek to qualify rather
than deny the skeptics' view of the text. They do not regard the text as
completely arbitrary, nor do they believe all interpretations are of equal
value.

The post-modern text is a plural text, so open (or vague) as to yield to
an infinite number of interpretations. It is called a "writerly text" (*scriptible*)
because it is rewritten with every encounter (reading). This is the opposite
of the "readerly" text (*lisible*), which is to be read for a specific message,
destined for a passive reader, and which resists being rewritten by the
reader.[10] A writerly text is assumed superior (though post-modernists
avoid such hierarchical terms) to a readerly text because "the more plural a
text is, the more it will make it impossible for the reader to find any origin
for it, whether it be in the form of an authorial voice, a representational
content or a philosophical truth" (Jefferson 1982: 103). The more open
the text, the greater is the range of potential interpretations. The post-
modern text "is a machine for generating interpretations" (Eco 1983a: 2).

Post-modernism is text-centered. Everything is a text including a life experience, a war, a revolution, a political rally, an election, a personal rela-

[9] Bauman claims that what Derrida really means here is that "anything we can possibly
know is a text; the only thing a text can refer us to in our effort to grasp its meaning is another
text; nothing we can possibly know of may claim a status better, more solid, or in any other
way different from that of the text" (1990: 427).

[10] Some claim the distinction between writerly and readerly texts developed by Roland
Barthes is structuralist rather than post-modernist (Culler 1983). Whatever the case, the
terms are exceedingly relevant to a post-modernist view of the text.

tionship, a vacation, getting a haircut, buying a car, seeking a job. Even speech is assigned the status of text (an oral text).[11] Critics charge that post-modernism eliminates "all external factors related to a text" (Harari 1979: 41).[12] In the humanities this means that texts are analyzed as if they were removed from their setting. In the social sciences it means phenomena are studied without regard to their historical, social, political, or economic context. Post-modernists respond to this criticism with the concept of in-tertextuality.

Post-modernists argue that every text is related to every other text, and this makes for "intertextuality" (Kristeva 1980: 36, 65; Morgan 1985: 8–12). Effects radiate out from a text and have an impact on all other texts. There is a global mixing, a simultaneous connection similar to the medieval carnival where every element refers to every other element (Bakhtin 1973). All texts are repetitions of other texts in a most profound sense. Inter-referentiality of texts characterizes everyday life (Lipsitz 1986–87). Noth-ing is original in the last instance. "Every text, being itself the intertext of another text, belongs to the intertextual" (Barthes 1979: 77). Finally, in an almost metaphysical stance, the skeptics conclude that the text is every-where and yet not fully present anywhere. It has little definitive substance, no concrete content. The affirmatives are not ready to eliminate textual content in such an absolute fashion and show more concern about the ac-tual substance of a text than do the skeptics.

Most post-modernists, however, would agree that in examining a text we should not focus exclusively on what the text says but rather on what it

[11] In recent history, speech is generally assumed superior to writing because it is more immediate, more direct. Listeners understand immediately what is said to them. Writing is assumed more remote, indirect, mediated by the pen or the printing press. A speaker can answer questions, qualify, and clarify for an audience, but the writer is absent, distant, and remote. No direct interaction or feedback occurs with readers. Derrida, a post-modernist, attempts to overthrow the hierarchy of speech over writing; he calls this position phonocen-trism or phonologism (Derrida 1981: 24) and criticizes it severely. He argues that writing, more demanding than speech, involves rigor and intellectual activity. Writing has the advan-tage over speaking because it offers a permanent record of what was thought and is not tran-sitory and lost immediately as is speech.

It might appear that modern technology—television, radio, video—privileges speaking, that it has made the act of speech-giving even more important; but appearances are deceptive. If we examine the televised political act of speaking, we realize that to a certain extent the distinction between writing and speaking has been extinguished; the two are now collapsed one into the other. Ronald Reagan read most of his "speeches" on a teleprompter; he was "speaking" a written text.

[12] Not all post-modernists are committed to considering the text in absolute isolation. Fou-cault called for balance and criticized Derrida for attributing too much autonomy to language and missing the historical and political implications of the text. Foucault (1972) emphasized the relationship of the text to power and to the many forces that influence its production and its final form.

fails to say, what it suggests by innuendo. For the skeptics, its apparent content is of little interest. The ideas it purports to express are not their focus of attention. As we will see in Chapter 7, texts self-deconstruct to reveal what is left out or forgotten. In doing so they generate their own "multiplicity of meaning." The reader may be a witness to the whole process, but the text unravels itself (Cantor 1989: 363).

b. Re-orienting the Reader

Reader-oriented post-modernism implies that meaning originates *not* in the production of a text (with the author), but in its reception (by the reader). Anyone may read a text and in so doing recreate it: journalists, social scientists, and citizens among others. This suggests there must be private, multiple readings or interpretations of any text. In the extreme the post-modern reader "writes" or interprets the text in the act of reading, without claiming special author(ity) (Derrida 1974b). The reader is more of a plural rather than a singular concept because post-modern readers are a diverse, spirited, and contentious lot.

Historically, the modern reader has been taken for granted. Readers were on the receiving end of this complex relationship between the author and the text. Theirs was a passive posture: to reconstruct the author's "aims and attitudes in order to evolve guides and norms for constructing the meanings of his text" (Hirsch 1967: 227). Life might be much richer as a result of reading, but readers were not expected to make a serious positive contribution in the process of communication beyond paying the price of the book and taking the time required to read it. In the extreme the modern author was assumed to be intent on "capturing the reader and his or her commitment." Some say this makes the reader "a potential victim" (Fortin 1989: 28–29).[13]

The post-modern reader in the humanities was not so much a dramatic innovation as the result of an incremental evolution (Suleiman and Crossman 1980). The role attributed to the reader in the text-centered world of New Criticism, in the 1940s and early 1950s, was substantial. But by the late 1950s, the text was increasingly viewed as having an objective content that could be determined by scientific procedures; therefore, what the

[13] Modern political writers have been sensitive to how readers are exploited, but post-modernists defend the reader from a different point of view. For example, a modern critic might argue that the Hollywood cinema industry "engages its viewers covertly, making them unseen observers of the world that always appears fully formed and autonomous." The devices employed to give viewers (readers) the impression that they are free although their "readings" are in fact quite controlled are as extraordinary as they are subtle (Allen 1987: 89–96). Post-modernists, especially the skeptics, would find this modern assessment mechanical, conspiratorial, left-wing, and logocentric.

reader thought mattered less. The study of literature was said to be "founded on a progressively accumulating body of knowledge, an aggregate of concepts, tools, taxonomies, and procedures of discovery which enable the critic to define the object of his study precisely and to deal with it in a 'scientific' fashion" (Freund 1987: 69).

In the 1960s and 1970s the pendulum was once again on the move, and the structuralists' view of the reader (Formalist literary criticism) moved toward the post-modern concept of the reader. It continued, however, to accord the text an objective, even scientific status (Freund 1987: 69). The structuralists emphasized that the reader was not a real person, not a "conscious, purposeful, and feeling individual." Although s/he is a culturally engaged human being, actively encountering the text rather than passively receiving it, s/he is "dissolved into the impersonal activity of 'reading' " (Abrams 1981: 189). Wolfgang Iser (1978) argued that a text calls for an "Implied Reader," and this involved an interaction, phenomenological in character, between the text and the actual reader, a two-sided relationship of communication. Inspired by Ingarden, he suggested that a text has gaps, and in the act of reading the reader clarifies the ambiguities. The "reader is free to fill in the blanks but is at the same time constrained by the patterns supplied in the text; the text proposes, or instructs and the reader disposes, or constructs" (Ingarden 1973; Freund 1987: 142). Within Iser's form of structuralism the text surrenders some of its objective status, and the increasingly relevant reader assumes a glimmer of initiative, constrained only by "implicit codes of the interested system" (Abrams 1981: 189). Stanley Fish (1980) has taken the process even further, approaching an understanding of the text as actually constructed by the reader. But Fish sets forth one major qualification: readers do not have absolute freedom in their readings. He argues they are guided by professional communities, what he calls "interpretive communities" (not individuals so much as collective strategies or sets of communal norms). The reader "creates" the text, but within the context of what s/he has learned from an "interpretive community."[14]

The post-modern reader takes the final step and assumes control. The skeptical post-modernists permit the reader unlimited freedom in reading, complete autonomy, the liberty or license to interpret the text without restraint. Once the text is empty of any objective content, it is open to any number of readings. Their post-modern reader, critical and creative, takes on an unprecedented significance by subjectively constructing meaning. In the last instance post-modern readers "write the text" (Derrida 1976). In the extreme each reader has absolute power, holding the right to any inter-

[14] Lakatos (1978) criticizes this "community of scholars" approach and calls it elitist. Bauman (1987) applies it in the form of "communally grounded meanings."

pretation without restraint of evidence, objective cues from the text, or the wishes of the author. The affirmative post-modernists differ more in degree than kind. They too enhance the power and autonomy of the reader. Few of them, however, would agree to the exaggerated powers the skeptics accord the reader.

But, one might ask, do the post-modernists not give over to the reader all the power and authority they previously found so objectionable in the hands of the author? Such a question may bother affirmative post-modernists, but it troubles the skeptics far less. The skeptics argue that while the modern author claimed special privilege and expertise, all post-modern readers are equal. The post-modern reader makes no truth claims for his/her reading, but rather agrees that other interpretations are all equally interesting. This, the skeptics continue, merely reflects that there is no real, objective world independent of the observer. Different readers are expected to offer divergent interpretations of a text because there are multiple realities in a post-modern world. Reading is textual construction, not knowledge building.

Post-modern efforts to expand the definition of the text by defining everything as a text incur certain disadvantages. Post-modernists are said to mystify the text, make a fetishism of writing, and produce a narcissistic reader who, like the post-modern individual (discussed in Chapter 3), seems excessively arrogant, smug, and vain. "The privileged reader looks everywhere and finds only texts, and within the texts only himself" (White 1978: 265). By centering on the text so completely the post-modern reader also risks eliminating "all external factors related to the text" or reducing them to a textual function (Harari 1979: 41). If everything is a text, then the word becomes imprecise, so global and inclusive as to be of little value. "Reality is nothing but words" (Graff 1989). In such a world we encounter texts "only through interpretive systems whose choices and exclusions 'inscribe' themselves in the results of interpretation" (Graff 1989). Such a world may be filled with mystery and intrigue, but it may also frustrate and outrage.

c. Consequences of the Post-Modern Text and Reader for the Social Sciences

Conventional social scientists read to discover the author's intent. They do not read for the pleasure of rewriting the text in the absence of any authorial intention. Few, if any, attribute as much authority, liberty, credibility to the reader as do post-modernists. Many would jealously guard against readers who expect to participate in the attribution of meaning. They are hardly likely to encourage readers to recreate the text according to how they personally experience the play of language, symbol, and signs. Few

social scientists seek to cultivate openness or ambiguity in a text as a creative end in itself, especially if policy questions or practical applications in
the social sciences are at stake. Their goal is the closely written text that
restricts the play of language and limits the possible meanings available to
the reader. Furthermore, unlike post-modernists, modern social scientists
seldom examine a text in the absence of its origins or context. Although
structural analysts and systems analysis may have permitted this, neither
approach ever successfully eliminated origins, history, or context.

The implications of a post-modern view of readers and texts for the social sciences range from dramatic to commonplace. In the extreme form
the post-modern view appears incompatible with conventional social science. Much also depends on whether words, text, and reader are assessed
in their literal significance (author as author-writer) or in their larger sense
(author as author-agent). Broadening the definition of text enlarges the
potential applications of post-modernism to the social sciences; if all the
world of human thought and action can be understood as a text, then the
whole of social science becomes a candidate for post-modern analysis. Expanding the interpretative power of the reader functions in much the same
way. Some of the most important consequences of the post-modern revision of text, author, and reader are methodological in nature (see review in
Chapter 7).

Post-modern reading re-focuses social analysis. "Rather than seeing political news as an account of events to which people react," for example,
post-modernists treat political developments (or texts) as readings, as "cre-
ations of the publics concerned with them" (Edelman 1988: 2). This re-
orients intellectual production in the social sciences. Sociology is no longer
an attempt to understand and bring objectivity to a topic; rather, it is vivid
narration of a novel variety, if it is anything at all. And in the context of
this narration-description, ambiguity and subjectivity are "neither deviation nor pathologies" (Edelman 1988: 95).[15]

The affirmative post-modernists look to these revisions of the reader role
in the social sciences to make for greater interest on the part of a wider
audience and even to enhance social science activity, including the participation of the general public. In anthropology the post-modern reader "is
in on the dialogue between ethnographer and subject." Post-modernism
"allows the reader to interact directly with . . . exotica itself" (Hatch 1987:
171). This is hands-on anthropology where Every-citizen becomes his or
her own anthropologist.

Giving more power to readers may be interpreted as encouraging critical

---

[15] Post-modern fiction has been described as "jumbles of confusing descriptions without
recognizable plots or engaging characters" (Culler 1983: 10; Harland 1987: 136). Discount-
ing content is perfectly consistent if one estimates, as post-modernists do, that there is no way
to arbitrate the adequacy of substance.

citizenship in the sense of stressing that each individual has a valuable and viable opinion on a candidate's speech, a government policy on social security, a foreign policy decision (all text-events).[16] Post-modernists might go on to suggest an equality of all citizen assessments (readings) of, for example, the outcome of an election. Power generally makes people feel good, and post-modern readers may feel they have more influence, at least until they realize that any increased sense of power is pretty much an illusion if it is accorded to Every-reader.

Post-modern views of the text shift social analysis away from conventional sociological variables such as age, sex, and race, away from historical determinism and Marxist economics. Rather than imposing order and understanding on a text, rather than seeking to choose between different analyses, we are asked simply to admire its disorder and appreciate it as an "infinite play of [intertextual] relationships with other texts" (Morgan, 1985: 2). If U.S. policy in Central America is understood to be an open, plural, post-modern text, then a variety of readings are available. Some skeptical post-modernists would place the following readings on an equal footing: (i) the Contras were "freedom fighters," advancing democracy in Nicaragua; and (ii) the Contras were anticommunist mercenaries financed by the United States for its own imperialist ends. Neither statement, or any between them, could be judged superior to any other. Nor are the post-modernists surprised if "the same people who see American military interventions in the third world as dangerous to peace and as repressive of the poor also see them as defenses against communist aggression" (Edelman 1988: 93). Such texts have "at their center a relativism of meaning which can be demonstrated consistently and insistently to undermine all claims to objective knowledge and meaning not determined by prior assumptions" (Wortman 1987: 171).

The text itself, not facts, is what counts for the post-modernists. The post-modernists are satisfied to conclude that what is actually going on can never be stated definitively; in any case, it matters little because there is no single meaning for any text, for any political, social, economic event. An infinite number of interpretations of any scenario is possible.

In this chapter we have seen how the post-modern redefinitions of modern concepts such as author, text, and reader are directly applicable to the social sciences. In the next chapter a case of more contested conceptual transfer is examined. As we will see, post-modern social scientists may prefer their own reformulation of the subject to any suggestion, originating in the humanities, that it be abolished altogether.

---

[16] The skeptical post-modernists argue that the modern political context today makes people feel powerless and everyone knows their vote counts for little, that public policy decisions are remote and impervious to influence by ordinary citizens.

3

SUBVERTING THE SUBJECT

The subject cannot be regarded as the origin of coherent
action, writing, or other forms of expression. . . . The language
that interprets objects and actions also constitutes the subject.
(Edelman 1988: 9)

WITHIN THE TERMS of post-modernism, "subjectivity" refers to "individuality and self-awareness—the condition of being a subject" (Henriques et al. 1984: 3; Hohendahl 1986: 59). When post-modernists say they are "post-subjective" and when they talk about the decline of "subjectivity," they do not mean that they wish to be objective. They are, rather, calling for less emphasis on the subject as a focus for analysis as the "preconstituted centre of the experience of culture and history" (Giddens 1984: 2). They mean the point of view of the thinking "subject" is not to be given much weight. Modern philosophy of science discourse defines "subjective" as referring to feelings (the normative) and "objective" as referring to some independent, external reality. Not the post-modernists.

Post-modernism offers a primarily negative assessment of the modern subject, but there are substantial internal variations. We will see that the skeptical post-modernists are generally anti-subject, while the affirmatives are of more mixed opinion. Both, however, have had to reach some accommodation with the subject because although the death of the subject may be feasible in the humanities, the absence of the subject makes the very concept of social science tenuous.

The skeptics question the value of a unified, coherent subject such as a human being, a person, as a concrete reference point or equivalent character (Baudrillard 1983a: 167; Booth 1985; Derrida 1978; Foucault 1970: 261–62; Wellmer 1985: 436–49). The subject, they contend, is fictitious, in the extreme a mere construction (Edelman 1988: 9), "only a mask, a role, a victim, at worst an ideological construct, at best a nostalgic effigy" (Carravetta 1988: 395). They criticize the subject for seizing power, for attributing meaning, for dominating and oppressing (Henriques et al. 1984). They consider the subject to be a fossil relic of the past, of modernity, an invention of liberal humanism, the source of the unacceptable object-subject dichotomy. They argue that personal identity of this sort, if it ever existed, was only an illusion, and it is no longer possible, today, in a post-modern context.

The most extreme of the skeptical post-modernists consider the subject to be a linguistic convention or an effect of thinking on language (Edelman 1988: 9; Flax 1990: 219; Schwartz 1990: 38).[1] The subject is not the origin of "action, writing or other forms of expression"; rather language constitutes and interprets subjects and objects. Post-modernists such as Foucault and Derrida argue that the self is only a "position in language," a mere "effect of discourse" (Flax 1990). The subject is nonessential to their own analysis that concentrates on language, free-floating signs, symbols, readings, and interpretations, all of which escape the concrete definitions and reference points required by the subject.

But who is this modern subject the skeptics seek to dissolve and eliminate from their analysis? How do they describe him/her? The skeptics seldom discuss the precise character of the subject in any detail. However, certain assumptions about the subject's personality pervade their analysis: in the end the subject becomes a vehicle for a general critique of modernity. The skeptics describe the modern subject in what, for them, are strictly pejorative terms though such characteristics might commonly be considered complimentary within a modern point of view. The skeptics report that the modern subject is a hardworking, personally disciplined, and responsible personality. S/he is constrained by "effort" and has a self-image of "trying hard" and doing his/her "best." S/he has no personal idiosyncrasies, or at least s/he does not dwell on such issues. S/he plans ahead, is organized, and defers gratification. The modern subject may become committed to political projects and work for goals of an ideological character. S/he may believe in free will and personal autonomy, but s/he will follow majority opinion (or the party line) once the vote has been taken and a decision is made. The modern subject is, in other words, willing to subordinate her/his own interests for the good of the collective. S/he respects rational rules, the general will, social conventions, fixed standards that seem fair. S/he searches, in good faith, for truth and expects that ultimately such a quest will not be fruitless. This means the modern subject has confidence in reason, rationality, and science and puts all these ahead of emotion. S/he is optimistic about the future of mankind and the possibility of progress (Lipovetsky 1983). S/he claims to be a knowledgeable human agent, and s/he has a distinct, set personal identity.

The skeptics are quite critical of the modern subject. They understand him/her to be "puritanical" and overly preoccupied with "self-authentica-

---

[1] If the skeptics appear to crush "the individual beneath the yoke of the tyranny of language," as we shall discuss in Chapter 7, then they empower the post-modern individual to turn this around and "to tyrannize language by freely interpreting words and making it what they will" (Schwartz 1990: 38).

tion." S/he pursues a "righteous life" of "self-denial" (Sennett 1977). They object to the philosophy, the knowledge claims, the action orientation of this particular subject-form, so characteristically a product of modernity itself and so deeply at odds with the post-modern view of the world. As we will see, some skeptics endorse a specific individual—the post-modern individual—as an alternative to the modern subject.

The affirmatives' understanding of the subject is neither unified nor entirely coherent. Some affirmatives give no special priority to the subject at all but rather look to a broader frame of reference; they focus on nature at the center. Others are quite sympathetic to a human-centered post-modernism, and they applaud the return of the subject in a new form, described below. Critics argue that this return of the subject is merely an effort to salvage some aspects of the humanist tradition. But the affirmatives consider it to be a re-positioning rather than a simple re-cycling of the modern subject.

1. Precursors and Antecedents: Origins of Post-Modern Anti-Subject Stance

The skeptical post-modern opposition to the subject is not entirely original. Two sources, Freud (Blonsky 1985: 264–65) and Nietzsche (Booth 1985; Miller 1981), are particularly important. Many post-modernist theorists, including Foucault and Derrida, were influenced in developing their own opposition to the subject by the philosophical writings of Freud and Nietzsche.

Nietzsche questioned the existence of a thinking, feeling subject who reasons logically and causally. He disputed the validity of the "fixed, substantial, selfhood" (Miller 1981: 247, 258). He discussed the subject as self-deceptive, lacking in consciousness, willful, vengeful, and power-seeking (Nietzsche 1979: 79–97) and as manifesting a "repressed, nihilistic will to power" (Booth 1985, 132–33). In the end Nietzsche proposed that the subject is a fiction (Laffey 1987: 93), a view that is central to his "end of man" philosophy (Schrift 1988b: 131–34). Anticipating the post-modern death of the subject, he performed "a wholescale [sic] dissolution of the idea of self, character or subject." Nietzsche's complaint about humanism in his own day included its association with the subject, Christianity, and transcendence. He saw the subject as one of the "ruses by which decadence has attempted to stifle the innocent spontaneity of strength." The subject imposes the "ideal of Being on the fact of becoming" (Booth 1985: 132–33).

Freud also questioned the status of a coherent, integrated, unified, modern subject. He eliminated the self-conscious subject and substituted a decentered, fragmented, and heterogeneous subject who was often unaware of his/her unconscious (Flax 1990: 59). His was not a "knowing" subject but rather a psychoanalytic subject better characterized by multiplicity, disunity, and self-deception than anything else. Post-modernists have been quick to employ Freud's view of individuals (as irrational and incapable of objective reasoned argument) to support their own parallel conclusions about the subject. But there are limits to the support Freud offers the post-modernists. He would never have abandoned the subject completely.[2] Neither did he repudiate the Enlightenment, science, material reality, or cease to believe in the liberating capacity of rational reflection (Flax 1990: 53–55, 208, 218, 228; Schwartz 1990).

In announcing the death of the subject the skeptics are also influenced by more recent structural precursors in literature and the humanities. For the structuralists, relinquishing the subject meant reducing the role of individuals and character development in literature. Subjects were stripped of any real identity, and they became mere codes or the fleeting, illusory product of codes. Structuralist fiction, then, is not concerned with "real" people but rather with the "effects produced by the semantic code through its naming of qualities, which are then given an appearance of individuality and reality through the attribution of a proper name" (Jefferson 1982: 103). Similarly, characters and character development in post-modern novels, plays, and poetry, at least in theory, do not count for much.

Post-modernists in the humanities followed the lead of the structuralists. There are no long character descriptions in post-modern literature. We are not told about a specific individual having a certain color hair and being of large or small stature. Post-modern literature is not about individuals in the sense of focus or form. As Umberto Eco puts it in *The Name of the Rose*, "In the pages to follow I shall not indulge in descriptions of persons . . . as nothing is more fleeting than external form, which withers and alters like the flowers of the field at the appearance of autumn" (Eco 1980: 7).

Where post-modern authors in the humanities retain the subject, s/he is conscious, aware of his or her "own fictionality." Such subjects misbehave in a comic fashion. They refuse to hear the author's voice or to recognize his/her authority. These subject-characters try their best to evade, defy, or resist their author. They do what their author does not intend or may even prohibit. Sometimes these subjects express regret and pain at being written into a text (McHale 1987: 120–23)!

Structuralism prepared the way for the death of the subject, just as it had for the demise of the author, in not only the humanities but also the social

---

[2] Jacques Laçan inspires post-modern psychology, but he retains the subject, probably because of "his prior philosophical formation, essentially Hegelian rather than Nietzschean or Heideggerien" (Anderson 1984: 55).

sciences. Structuralists argued that the subject is a mystification because s/he is presumed to be an agent independent of social relations. Structuralists initiated the trend away from the author/subject by deemphasizing the individual and focusing on larger structures, on the formal laws of a system's functioning, on the linguistic construction of these structures, on the symbolic meaning they carry, and/or on change as manifest in structural transformations. Structuralism and systems analysis, then, deny the possibility of a subject with any personal capacity to maintain or change social relations (Althusser 1971: 160). The subject was a "missing person" in the structuralist tradition. Lévi-Strauss, for example, suggested that the ultimate goal of his own research was not "to constitute man but to dissolve him" (Lévi-Strauss 1966: 247–55) and post-modernists agree.[3]

The post-modernist social scientists, therefore, were predisposed to examine society without subjects or individuals. Subjects get lost in the flood of structures that overpower the individual. The absence of the structuralist subject conditioned post-modern social scientists to the idea that individual subjects were not the building blocks of social processes. The structuralist view encouraged them to question the efficacy of human beings as agents with the power to determine the conditions around them or to effect political outcomes. "Human agents act in a world constituted by large-scale social structures that are not the products of anyone's plan or intention" (Ball 1987: 7). Structuralists defined structures as beyond the reach of human intervention, and post-modernism, especially in its skeptical forms, does the same.

2. Skeptical Post-Modernist Opposition to the Modern Subject

The skeptical post-modernists oppose the modern subject for at least three reasons. First, s/he is an invention of modernity. Second, any focus on the subject assumes a humanist philosophy with which the post-modernists disagree. Third, the subject automatically requires an object, and post-modernists renounce the object-subject dichotomy.

a. The Subject is a Symbol of Modernity

Skeptical post-modernists associate the subject focus with modernity and modern values, and this itself is sufficient reason to treat it with suspicion.

---

[3] While structuralists prepared the way for a subjectless post-modern social science, postmodernists push the point further; they employ the death of the subject as a device for removing the constraint of science, reason, and rationality.

They argue that the subject is an invention of modern society, a child of the Enlightenment and rationalism (Wellmer 1985: 349; Derrida 1978). As modern science replaced religion, the rational individual (the modern subject) supplanted God. Modern concepts, whether scientific (external reality, theory, causality, scientific observation) or political ("politics of rights," democratic representation, emancipation, and liberation), assume an independent subject (Hawkesworth 1989); all are "posited on the positing of the ego" (Miller 1981: 261). Cancelling the subject simultaneously banishes all the objectionable modern concepts associated with it. For example, without a subject the importance Marxists, Liberals, or others attach to the modern categories of position, group, person, or class is meaningless, and power is dispersed in intertextuality (Henriques et al. 1984). Eliminate the subject, and, as with the author, the tools central to modern inquiry such as causality and agency vanish. In addition, denying the subject affirms post-modern pessimism as to the efficacy of human intervention, human design, rationality, and reason in the modern world because the subject is essential to each (Wellmer 1985: 346).

The skeptical post-modernists are critical of the central role the subject holds throughout the social sciences. For example, the skeptics criticize mainstream political scientists for assuming that the subject is the center, a "sovereign," the "hero" of analysis, an individual "possessing unparalleled powers of clairvoyance affording direct apprehension of external and internal reality" (Hawkesworth 1989: 551). Post-modern political scientists reject this, arguing that subjects are actually "contingent effects" of language or political activity in a particular historical context (Ashley 1988: 94). They also argue that individuals have little opportunity to create or modify those forces that control them; and political science would be more interesting without the modern subject (Ashley 1989a; Ashley and Walker 1990a: 261–62).

b. The Subject Is Humanist

Skeptical post-modernists reject the subject because it is central to humanism, and humanism has failed them in a number of ways. They considered humanism a logocentric meta-narrative, seeking to provide answers based only on its own unquestioned, internally validated, fixed frame of reference. It propels the human subject to the center (Hoy 1985a: 46–49) and implies "man as master of the universe, dominating, controlling, deciding" (Vattimo 1988). Post-modernists charge that humanism assumes an almost metaphysical presence or essence of "man." It fraudulently underscores the individual as a potentially effective, rational agent. Humanists are said to be naively optimistic about the nature of humankind, the potential for improvement in the human condition, and the scope of human accomplishments. A post-modern view of human nature disallows these orientations and the moral good/bad hierarchy they imply.

The skeptics argue that humanism is hypocritical in its emphasis on the dignity of human beings and the value of the individual. They are disappointed by humanist philosophy and practice and find them "oppressive," and the subject, by association, stands condemned (Kellner 1987: 1). Although claiming to seek justice and equality, they argue, humanism has been employed by liberal society to legitimate injustice and inequality. It has been "both a disguise for and a manifestation of social privilege; it has also been almost exclusively male-centered." They also point to the discrepancy between the stated goals and the actual practice of humanism. While claiming to better the human condition, the skeptics argue, humanism has misled humankind into Marxism, National Socialism, and Stalinism (Foucault 1987: 168–69; Touraine 1988a, 1988b).[4] It certainly "no more worked as an effective shield against Fascism than did the Christian Churches" (Laffey 1987: 89–90).

Humanism is a complex phenomenon, and, although it takes on many different, sometimes overlapping, often contradictory forms, the skeptical post-modernists have serious reservations about all of them because each requires a subject and attributes special attention to human beings, individuals. Some examples help to illustrate this perspective. First, liberal humanism proposes to reward and encourage those who accept the modern challenge of competition and achievement, but humanists also view society as responsible for providing the basic necessities for those who try but fail in their efforts. This responsibility extends, in the case of the liberal welfare state, even to those who do not appear to be trying very hard. Humanists assume that modern subjects have differing abilities and can only ask that each human subject make his or her best effort, take full advantage of all opportunities for human development. Equality of opportunity exists in a world of unequal subjects. Second, what has been called "technical fix" humanism (Soper 1986: 14) expresses confidence in the powers of modern science to solve the problems of humanity. Technical fix brings in the subject, for example, in industrial relations; it advocates efficient management that employs the most technologically advanced equipment to increase productivity and improve the quality of life and general prosperity of each individual (subject) in the workplace and society. Third, "Enlightenment humanists" oppose the narrowness of church dogma and elevate humankind above the control of church authorities; thus, they combine atheism and a commitment to the search for truth through reason and rigorous inquiry. This Enlightenment project requires subjects to implement its design, to affirm its significance, and to confirm its successes. Finally, post-

---

[4] Some post-modernists assimilate Nazism and humanism. Nazism becomes humanist in the senses of having a "universal vocation" and attributing a special essence to Aryan man (Lacoue-Labarthe 1987; Ferry and Renaut 1988: 12, chap. 3).

modernists are equally unhappy with "Renaissance humanists" who argue not for modern science and technology or reason so much as for individual freedom and liberty, for the full development of each human being's (subject's) potential.

The skeptics contend that humanism has been used to justify Western superiority and cultural imperialism. Although bringing modern medicine to primitive people, for example, may have appeared altruistic, compassionate, "humanist" in design, it had the unintended disruptive consequences of introducing all the other aspects of modernity. It often resulted in loss of language and culture. Neo-colonialism was humanist in that it asserted a responsibility to educate primitive peoples, to teach them to read and write. But in most cases education translated into assimilation to the culture of the colonial power, teaching the reading and writing of a foreign language. Similarly, native people in America were moved to reservations because it was said they could not take care of themselves. But along with this "humanism" went a dramatic change in life-style, a decline of population, reduced pride in ethnic identity, and increased disease.

Post-modern social scientists argue that although humanists have criticized the abuses of positivism their critique was superficial, and therefore they are directly responsible for the undesirable results. For example, although the "humanist approach in race-relations" personalizes work relations, it also "unwittingly reproduces existing power relations" (Henriques et al. 1984: 13).

c. The Subject Implies an Object

The skeptical post-modernists contend that the modern subject automatically requires an object. Erasing the subject, then, also suspends any division of the world into subjects and objects. It explodes the object-subject dichotomy, thwarts the authority of the one over the other, suspends the arbitrary power relations associated with the subject category, and thus abolishes this implicit hierarchy. The epistemology and methodological dimensions of this matter are discussed in greater detail in Chapter 7, but the implications for the subject must be addressed immediately.

Post-modernism rejects the subject-object distinction of modern social science that designates the observer as subject and relegates those being studied to object status.[5] This implies unfair characterizations of the subject, the skeptics argue, as active and human, while the object is passive and

---

[5] Post-modernism suspends object and subject, so central to modern science, as separate knower and the known. Modern science retains the subject and object of inquiry even as it does away with "me," "I," "we," in professional communications. Post-modernists argue that this merely creates the illusion that there is no omnipotent narrator, as scientist, to give the illusion of objectivity (Richardson 1988: 203), when in actuality the researcher as subject is always present.

treated as a "thing" (object). Many affirmative post-modernists argue that scientific classification of humans leads to objectification. The existence of the subject implies one human being is under the control of another, dependent on the other; a social science researcher (subject) guides the students (objects) participating in an experiment, and the interviewer (subject) directs the respondents (objects) in filling out a questionnaire in a public opinion poll.[6]

For the affirmative post-modernists this subject-object distinction allows humans to be transformed into subjects in an unacceptable fashion, in ways that all involve, directly or indirectly, humiliation and oppression (Rabinow 1984: 7–10). This is not a simple mechanistic theory of rulers lording it over an oppressed underclass. Post-modernists suggest that the dichotomy itself promotes "dividing practices," encouraging people to see themselves as mere members of groups and to categorize themselves in a simplistic fashion. "Self-subjectification" results, and people actively define themselves as objects. The subject "is either divided inside himself or divided from others" (Foucault 1983b: 208–13).

Skeptical post-modernists also challenge the subject and what s/he produces in terms of knowledge and truth claims. Without a subject to announce logocentric meta-narratives, and without other humans with subject or object status to register recognition or approval, such devices are deprived of any voice, and theory cannot endure. This is consistent with post-modern skepticism about the possibility of theory altogether (this idea is discussed in Chapter 5).

3. Social Science without a Subject

Post-modernists in almost every field of the social sciences have been experimenting with a subjectless approach in their inquiries. The results vary from discipline to discipline. In general, reaction to the "death of the subject" has been far less enthusiastic in the social sciences than in the humanities.

[6] Subject and object are sometimes used in a contradictory and opposite fashion in psychology. The word subject can also refer to those participating in an experiment. Here the subject(ive), the person being studied, is assumed nonrational (relating to the inner, but active) while the object(ive), the researcher, is rational, distanced, and uninvolved. Consider another contrary example: Monarchs rule over subjects. In literature and language, however, the grammatical subject of a sentence is "active," and the object is "passive." R. W. Cox suggests a number of different and conflicting definitions are attributed to the subject. "I can think of (1) the Cartesian or Kantian mind through whose categories the world (supposed to be external) is perceived, i.e., the subject who is the basis for modern epistemology: (2) the maker of history (subject of history) as individual or social class; (3) the realm of feeling or emotion (subjectivity); (4) the subordinate person, e.g., subject of the monarch, and Foucault's condition of subjection or the subject as object" (personal correspondence, December 13, 1990).

In the field of psychology, post-modern psychologists seek to do away with the view of a rational, unified subject and to re-theorize "subjectivity" as multiple and contradictory, largely irrational. Some contend that discursive practices constitute or produce "subject positions" or "sites" rather than an individual, a "subject" as an agent. Psychoanalysis and certain subject-free readings of theorists such as Reich, Lacan, and Freud inform and encourage this process of de-centering the subject (Sheridan 1980: 93). Post-modernism dissolves the essential difference between I and me, between the analyst and the patient. The analyst is not detached, but rather is susceptible to being caught up in the figures of speech, of having his or her unconscious structured by the "text," just as the patient is caught up in his or her own fantasies (Kugler 1988). In addition, post-modern psychologists conclude that the subject is never "entirely accessible because it is buried so deeply in the unconscious" (Henriques et al. 1984: 225).

In sociology and anthropology the absence of the subject has been a burden. Bauman provides an example of a post-modern sociological approach without a subject (1989). George Marcus and Michael Fischer do the same for anthropology. But historically the subject has been central to many subfields in sociology, where methodologies such as the life history approach (Bertaux 1980, 1985), ethnomethodology, and symbolic interaction (the work of Harold Garfinkel and A. Cicourel) require it. For these sociologists, the subject should return fully developed. S/he is what s/he "thinks, says, and does." Behavior and meaning constitute a whole, gathered together around a specific person-subject without any preestablished categories (Rafie 1987). The same is true in modern anthropology, where so many believe that the very existence of the ethnographer implies a subject status. But some feel that to erase the distinction between the ethnographer and the subject being studied would be to do away with the field itself.

Post-modern political science has also sought to reach beyond the autonomous subject,[7] beyond relations between individuals or individual agents in an effort to provide new openings for creativity and innovation.[8] Post-

[7] As with other social sciences, a subjectless political science was not the unique innovation of post-modernism. For example, regime theory in international relations argues for the viability of a subjectless international relations (Kratochwil and Ruggie 1986: 764). It looks to the structure of international relations in specific thematic or content areas rather than to the role of formal manifest agencies and organizations staffed by visible individuals.

[8] Some post-modernists argue that the subject can be a source of deliberate misinformation and manipulation. For example, enemies, as subjects, are assumed threatening. They are employed to direct public attention from other matters or to "marshall support for a regime or a cause" (Edelman 1988: 66). Enemies "who are targets of the most intense animus may threaten no harm at all," and people who "demonstrably hurt others severely are often not defined or perceived as enemies." Much depends on "ideology or symbols" (Edelman 1988: 86, 91). The conclusion of these post-modernists is that political science would be better off without subjects.

modern political scientists doubt the adequacy of locating actors and people in structures. Rejecting the subject permits them to shift the focus of inquiry elsewhere, away from any of the multiplicity of forms the subject might take in this discipline, including "the possessive individual, the national state, the national community, the scientific man, the conscious proletariat, the father of the family, the feminine voice, the general will, immanent imperatives of humankind, the West, . . . God, King, phallus, or womb" (Ashley 1988: 93–94). Post-modern political scientists also call for a revision of the concept of the potential subject category of political leader. Language and social situation constitute the leader as well as the meaning of any text. Leaders are judged not to be acting as "persistent selves," not to be speaking for themselves, but rather as reflections of a situation they confront (Edelman 1988: 9). Neither can leaders be viewed as "originators" of political actions or political discourse or coherent policies. But it is hard to conceive of inquiry in the absence of the individual subject in some subfields of political science such as American government. Most, but certainly not all, quantitative research techniques posit the individual subject. Erasing the subject in these cases would cripple this subfield that is so dependent on the individual-specific data of survey research.

Women's studies reflect ambivalence about the death of the subject. Some feminists conclude that the anti-subject strand of post-modernism is "gender bound and biased" (Flax 1990: 225). The debate between the post-modernists and the feminists crosses every topic imaginable. Even feminists who are sympathetic to post-modernism argue that "postmodernist narratives about subjectivity are inadequate" (Flax 1990: 210). The demise of the subject may be interpreted as denying any special status to women's experiences. Deconstruction is said to "empty subjectivity of any possible meaning or content" (Flax 1990: 231). Post-modernism abolishes the subject at the very moment that women (and other marginal groups) for the first time in history are constituting themselves as empowered subjects (Hartsock 1987). If the subject has no voice, then there is no place in social science for special attention to a women's perspective.

Given the above examples it is hardly surprising that enthusiasm for a subject-absent social science has not been unanimous. Despite the structuralist precedent, there is a certain ambivalence about eliminating the subject in post-modern social sciences. Both skeptical and affirmative post-modernists have been obliged to take a second look, not readopting the subject so much as repositioning it. This trend is unusual because it originates in the social sciences rather than the humanities, which have been the major source of inspiration for post-modern social science. And so we see that some skeptics propose a substitute for the modern subject—the post-modern individual—while the affirmatives are more inclined to revise the modern subject by calling for its return in new and innovative forms. To these efforts we now turn.

4. The Post-Modern Individual: The Skeptic's Alternative to the Modern Subject

Some skeptical post-modernists argue that the modern subject has little relevance in a post-modern world but that there is a central role for the post-modern individual if it is not humanist and if it does not imply that people are free, conscious, self-determining human beings.[9] These post-modernists seek not to resurrect the modern subject but rather to replace it with another character or *personage* in a different form. Inventing the post-modern individual will not be easy. It is a delicate task because it must be accomplished within an anti-humanist philosophy and without resurrecting the object, the alienating shadow that so burdens the modern subject. The skeptic's post-modern individual will have an almost anonymous existence. S/he will be a person but will not be held accountable for events, actions, outcomes; nor will s/he be the author of "caring" relationships (humanist) or creative individualism. S/he will be so independent of all identifiable truth-seeking perspectives that s/he is, in short, no subject at all!

The invention of the post-modern individual provides a means for post-modernists to abandon the subject while retaining an individualist perspective; but to do this the meaning of subject and individual in the social sciences must be kept analytically separate (see Lipovetsky 1983). This device makes it possible to announce that the modern subject is dead even as the post-modern individual is very much alive (Ferry and Renaut 1990: 66–67).[10]

The post-modern individual is relaxed and flexible, oriented toward feelings and emotions, interiorization, and holding a "be-yourself" attitude. S/he is an active human being constituting his/her own social reality, pursuing a personal quest for meaning but making no truth claims for what results. S/he looks to fantasy, humor, the culture of desire, and immediate gratification. Preferring the temporary over the permanent, s/he is contented with a "live and let live" (in the present) attitude. More comfortable with the spontaneous than the planned, the post-modern individual is also

[9] See Ferry and Renaut (1988: 98–103) for an excellent synthesis of Lipovetsky's (1983) view of the rise of the post-modern individual and (Ferry and Renaut 1990: chap. 7) for a review of the "return of the subject."

[10] Ferry and Renaut argue that in France the post-modern individual emerged as a philosophical and intellectual construct in the 1960s and this set the stage for the rest of the twentieth century (1990: 64–67).

fascinated with tradition, the antiquated (the past in general), the exotic, the sacred, the unusual, and the place of the local rather than the general or the universal. Post-modern individuals are concerned with their own lives, their particular personal satisfaction, and self-promotion. Less concerned with old loyalties and modern affiliations such as marriage, family, church, and nation, they are more oriented toward their own needs.

The post-modern individual, shying away from collective affiliation and communal responsibility in modern terms, considers them a hindrance to personal development and a threat to privacy (Bauman 1987). Modern community is said to be oppressive; it demands intimacy, giving, self-sacrifice, and mutual service. Inasmuch as it is "reasonable," it also is "domineering and humiliating." Post-modern community is possible, but it must be based in "community without unity" (Corlett 1989: 6–7). Only in this condition can it be considered acceptable to the post-modern individual.

The post-modern individual is characterized by an absence of strong singular identity. This step-child of Freud, a subject characterized by fragmentation, lacks much self-awareness and makes no claim of self-consciousness. S/he is a floating individual with no distinct reference points or parameters (Lipovetsky 1983: 60, 80, 125). What the modern subject characterized as indifference, the post-modern individual calls tolerance. The modern subject may be politically conscious, but the post-modern individual is self-conscious. The post-modern individual favors dispersion over concentration, the unrehearsed rather than the carefully organized. S/he emphasizes choice, free expression, individual participation, private autonomy, personal liberation, without any need of universalistic claims or ideological consistency. The post-modern individual seeks freedom (from coercion by others) and liberation (from self-denial). S/he relinquishes all normative assumptions, any possibility that one value or moral norm can ever be demonstrated to be better than any other. The post-modern individual is wary of general rules, comprehensive norms, hegemonic systems of thought.

Post-modern individuals are comfortable with personalized politics. These views are characteristically free of totalizing global projects such as those of socialism. They are skeptical about the intentions and motivations of committed activists. Despite a general political disaffection, the post-modern individual may from time to time affirm struggles against the state and the system. S/he is open to participation and recruitment in diverse and contradictory causes and social movements with fleeting existences. This is not surprising because the post-modern individual is comfortable with multiple realities, without requiring coherence (Lipovetsky 1983). And this makes sense given the post-modern individual's fluctuating, ever-changing personal identity.

What future awaits the post-modern individual? There are good reasons to worry about him/her. If the post-modern individual understands being to be only "scattered traces and fragments," or a "fading signal from the past" (Vattimo 1988), then s/he has only an "anonymous" existence, no positive identity of any substantive character (Megill 1985: 203), along the lines modernity encouraged. S/he is rather the disintegrating patchwork of a *persona*, with a disparate personality and a potentially confused identity. S/he submits to a multitude of incompatible juxtaposed logics, all in perpetual movement without possibility of permanent resolution or reconciliation. In a post-modern context no new integrated personal styles are conceivable. Everything has "already been invented"; all one can do is to imitate (Jameson 1983: 114–15). In the extreme the post-modern individual may succumb to questionable, perhaps darker, realms of thought and action. In some cases s/he tends to excessive self-criticism, cynicism, indifference, narcissism, hedonism, apathy, egotism, anti-intellectualism (Agger 1990: 11; Hassan 1987: 17). The views of the post-modern individual are likely neither to lead to a post-modern society of innovative production nor to engender sustained or contained economic growth. And that is no surprise because these are not post-modern priorities.

Can the subject be reintegrated into post-modern social science without introducing serious contradictions and undermining the internal consistency of post-modernism itself? As indicated by the post-modern objections to the subject outlined at the beginning of this chapter, it would be very difficult to reconcile the return of the modern subject to post-modernism. But integrating the post-modern individual has far fewer consequences and presents less of a threat to the intellectual integrity of skeptical post-modernism.

The presence of the post-modern individual is compatible with a post-modern focus in a number of ways. This individual confirms post-modernism's emphasis on phenomena at the margins because s/he is often a member of the various groups that populate the margins. S/he is nonjudgmental rather than dogmatic. The same tenor assures that the post-modern individual can readily be reconciled with post-modern epistemology. S/he relinquishes the need either to base attitudes or action on reason or to lay claim to truth. S/he does not attempt to arbitrate among the various coexisting multiple views of reality. The post-modern individual calls for the end of certitude, reasoned argument, modern rationality, objective modern science, law grounded on jurisprudence, and art subject to evaluation on the basis of standard criteria.

The return of the subject in the form of the post-modern individual is consistent with post-modernism's anti-humanism. The post-modern individual is shaped by the contemporary culture (Lyotard 1984). S/he has little affection for a humanist stance, for any belief in the idea of progress, for any need to contribute to society. The post-modern individual repudiates the responsibility imposed by humanism, that each modern subject carries on his/her shoulders. S/he adopts a post-modern anti-causal point of view because s/he has no desire to assume responsibility or insist on his/her role as agent. The end of the twentieth century is a time when it is more popular, perhaps even more reasonable, to deny personal responsibility. The political landscape includes world wars, environmental disasters, the Holocaust, Vietnam, the rise of religious fundamentalism, worldwide poverty, and unanticipated famine. In the absence of cause and effect, the post-modern individual cannot be held personally accountable because these things "just happen."

The post-modern individual resolves certain potential contradictions within skeptical post-modern analysis.[11] First, we have seen that post-modernism gives priority to readers over authors, expanding their freedom to interpret texts. This appears contrary to the post-modernists' call for an end to the subject, for at first glance the reader certainly appears to be a person, a subject. How then is it possible to talk about the death of the subject and elevate the reader at the same time? The contradiction is removed if the reader is understood to be a post-modern individual, not a subject in search of authority. The reader, defined as a post-modern individual, would willingly accord the freedom of interpretation that a post-modern reading requires. Second, the death of the subject seems to abolish modern individual identity, for if the subject no longer exists, it could then be argued that individualism is a theoretical impossibility. The end of the subject has even been interpreted to indicate post-modern "selflessness." But this would be too simple, for the post-modern age is not one of self-sacrifice; and some even characterize it as the "Golden Age of the individual" (Lipovetsky 1983; Hassan 1987: 17). The invention of a post-modern individual in a subjectless social science resolves, at least in part, the apparent contradiction between the skeptical post-modernists' anti-subject stance and their sympathy for individual rights and liberties. Inconsistency disappears if the responsible, self-sacrificing, collectivity-oriented, modern subject is distinguished from and replaced by the self-centered, post-modern individual. Individualism may then still exist in the absence of a modern subject.

The invention of the post-modern individual does not quiet all modern social scientists' objections about the absent subject. S/he is certainly more congenial to the skeptical post-modernists than to the affirmative post-modernists. Many affirmatives offer another, alternative response to the demise of the conventional modern subject, one many social scientists find more appealing.

---

[11] This should not be taken to mean that all skeptical post-modernists will embrace the post-modern individual. S/he remains, after all, an individual, and even if her/his views are uniquely appropriate for the post-modern age, many will remain uncomfortable with him/her.

5. Affirmative Post-Modernists Propose the Return of the Subject

There are indications that at least in the social sciences the death penalty may be too extreme a punishment for the subject. If there has been a period of "temporary death of the subject," then that interval is coming to an end (Agger 1990: 20),[12] and support for a radically more lenient attitude is on the rise, particularly among affirmative post-modernists who oppose the total destruction of the voluntary, meaningful, and communal subject identity.

Some of these post-modernists call for a return of the subject as a person and a renewed recognition of the subject in society. They assert that the return of the subject is not inconsistent with the other intellectual orientations of post-modernism. Their goal is not to re-install the subject-object distinction, to reaffirm humanism,[13] or to revitalize modernism. They argue that giving attention to either the marginal and excluded or to the new social movements is not necessarily incompatible with the subject status. In fact, as will be discussed in Chapter 8, the affirmative subject may be necessary to assure the "resistance" required by the new post-modern social movements. Why, they ask, cannot post-modernists be dubious about theory (see Chapter 5) and retain a subject who does not seek to validate it? Why cannot a renewed subject reject logocentric, totalistic explanations? Would it incur serious epistemological or methodological pain or contradiction to bring back the subject?

If a post-modern subject returns as the affirmatives suggest, it will not be the same subject who was banished, and s/he will not take on a single form or personality. The returning subject will not be "a conscious, purposeful and feeling individual." S/he will be a decentered subject, an "emergent" subject, unrecognizable by the modernists, empiricists, and positivists. S/he will be a post-modern subject with a new nonidentity, focused not on the "Great Men" of history, but rather, on daily life at the margins. This subject will reject total explanations and the logocentric point of view that implies a unified frame of reference, but s/he need not oppose all dimensions of humanism (Megill 1985: 203).

Reviewing a number of efforts to revitalize the subject in the social sci-

---

[12] Agger suggests a post-modern moratorium on the subject is necessary to provide a period to "re-conceive of politics in a way that we can formulate and enact new modes of opposition and reconstruction . . . rethink the modalities of personal and public life in an energizing way" (Agger 1990: 20). It is, of course, too soon to evaluate whether his aspirations have been realized, but the return of the subject is certainly underway.

[13] Some post-modernists in the social sciences are either refugees from the 1960s New Left or disillusioned Marxists. This group is particularly uncomfortable with anti-humanism and the denial of the subject.

ences illustrates these points and suggests that this movement is recent in origin and broad based in orientation. Not all efforts to re-invent the subject considered here are synonymous with affirmative post-modern approaches. Some attempts to formulate a new and innovative subject focus, such as those of Pierre Bourdieu and Alain Touraine, may be motivated more by their discontent with structuralism's neglect of the subject than with any need to make post-modernism more viable. Their work is reviewed because, whatever their intentions, they have had an important impact on those more closely associated with an affirmative post-modernism.

There is a trend toward a return to the politically involved subject as well, not just among political scientists but throughout the social sciences. Richard Ashley's post-modern subject is one such "emergent" subject, the consequences of the "political struggle among concepts, themes, interpretations, and modes of practice." This subject can be "identified" only in "the precarious balancing and dispersal of plural interpretive elements resulting from the continuing strategic interplay of multiple alien forms" (Ashley 1987: 410). Alain Touraine speaks along the same lines for the revival of the subject based on "resistance" in a world where autonomous self-definition apart from society has become very difficult. His subject struggles for autonomy and seeks to construct a new identity by appealing to life, personal freedom, and creativity. His activist subject, an actor—at once sexual, emotional, political, and spiritual—seeks freedom from "both transcendental principles and community rules" (Touraine 1988a: 38–41; 1988b). This new subject is not a "modern" subject in search of conquest. On the defensive, s/he looks rather for self-defined affirmation apart from any vast global project or modern collective. Such subjects take part in fluid coalitions, temporary issue-oriented alliances that unite rich and poor, men and women, and diverse ethnic groups. Manfred Frank argues that the study of process requires the return of the self-conscious subject to social analysis. His subject, belonging to society, is immersed in broad-gauged structures of shared spontaneous consciousness (Frank 1988).

Fred Dallmayr seeks to go beyond the domineering individual (subject) who looks to mastery and submission. He substitutes a vision of an "open-ended, non-possessive individuality" capable of communalism, association, community, anticipative-emancipatory practice. At the same time his new subject is not the reasoning humanistic citizen of the Enlightenment (Dallmayr 1987).

Julia Kristeva does not deny the subject, but she also theorizes it as a "subject-in-process" emerging from her psychoanalytic practice, where subject as either analyst or patient is "real and necessary." In the psychoanalytic situation interpretation itself leads to a subject (Kristeva 1986: chap. 3). Kristeva turns the modern subject into what she calls "a work in progress," a "speaking subject," both "imagination and imaginary." In this form the subject offers a basis for identity (Kristeva 1974: 142–45; Moi 1988).

In the mid-1980s Anthony Giddens formulated "structuration" analysis, which sought to reconcile the subject as agent with the limitations modern structuralism places on this subject role to constrain an action. Giddens argues for "decentering" the subject but not for its "evaporation." Human beings employ language to communicate. Subjects, as agents, affect structure, but no action by an agent is meaningful in the absence of structure. The two are said to be mutually constitutive. This, we might say, is a call for the half-return of the subject (Giddens 1984). In 1990 Giddens went further by arguing that active processes of reflective self-identity are possible today.[14] He proposes a subject who looks for "freedom to" have a fulfilling and satisfying life rather than "freedom from" inequality or servitude. This subject does not conceptualize life as a zero-sum game where my gain is your loss. It is rather a subject-appropriate post-scarcity world where "self-actuation," so fundamental to self-identity, is possible without asking anyone else to bear the cost (1990: 150, 155–57). Sociologists Wood and Zurcher undertake a more empirical analysis to establish the transition in self-concept associated with post-modernism. They see the new post-modern subject as one in touch with "impulse and process" rather than as an "institutional end-product" (Wood and Zurcher 1988).

The subject returns via the conceptual grounding provided by Pierre Bourdieu's "habitus" whether this is his intention or not. Habitus, a summary term, refers to the cumulative, durable totality of cultural and personal experiences that each human being carries around as a result of life experiences (speech, mannerism, stye of dress, table etiquette, posture, body shape). All these are found to have an impact on how one is perceived, on the patterns of interaction involving others, and on the formation of the parameters that govern social outcomes. Habitus, a subject-specific concept, cannot be structuralized or aggregated: it is unique to each individual; it requires a specific, noncollective subject. This concept encourages and transforms the object of research and directs it toward a renewed subject. Although it is empirical, it defies scientific generalization and is therefore anti-positivist or post-positivist. Nevertheless, the habitus of the specifically produced subject is the focus of research (Bourdieu 1984: 179, 191, 210; see also Angenot 1984: 21).

David Griffin calls for a return of the subject and at the same time strives to retain the categories of object and subject. He does this by denying the power differences that separate them and make them objectionable to post-

---

[14] He refers to the present as "radical modernity" rather than post-modernity.

modernists. He says subjects and objects "are not different in kind, merely different in time." These categories are not enduring but rather in flux. Objects can affect subjects. "The very nature of a subject, as a momentary experiencing event, is to prehend or receive feelings from previous events into itself as the basis for its own self-creation in time" (Griffin 1988b: 155). Defined in this way, Griffin concludes, the subject returns in an acceptable guise and can be sustained within a post-modern approach. Post-modern anthropologists reason along the same lines as they elevate the subject to be studied to a position of equality with the ethnographer and thus overcome object-subject power differentials. They conclude that a renewed subject develops if there is reciprocity between the informant and the ethnographer (Clifford 1988: chap. 2; Strathern 1987).[15]

6. Conclusion and Summary

The subject generates considerable debate within post-modernism, and in the end her/his status remains an unsettled question, any final identity an unknown dimension. The death of the subject has not taken hold in the social sciences as it did in the humanities. Post-modernists generally reject the modern subject, but the viability of a subjectless social science remains contested. Skeptical post-modernists are anti-humanist, and although they speak of the death of the subject, some of them offer the post-modern individual as an appropriate substitute. The affirmative post-modernists compromise and suggest a number of ways to re-position the subject. The

[15] Anne Norton, Mary Hawkesworth, Michael Gibbons, and Michel Foucault offer other forms of a renewed subject that resemble the skeptics' post-modern individual more than the affirmatives' returning post-modern subject. Gibbons's subject is not "a reflection of correspondence or representation" of individual human desires, beliefs, and feelings vis-à-vis some objective reality. The subject is rather the absence of such correspondence. It is apparent in self-reflection and the act of choosing and cultivating life-styles, in self-clarification, and in the articulation of self (Gibbons 1987: 161). Norton's subject returns grounding identity on the difference between self and polity, body and mind, friends and enemies. She is indebted to Nietzsche, Freud, and Melanie Klein for insights into the importance of violence in establishing whatever self-definition exists. In the end Norton is ambivalent as to any final personal definition as befits the post-modern era (Norton 1988: 6–7). In a similar vein Hawkesworth develops the subject as an "unstable self, a constellation of unconscious desires, fears, phobias, and conflicting linguistic, social, and political forces" (1989). Foucault campaigned against any special status for the human individual for decades, but he expressed a nostalgia for the subject in his later writings; this represents a major revision in his thinking. He resurrected the subject in terms of "bodies and pleasures," as the "object of an aesthetic attitude" to spontaneity and expressiveness. He applauded the struggle against "subject status," oppression, humiliation, and "subjection" (Foucault 1983b: 207–9). Although all these authors refer to a subject, the substance of what they are talking about is closer to the skeptics' post-modern individual than to the affirmatives' post-modern subject.

"return of the subject" movement both inside and outside the ranks of the post-modernists signals that the elimination of the subject is, possibly, unnecessary. It is a means of retaining the subject in new and novel forms while at the same time avoiding those aspects of the modern subject that the post-modernists find most objectionable.

4

HUMBLING HISTORY, TRANSFORMING TIME, AND GARBLING GEOGRAPHY (SPACE)

History is the Western myth.
(Descombes 1980: 110)

If only art could accomplish the magic act of its own
disappearance! But it continues to make believe it is
disappearing when it is already gone.
(Baudrillard in Tomkins 1988: 241)

POST-MODERNISTS have developed a unique counterintuitive view of time, geography or space, and history, all of which are re-defined and reconstituted in a mutually reinforcing, if not entirely unified, perspective.[1] They question almost everything that is taken for granted about these concepts: a knowledge of history is essential for com-prehending the present; time is linear; and space is fixed, constant, mea-surable. Post-modernism reverses the priority accorded to these terms by calling for more attention to time and space and less to history. Post-mod-ernists propose modifications they consider audacious and daring for all these dimensions. But their critics deem post-modern versions of time, space, and history frivolous and nonsensical. In this chapter I first examine post-modernist complaints about modern notions of space, time, and his-tory. Next I explore parallels between post-modern views and those of the End of History philosophy and the New History movement. I then look at post-modernist proposals for re-conceptualizing modern conceptions of time, space, and history.

1. Conventional History—Hopelessly Modern

History is both a discipline and an approach to many other social science fields. Thus, most of what is said here about history is equally relevant for the historical approaches to sociology, political science, psychology, and the other social sciences. Although an academic discipline, history falls be-

[1] The arrangement of time, space, geography, and history employed here is not the only one possible. Time and history are sometimes grouped together by post-modernists as are geography and space (Dear 1986; 1988; 1989).

tween the humanities and social sciences; the post-modern critique of history applies no matter where one chooses to locate it.

Post-modernism is only one of a number of efforts to challenge conventional views of history. Most of these challenges overlap; nearly all assume a monolithic, unified, singular, "old" history that post-modernists criticize as inadequate (Scott 1989). Generally they question (1) the idea that there is a real, knowable past, a record of evolutionary progress of human ideas, institutions, or actions,[2] (2) the view that historians should be objective, (3) that reason enables historians to explain the past, and (4) that the role of history is to interpret and transmit human cultural and intellectual heritage from generation to generation. Thus, besides post-modernism, the New History movement and the End-of-History philosophy are important centers of opposition to conventional history. We will see that the skeptical post-modernists have much in common with the End-of-History movement, whereas the affirmatives are closer to the New History current.

a. The Skeptical Post-Modernists on History

The skeptical post-modernists criticize conventional history and relegate it to a peripheral role in the larger scope of human affairs. They attribute little importance to history for its own sake: as witness to continuity, as testimony to the idea of progress, as the search for origins, or as evidence of direct causal understanding (Baudrillard 1983a; Derrida 1976). Nor do these post-modernists view history as periods of time that unfold with regularity, that can be isolated, abstracted, represented, and described in terms of essential characteristics (Benhabib 1984: 104). They reject history as reasoned analysis focused on the particular or the general because both assume "reality, identity, and truth" (Foucault 1977: 151). They are especially critical of humanist history, that is, the view that human agents form the individual and collective experiences of societies, that human intervention can direct the course of history.

Skeptical post-modernists can hardly be called history-friendly. They contend that history is logocentric, a source of myth, ideology, and prejudice, a method assuming closure. History privileges "one or another subject as the sovereign center, the ultimate origin and register of truth and meaning, in whose terms all else must be interpreted" (Ashley 1989ab: 282). History is a creature of the modern Western nations; as such it is said to "oppress" Third World peoples and those from other cultures.[3] History has no reality. It is either considered indeterminate (Himmelfarb 1989a) or determined by "catastrophe," "broken off" from the present. It repre-

[2] Progress in history is objectionable to the post-modernists because it implies a "pregiven goal toward which Man is steadily moving" (Flax 1990: 33).

[3] Salaman Rushdie (1989: 210) presents a fictional but revealing example of Third World discourse on this point.

sents the "loss of eternity" (Kamper and Wulf 1989). The skeptics argue that history is exhausted, and humankind is at the present moment striving actively to forget the past, to go beyond history, beyond any universal basis for knowledge. According to this analysis, as Jean Baudrillard argues, "everything has already happened . . . ; nothing new can occur." It is no surprise, then, that he and many other skeptics ask, Why history? (1983a, 1983b).

The skeptics' critique of history applies to all its various contemporary forms. They reject history as *longue durée* (slow time—the structuralists' long-term view of history) (Braudel 1972: 20–21) because it claims to discover a set of timeless relations existing independent of everything else. History, in this case, is a theory that registers "an abstract logical truth characteristic of a social whole." It is assumed, the skeptics argue, to be a search for "deep, enduring, and autonomous structures"; it is an effort to establish a broad, totalizing, universalistic explanation linked to a single theme or essence. It assumes a material world, an external reality unappropriated by the cultural and aesthetic, where "some meanings at least might be initiated directly from nature" (Clark 1985: 192). The skeptics also criticize *evenementielle* history (instantaneous time—the analysis of fixed events) (Braudel, 1972: 20–21) because it emphasizes history as dramatic events, event-bound practices, important individuals ("great men"), diplomats, heads of state, battles, dates, wars, and treaties. In this form history claims to be empirically grounded, objective and scientific. From the postmodern point of view it fraudulently appears to recapture and represent the past. Nor do the skeptics accept historical contextualization, an approach assuming that although it is impossible to empirically reconstitute historical events, ideas, and institutions, one can meaningfully examine them on their own terms in their own specific historical setting (Hollinger 1989: 618). The skeptics are equally dubious about historical theories of revolution, social change, and progress (Kellner 1989b: 212).

For skeptical post-modernists, history, if it exists at all, is a humble discipline, dependent on the present, without any integrity of its own. The contemporary is the time frame that counts most; we live in the present-as-text, in a fragmented "series of perpetual presents" (Jameson 1983: 125), where the future is only an "anticipated presence and the past a former presence" (Culler 1979: 162). History is only important to the extent that its traces have an impact on the contemporary, and even then, those traces are complex and intertextual. We are told that it is sufficient to let "the present interrogate the past" (Harlan 1989: 608).[4]

What role, then, is left for history? Some skeptics, inspired by post-mod-

---

[4] This is consistent with the skeptics' understanding of social phenomena in terms of language and discourse. The skeptics, however, are criticized for replacing history with "irregularly emerging and disappearing islands of discourse" (Habermas 1987a: 251).

ern eclecticism in the humanities, try to select and recycle previous notions of history, and in so doing they refuse to attribute any special value to the "new." They manifest a deep respect for the primitive and an attraction to tradition. In this sense one might say that post-modernism "recollects" (Vattimo 1988: chap. 6).

The skeptical post-modernists, such as Vattimo (1988), are not alone in arguing for the end of an identifiable direction to history. The End-of-History, post-history, or post-histoire movement concur (Baudrillard 1983a, 1983b, 1989b; Kellner 1989b: 212). The End of History means an end of the idea of progress, an end "to the evolution of human thought about . . . first principles." Fukuyama, one contemporary End-of-History theorist, suggests that in the future it will "be impossible to state a philosophical proposition" that is both "true and new" (Fukuyama 1989–90: 223). As he presents it, the End of History means the triumph of Western ideas, liberal pluralist democracy, consumer society, the "universal, homogeneous state" and the defeat of all other ideologies including communism and fascism. The skeptical post-modernists would disagree with him on this point. For the skeptics the end of history does not mean that some superior Good has won a final victory, or that some final truth has been revealed (Flax 1990: 34–35).

The End-of-History philosophy coincides with skeptical post-modern perspective on many points. Both argue against privileging meta-narratives in history. Both agree on the centrality of culture, ideology, consciousness, and assume that ideas have a power of their own in determining life conditions. Both reject materialists of the right (for example, the *Wall Street Journal*) and the left (materialist Marxists). Neither pays much attention to economics, policy making, or prediction of the future (Fukuyama 1989: 12). The End-of-History theorists agree with the skeptical post-modernists about the end of ideology, the end of any motivation to struggle for "just causes" (Fukuyama 1989: 18), the end to "redemptive politics of any kind and of all utopianism or messianic movements" (Heller and Feher 1988). The major point on which they differ concerns rationality: the End-of-History theorists are more confident about human reason than are the post-modernists.[5]

[5] Fukuyama can be read as advancing the meta-narrative of liberal democracy, and this, of course, is a point of disagreement with the post-modernists. But he can also be read as merely observing its ascendancy rather than advocating it. He certainly does not paint liberal democracy in an idealized unequivocally positive light; he is not an apologist for it so much as an advocate of Hegelian views. Fukuyama suggests that the victory of the West is a mixed blessing: the end of history will be a gloomy, dull, and boring period without the necessity of risk, without any need for personal courage or imagination, without places for heroes, generals, or diplomats (Fukuyama 1989: 5). Fukuyama's reply to his critics could be read to suggest that he does indeed believe in the superiority of Liberalism (1989–90: 28), but this was not the case in the initial presentation of his ideas (1989).

b. The Affirmative Post-Modernists on History and Genealogy

The affirmatives are almost as critical of conventional history as the skeptics, but they seek to revise and relativize it, salvage it, re-draft it, or re-invent it rather than simply abolish it. For example, Fred Dallmayr talks about history as "a succession of partially discontinuous frameworks or temporal and spatial world-contexts" (Dallmayr 1987: 181). Other affirmatives also call for the radical revision of history as a focus on the daily life experience of ordinary people, on "small" topics (Zagorin 1990: 273), or they substitute traditional narratives for more conventional forms of history.[6] Their version of post-modern history is not a truth-seeking activity so much as "storytelling" (Ankersmit 1989).[7] "Description" in the form of such stories becomes as valuable as "explanation." Post-modern historians also accept contradictions because they expect that there will be many different "stories" about history (Scott 1989).

The affirmative post-modernists are influenced by "New History" in their quest for an alternative to the more established versions of this discipline.[8] New History employs deconstruction, subjective interpretation, and a symbolic construction of reality, rather than quantitative, structural, or functional methods. Like post-modernism, it seeks to unravel texts, raise questions about meaning in the text, and invent micro-narratives as alternatives to history (Hunt 1989).

Substantively, New History locates meaning in the social. It focuses on the ordinary, what is taken for granted, daily life, all that is "Petite Histoire" (Hassan 1987: 91–2). One New Historian, for example, argues that "Mickey Mouse may in fact be more important to an understanding of the 1930s than Franklin Roosevelt" (Susman 1985: 103, 197). New History is populist, emphasizing ordinary people rather than the elite; it privileges the point of view of the victims rather than the victimizers.[9] Sometimes it

---

[6] Following the lead of New History, post-modernists talk about history-as-narrative, but by this they do not mean history as narrative in the modern sense (Jameson, 1984a: 54), as grand theory (Hassan 1987: 91–92), or as a "recounting of a series of facts or events and the establishing of some connection between them" (Fowler 1987: 156). History as narrative is merely the telling of a story, an unassuming form of history or a radical substitute for it (White 1978).

[7] In Chapter 5 we will see how "small" post-modern narratives substitute for theory.

[8] New History is not a singular invisible college with a specific set of ideas. It includes feminist historians, Black History social historians, neo-Marxists, post-Marxists, psychoanalytical historians, discourse-oriented historians, and post-modernists. This makes for a rather conflict-ridden family, which agrees on little other than discontent with the "old" history. For example, the neo-Marxists criticize the post-modernists for eliminating class and state from history. The feminists say New History forgets male dominance. The Black historians argue it overlooks the white oppressor. For a review and critique of New History, see Himmelfarb 1987.

[9] Skeptical post-modernists would criticize this aspect of New History because it requires a subject and sets up a hierarchy of good/bad, superior/inferior, victim/victimizer.

is oriented to the margins. Feminist New History offers one such special perspective, with the history of menarche assumed to be as meaningful as the history of monarchy (Stearns 1976: 250). New History makes no claim to special truth; it erases the difference between history and fiction (Foucault 1980: 193) and holds that there is as much to be learned about life from the one as from the other.

Foucault's genealogy is also a source of inspiration to the post-modernists, especially the affirmatives, as a substitute for more modern versions of history. Genealogies are "constituting," engendering processes that refer to historical knowledges, struggles, reversals, popular lore, the memory of hostile encounters, the interrelationship of constraint and discourse (Fraser 1989: 20) and strategies of domination. But in describing them Foucault underlines that they are all constantly changing. His genealogy focuses on rupture, breakthroughs, on "local, discontinuous, disqualified, illegitimate knowledges against the claims of a unitary body of theory which would filter, hierarchise, and order . . . in the name of some true knowledge and some arbitrary idea of what constitutes a science and its objects" (Foucault 1980: 83). It has no room for representation, for individual or collective actors (subjects), but it does focus on the excluded and the marginal (Foucault 1980: 83, 117). It looks to the relationship of forces, not to make normative judgments or to offer ideological assessments (Fraser 1989: 20–21), not to find deep meaning, but to be in touch with the "singularity of surface events, . . . small details, minor shifts and subtle contours . . . discontinuity and arbitrariness" (Burrell 1988: 229).

Genealogy, as with a post-modern approach, has no use for origins, causality, synthesis, truth (laws of history), hidden significance, depth and interiority, belief in progress (Dreyfus and Rabinow 1983: 105–23; Harlan 1989: 608). Genealogical analysis, unlike modern history, does not interpret the past through a present-day perspective. Genealogy is rather a "history of the present in the sense that it finds its point of departure in problems relevant to current issues and finds its point of arrival and its usefulness in what it can bring to the analysis of the present" (Henriques et al. 1984: 104). It searches for neither universal structures nor universal value. It "campaigns against science and humanism" (Foucault 1973: 95; Harland 1987: 155).

2. Displacing Modern Time and Space

The skeptical post-modernists reject any understanding of time as chronological or linear; they attribute to this conception the pejorative term, "chronophonism" (Derrida 1981). The modern understanding of time is said to be oppressive, measuring and controlling one's activities. It "belongs to the imperative of productivity and is substituted for the rhythms of work and celebration" (Baudrillard 1987: 67). Linear time is viewed as offensively technical, rational, scientific, and hierarchical. Because modernity is excessively conscious of time, it somehow removes joy from human existence. In addition, time is a human creation (Latour 1988), a function of language, and as such it is arbitrary or indeterminate.

The skeptics offer a view of time as anarchical, disconnected, and misaligned rather than linear, evolutionary, or intentional (Dallmayr 1987; Derrida 1976; Megill 1985; Vattimo 1988: chaps. 6 and 7). Time can never be controlled or located in a definitive manner in either discourse or discussion (Lyotard 1988). The skeptics set out to violate all that is taken for granted about time in their own analysis. Baudrillard, for example, suggests that if we are unhappy with the world as it is, "could we not just skip the rest of this century . . . pass directly from 1989 to the year 2000?" (1988: 17). He also claims the nuclear holocaust and the Third World War have already taken place; in so doing he violates all modern concepts of time (1989b).

The most extreme skeptical post-modernists set time aside altogether, and with it they relinquish the idea that something is ever entirely present or absent. Derrida, inspired by Heidegger, defies and denies the present/absent in his own writing. Some of his published works look like printed rough drafts with certain words strategically and symbolically crossed out (Derrida 1976: 19, 33, 44). He creates a "world under erasure," where language is a "trace-structure, effacing it even as it presents its legibility" (Spivak, in Derrida 1976: xviii). This means that what is erased somehow still exists; "the oscillation between two states of affairs, has been *slowed down* and *spread out*, . . . physically canceled, yet still legible beneath the cancelation, these signs, *sous rature* [under erasure], continue to function in the discourse even while they are excluded from it" (McHale 1987: 99–100). Only in a world without modern conceptions of time can such violations of presence and absence have any credence.

To dismiss this post-modern challenge to conventional views of time as absurd would be a mistake because, ironically, it receives unexpected support from modern science. New perspectives on time in the universe, such as light years and cosmic dimensions, were barely imaginable a few years ago, and they feed the skeptical post-modern feelings of vulnerability. "Individual lives with their limited time-spans become meaningless. As the traditional sense of time lost its significance, modern time has become boundless and human life seems to disappear in it all" (Wulf 1989: 52). In *A Brief History of Time*, Stephen Hawking, a theoretical physicist and mathematician, argues that "imaginary time is really the real time, and what we call real time is just a figment of our imaginations." In real time, "the universe has a beginning and an end at singularities that form a boundary to space-time and at which the laws of science break down. But in imaginary time there are no singularities or boundaries." He contends there is no "unique absolute time," that "clocks carried by different observers would not necessarily agree. Thus time became a more personal concept, relative to the observer who measured it." In addition, there is "no important difference between the forward and backward directions of imaginary time" (Hawking 1988: 139, 143–44).[10]

Space is the site of another dimensional mutation. The skeptical post-modernists see geography as tantamount to hyper-space (the dis-illusion of space altogether, as Jameson calls it). Post-modern hyper-space can be invented and with equal ease commanded to vanish, or it can be expanded with the aid of mental gymnastics by pure intellectual construction. A dislocation of post-modern spheres has taken over, and the proper co-ordinates for re-assembling them are not now known (Dear 1986: 380; Jameson 1985). Post-modern space and geography transcend "the capacities of the individual human body to locate itself, to organize its immediate surroundings perceptually, and cognitively to map its position in a mappable external world" (Jameson 1984a: 83).

These skeptics question every aspect of geographical space as normally conceived by turning it inside out and reformulating it as a mentally constructed set of relationships. Post-modern hyper-space is dramatically at odds with the philosophical material world of conventional science, where concrete objects, located in an objective geographical space, are charted in terms of latitude and longitude, where one inch on the map equals one linear mile on the earth. Conventional geography assumes that, once located, things either stay put or, if they move around, they do so in predictable patterns. Hyper-space makes no such assumption. It speaks to the "dissolution of things," and the unexpected is the order of the day. There is a loss of ability to "position ourselves within this space and cognitively map it" (Stephanson and Jameson 1988: 7).

The affirmative post-modernists share the skeptics' impatience with modern views of space and geography. But their feelings that conventional views are inadequate lead them to revise space in more political terms. They look to local space, the place for community. This coincides with their preference for regional resistance, their emphasis on the respect of others' "space," and their insistence on the preservation of their own "place." Their focus on the local and on the right to space and geography are highly political in character and adapted to the social context.

The affirmatives' concern is that modern assumptions about space and time are manipulated so as to confine and enclose, as tools of discipline.

---

[10] Although this may make Hawking sound like a post-modernist, such an interpretation might well be erroneous. Ultimately, Hawking might argue "imaginary time" is very likely to conform to rules just as current notions of time do, though the rules relating to "imaginary time" are not presently known and are likely to be very complex.

"Space can be made to hide consequences from us . . . And power and discipline are inscribed into the apparently innocent spatiality of social life" (Soja 1989: 6). Foucault argues that relational forms of space are important. He offers total institutions, such as the monastery or the school, as examples of how organizations employ space and time to control the lives of the individuals they supposedly "serve."

3. Post-Modern Views of Space and Time in the Humanities

Post-modern views of time and geography emerged in the humanities where modern assumptions about each can be removed without much consternation or consequence, though the same, as will be seen, is not the case with social science. For example, the literary utopian tradition and some forms of science fiction, such as Italo Calvino's *Cosmicomics*, regularly ignore history and geography, defy linear time, and Euclidean space. Such playful fantasy adds interest, arouses the imagination, challenges the creative intellect. But in the humanities hardly anyone takes these transgressions of normal time and space seriously.

Post-modern fiction sets the trend for violating conventional conceptions of both time and space. For example, event A, takes place at Time 1. Event B occurs at Time 2. But the discussion in such novels at Time 1 assumes B has already happened, and the narrative at Time 2 goes on as if A had not occurred. This reflects a post-modern fictional world where "all future and past times, all the branches of eternity, are already here, broken up into tiny morsels and divided among people and their dreams. . . . Time, then, does not exist here" (Pavic 1988: 314–15). Post-modern authors deliberately violate linear sequence. Stories "fold back upon themselves and endings turn out to be beginnings, suggesting an endless recursivity" (Trachtenberg 1985: 234). Tom Stoppard's *Artist Descending a Staircase* is an example. This play has an underlying linearity, but the author chops it into twelve parts and shuffles them (or re-organizes them) so that time and space cease to make sense. In post-modern fiction the story "doubles back, bends, loops around, an event is both antecedent and sequel." Stories also turn in upon themselves. They are "recursive." In Italo Calvino's *If on a Winter's Night a Traveler* the main story is broken into so often by "nested representations in such diverse media (novels within-the-novel . . .), that the fiction's ontological 'horizon' is effectively lost" (McHale 1987: 100). Or the elements of a novel are organized almost randomly, not sequentially. In the case of the *Dictionary of the Khazars*, alphabetical entries substitute (Pavic 1988). Characters leap across the centuries and across cultures where the space occupied by dreams is as real as that of waking moments. It is impossible to judge what is authentic. This is done to confuse and even mislead the reader, to encourage him/her to question what is real and what is invented. But its most important function is to require the reader to construct his/her own book. Because normal constraints of time and space are violated, any number of stories are viable. Indeed, it makes no difference where one begins and ends a reading because it is impossible or useless to argue about what happened when normal time and space are meaningless concepts.

4. Post-Modern Social Science—Without History, on New Time, Drifting in Space

Post-modern history, time, and space are potentially far more troublesome for mainstream social science than for the humanities. The greatest impact of abandoning these modern concepts occurs in fields such as urban and regional development, public administration, (urban) planning, international relations, and geography—all of which have special claims on time and space. In fact, the whole of the social sciences would need to be re-created if post-modernists were to eliminate all modernist presumptions about history, all assumptions about time, or all suppositions about space and geography.

If modern conceptions of time and space are completely overthrown as the skeptics propose, identifiable consequences follow. Without linear time, cause-and-effect relations within a scientific framework are impossible to specify because temporal priority must be established so as to separate one from the other. The probability of truth is reduced to zero as the significance of the present moment approaches at once both infinity and anti-infinity. Theory is equally effervescent, transient, and temporary, for this moment only, of little permanent consequence. Knowledge claims compete with the "unbearable lightness of being" (Kundera 1984).

In addition, efforts to abolish history altogether (the post-modern equivalent of the End of History) have severe consequences for the social sciences, especially if this is taken to mean that one can learn little or nothing from the past. Much of modern social science is contingent on evidence derived from previous human experience, all of which is fundamentally historical in character. Social science requires we use what we know from the earlier periods of time to improve upon the human record, to make action more effective in the present. But if there are no facts and if all interpretations are equally interesting (Chapter 7, section 2), then history cannot play this role.

Certainly those social scientists who look to history for inspiration in their own research must be wary, for they may find limited prospects within a post-modern social science; however, such a warning may be exaggerated. Eliminating history from the social sciences is, after all, not that revolutionary. Systems analysts and structuralist social scientists have long argued for a view quite similar to that of the post-modernists, at least as concerns history. In doing away with history, by emptying the past and future into the present, some skeptical post-modernists take one step further. Derrida goes so far as to argue that "the trace must be thought before the entity" (Derrida 1976: 47); he implies that the effect must precede the cause, and this notion too is consistent within post-modernism because it abolishes linear time.

The affirmative post-modern revisions of history, time, and space are not so threatening; they can in many cases be woven into the modern fabric of social science in an interesting and innovative fashion. Not every post-modern social scientist calls for eliminating all these dimensions; some look only to radical re-definition and novel deployment. But as will be seen, differences among post-modernists about how to reorganize and reorder these terms has led to substantial differences of opinion.

Modern social science anticipated the post-modern redefinition of space and time.[11] For example, Anthony Giddens breaks ground in the direction of space/time consciousness. He does not call for a post-modern reformulation of these concepts, and until recently he was quite hostile to post-approaches (Giddens 1987). In his more recent work (1990) he moves in a post-modern direction, especially as concerns the "disembedding of social systems . . . the 'lifting out' of social relations from local contexts of interaction and their restructuring across indefinite spans of time-space" (1990: 21). Giddens questions "clock time" and says it is "socially conditioned influence." He points out that space and time are generally taken for granted in the social sciences and calls for a renewed consciousness of their import (1984: chap. 3). Historian Charles Maier argues that time is political in both conception and terms of allocation (1987). Such a view is increasingly a center-piece of criticism directed at the liberal order. Harvey (1989) speaks of time-space compression, and this too inspires revisions of these concepts.

The application of post-modern time and space in some fields of the social sciences is well underway. In the field of planning and public administration where conceptual views assume modern controllable time and space, post-modernists are, today, arguing that concepts such as controlled growth and policy implementation have become meaningless. Post-modern planning looks rather to the political use of space and time. The city is a text, constituted of different interpretations by various readers. Post-modern planning dissolves space as a knowable, manageable constraint and replaces it with hyper-space, which conceives of space as fragmented and

---

[11] Henri Bergson (1896) distinguished *duree* from clock time long ago.

disorganized, as manifesting gaps of undecidability. Post-modern planning is pastiche, a hodgepodge, crazy-quilt composition (Dear 1986: 367, 379–80). Post-modernism signifies that "vernacular traditions, local history, and specialized spatial designs ranging from functions to intimacy to grand spectacle should be approached with a much greater eclecticism of style" (Harvey 1987).

In international relations post-modern redefinitions of time and space have also had considerable influence. Post-modernists reject the normal divisions of geography and space in terms of territory and population generally recognized by international relationists, such as nation states or commonwealths. Such political entities, they argue, employ a "universal narrative," each asserting "the right to a partially unique interpretation of the whole and each making good on that claim within some spatial, demographic, and temporal compass." Post-modernists in international relations argue that geography and space are not autonomous, isolated, separated, fixed identities, but rather are defined by the "plane of contest." Geographical exclusion, silence, and dispersal result from a "field of clashes" and from the "play of power among plural elements" (Ashley 1987: 409–10). These post-modern scholars employ post-modern conceptions of time and geography to erase the boundaries between domestic and international politics. They locate post-modern international relations at the border of both the domestic and the international, a site called a "nonplace" (Ashley 1989a: 39).

Ashley's consideration of "historicity" remodels history in a post-modern fashion by making it more appropriate for post-modern international relations. He scraps conventional history as a fabricated facade that legitimates hegemonic discourse and justifies arbitrary universalistic definitions of reality. He rejects the "production of historical narratives that brings the meaning of history to a close by privileging one or another subject as the sovereign center, the ultimate origin and register of truth and meaning, in whose terms all else must be interpreted" (Ashley 1989a: 33). Influenced by Foucault, he advances decentered history or genealogy as a substitute for history in international relations because it looks to struggles, discontinuity, and power plays in situations of constant change and movement and because it accepts diverse interpretations and the absence of truth (Ashley 1987: 409).

The tradition of questioning modern views of time, space, and history already existed in international relations before post-modernism arrived to air such complaints. Certain innovations as noncontroversial as "regime theory" in international relations have, for more than a decade, escaped traditional views of the geographical unit of analysis and established the legitimacy for denying and defying modern concepts of geography and history. Although post-modernists encourage such efforts, at the same time they criticize other aspects of regime theory and carry that questioning much further than regime theory.

Certainly political sociologists could accept a post-modern view of time if doing so meant examining yesterday's primary election results, not to assess who won, but rather to consider the impact of the primary election on another moment—the general election, for example. But mechanical conformity such as that offered in this illustration is unlikely to excite post-modernists. A more authentically post-modern consideration of time is Der Derian's post-modern analysis of speed in the modern context and its role in transforming international relations, especially espionage (Der Derian 1989b).

Drawing on the example of Los Angeles, Shapiro and Neubauer (1989) discuss space and geography in the city. Their goal is to make explicit the "shape of a society's spaces, e.g., leisure space, work space, public space, military space, etc.," all of which have been neglected in political science in the past. While demonstrating a new self-consciousness of these concepts and acknowledging their debt to the French post-modernist tradition, they do not reject all modern social science assumptions; rather they choose to work with many of them and question only especially objectionable elements of modernity.

The application of post-modern views of space, time, and history in the social sciences has engendered important disagreements among post-modernists, and this has led to some fascinating controversies. The discussion developing between post-modern geographers and political theorists over the comparative importance of space and time is particularly interesting; disciplinary differences are at the heart of the debate. The political theorists stress the importance of post-modern time over geography. Post-modern geographers advocate increased priority for the concept of post-modern space over history and time.[12] By elevating the weight given to the concept of post-modern space they hope to revitalize post-modern geography relative to post-modern history. Post-modern geographers complain that in the past geography (or space) has been unfairly misunderstood as fixed, dead, immobile, undialectical—a form of Cartesian cartography of spatial science (Foucault 1980: 170; Soja 1989: 4). Space, or geography, they argue, was unfairly subordinated in the study of social relations in the late nineteenth century and only began to return to its proper role in the mid-twentieth century.[13] They hope to employ the post-modern reorganization of the social sciences to "reassert" the import of geography.

[12] The post-modern geographers, scarcely distinguishing between the concepts of time and history, argue that the two overlap and are conceptually interdependent.

[13] Initially, they point out, the critical Marxists anticipated a post-modern view of space and geography and directed considerable attention to it (Soja 1989: chap. 2). Today, a small but growing group of post-modern geographers carry this project forward.

Political theorists, however, contend that post-modernism upgrades time (speed) as a critical variable over space and geography (Der Derian 1990: 297, 307). As they see it, there is no need for humans to move through space anymore, and thus the significance of geography is reduced. Film and audiovisual replace real spatial locomotion as they transport us to different places (Virilio 1989: 112–15). Time and speed are political, and "power is more 'real' in time than space" (Der Derian 1990: 295). Time in the form of speed is violence, the essence of war, that which has transformed the battlefield. Time supplants space; "the distribution of territory becomes the distribution of time" (Virilio 1983: 115; 1989). Post-modern political scientists believe "we have not given serious consideration to the political effects of excessive or insufficient speed, in our systems of weapons, communications, decision-making"; they call for elevating "chronology over geography, pace over space" (Der Derian, 1990: 307, 297). They argue for the primacy of time over space (Virilio 1989: 112–15).

There is no easy resolution to this budding debate; nobody "wins" in a post-modern argument anyway. But we do glimpse what is at stake. Post-modern concepts of space, time, and history are controversial, even when viewed from the post-modern side of the intellectual fence.

5. Putting It All Together

Post-modern views of history, time, and geography are closely intertwined: all are irreconcilable with modern assumptions. Rejecting linear time automatically casts a suspicion on the conventional history that presumes it. Similarly history is assumed to take place in a physical, spatial arena just as it presupposes a relationship with time and place. Without time there can be no precise beginning, and thus history, in terms of origins, is meaningless. It is no surprise, then, that post-modernists say they are preoccupied with "our one and only eternity," that is, the present (Heller and Feher 1989: 150). Time is related to the distances between geographical units, but in a post-modern context these are no longer governed by known rules and metric distances. Each dimension is dependent on the others; if conventional views of one fall, then all risk being simultaneously dislodged. Theory and reality, however, differ, and it is not uncommon in social sciences to see authors contest the modern view of one of these variables while leaving others untouched.

Post-modern dimensional permutations of history, space, and time are related to other substantive post-modernist perspectives in a reliable fashion. Charting any space (social, physical, or cognitive) raises questions about the adequacy of representation. As will be seen in Chapter 6, post-modernists conclude that there are no true maps because no representation is ever really authentic (Jameson 1984a: 90). The post-modern suspicion of the subject is linked to unhappiness with the role of this creature in conventional history. Conventional history collapses without subjects (Flax 1990: 32–33). Post-modernists reject Enlightenment science, a view consistent with a radical post-modern re-definition of linear time and its re-conceptualization of space or conventional geography.

5

A THEORY OF THEORY AND THE TERRORISM

OF TRUTH

The secret of theory is, indeed, that truth doesn't exist.
(Baudrillard 1986: 141)

The problems are the traditional problems of any philosophy
which leads knowing to a knowledge of ultimate
unknowability, and thereupon summons knowing to un-know
itself—as by an active forgetting.
(Harland 1987: 118)

TRUTH AND THEORY are closely linked within a post-modern perspective, and they are discussed together here. Theory implies truth, and truth, at least in the social sciences, is theoretical in character. Post-modernists are suspicious regarding modern versions of both. In this chapter I first discuss skeptical post-modern views of truth, especially the contention that because all knowledge is language-bound truth is forever arbitrary. The affirmative post-modernist re-conceptualization of truth as local, personal, community specific is examined. Next, post-modern objections to modern theory are outlined. I consider the diverse suggestions for theory, either discarding it (skeptics) or reconstructing it (affirmatives). Finally, examples from several social science disciplines are offered, and consequences of post-modern views of truth and theory for the whole of the social sciences are considered.

1. Life without Modern Versions of Truth: The Problem of Language

Almost all post-modernists reject truth even as a goal or ideal because it is the very epitome of modernity (Foucault 1984: 72–80; Ashley 1989a: 271–80). Truth is an Enlightenment value and subject to dismissal on these grounds alone. Truth makes reference to order, rules, and values; depends on logic, rationality, and reason, all of which the post-modernists question. Attempts to produce knowledge in the modern world depend on some kind of truth claim, on the assumption that truth is essential.

a. Why the Skeptical Post-Modernists Reject Truth

Skeptical post-modernists deny the possibility of truth (Lyotard 1984) or merely state their indifference to all projects designed to discover truth (Baudrillard 1983a, 1983c). As they see it, truth is either meaningless or arbitrary (Culler 1982: 22). For the skeptics, the result is the same: there is no difference between truth and even the most obvious, distorted forms of rhetoric or propaganda.[1]

Skeptical post-modernists object to the monopolistic claims made for truth, whatever the rationale. As Derrida suggests, "There is no such thing as a truth in itself. But only a surfeit of it. Even if it should be for me, about me, truth is plural" (Derrida 1979: 103). These post-modernists understand truth claims to be merely the product of power games, manipulated into position by those whose interests they serve. If this is so, if truth claims are really quite arbitrary, then they do not merit special privileged status or superior authority. As Foucault (1975) puts it, "We are subjected to the reproduction of truth through power, and we cannot exercise power except through the production of truth." He maintains that it is absurd to argue that there is a sharp distinction between truth and ideology, understood as false propaganda (Foucault 1980: 132). It is impossible to separate truth from power, and so there is no real possibility of any absolute, uncorrupted truth.[2]

For the skeptics, truth claims are a form of terrorism. They threaten and provoke (Baudrillard 1983c). Truth by its very existence is said to silence those who disagree. Truth claims "serve to justify the powerful and to make the weak feel at fault and inadequate" (Handler 1988: 1036). Lyotard argues that truth "eliminates" the argument of "the other," the point of view of someone else that upsets what we define as the truth even though it is only what we have come to take for granted (Lyotard 1984).

The skeptics' theory of language transforms truth into a largely linguistic convention. They argue that claims of truth can never be independent of language, that truth is an "effect of discourse" (Flax 1990: 35). The relationship between name and meaning, the signified and signifier, is problematic (Derrida 1974b; Graff 1979; Ryan 1988: 565). If, as post-mod-

---

[1] When pressed by an evident, truthful example, such as the statement that "the sky is blue," the skeptics might respond that such examples are trivial (Derrida 1981: 105; 1979: 103); or they might reply that the "sky is blue" only in a context of interpretation, and so this is not a statement of truth (Hoy 1989: 456).

[2] Nietzsche's influence on the skeptical post-modern understanding of truth is evident. He ridiculed love of knowledge and emphasized myth over truth, but he was equally dubious about the "creative lie" (Megill 1985: 54–58). For Nietzsche (1979) both truth and lies are fabrications. Neither truth nor falsity exist, and anyone who claims to know the truth is suspect.

ernists argue, language produces and reproduces its own world without reference to reality, then it is impossible to say anything definite because language is purely an artificial sign system and cannot assure truth (Flax 1990; Murphy 1988: 179). "What is communicated about events is determined, not by the character of events themselves, but by linguistic figures or forms" (Gergen 1986: 143). Linguistic meaning, always personal and idiosyncratic, can never be communicated from one person to another. Language has a will and a power of its own. It generates meaning quite independently of "human agency or will" (Norris 1988: 176). There are no precise meanings for words, no definitive versions of a text, in short, no simple truths (Descombes 1980: 182). Human institutions are all "predicated on the lie that is the word" (Norton 1988: 5). Nothing remains of truth, and it is only "a product of our willing bewitchment by language" (Norris 1988: 188). "If meaning in language rises not from the reference of signs to something outside words but from differential relations among the words themselves, if 'referent' and 'meaning' must always be distinguished, then the notion of a literary text which is validated by its one-to-one correspondence to some social, historical or psychological reality can no longer be taken for granted" (Miller 1971). The only skeptics who retain the concept of truth redefine it so that it would be unrecognizable in a modern context. For example, Vattimo (1988) suggests that post-modern truth would be without grandeur. Only traces of the past, reminiscences, myths, all of which "must lie," make up post-modern truth. Post-modern truth is, then, necessarily fragmentary, discontinuous, and changing. It is rhetorical and aesthetic, associated with experiencing art, and as such it is constantly reconstructed and ultimately linked to death, just as all art is destined to disappear.

The skeptics' understanding of truth is consistent with their view of the author, subject, presence, history, time, and space. Truth implies an author. Thus, rejection of truth conforms closely with their view that no single person (such as the author) can tell us what a particular text really means. Nor can one reader argue that s/he has the "true reading" of a text. Post-modernism abandons the subject, and this makes sense because truth requires a unity of subjects as to the contents of the truth statement. Truth requires a distinct object and subject so that someone can stand outside and discover what is true (Harland 1987). Truth assumes a belief in presence and the ability to distinguish between what is actually present and absent (Schwartz 1990: 32), and, as we have seen, post-modernists argue presence is never absolute: the absent is always present to some degree, and the present is always absent. Skeptical post-modernists reject truth as "completeness, adequation, transcendence, or self-identity. It cannot be the representation or mirror of an external or universal substance ('presence') or subject because none exists" (Flax 1990: 200). Modern history searches for the true account of the past, and the skeptics reject this effort, which is meaningless in the absence of modern versions of time and space. Modern definitions of time and space fall away in any case without a sovereign someone to testify to their veracity.

As will be seen in the chapters that follow, the skeptics' rejection of truth is also consistent with their views of representation, science, epistemology, methodology, and politics. A denial of truth is linked to post-modern anti-representationalism. Representation assumes the possibility of a true image being reproduced or represented; post-modernists say this is impossible (Chapter 6), and truth, to the extent that it strives to re-present reality, is fraudulent. Post-modernists question the value of truth because they consider it impossible to evaluate the adequacy of knowledge claims with any certitude. All criteria for distinguishing between truth and falsehood, for evaluating theory, require that one choose between categories, or they expect one to establish a hierarchy of values that designates some as good and others as bad. Post-modernists reject such distinctions and rather emphasize multiple realities and the view that no single interpretation of any phenomenon can be claimed superior to any other. If this is the case, if there is no single best answer to every question, then there is no room for truth.

b. The Affirmatives Re-define Truth

Affirmatives are as likely as the skeptics to reject universal truth and dismiss the idea that truth is "out there" waiting to be discovered. But many of them do accept the possibility of specific local, personal, and community forms of truth. The affirmatives are also less likely than the skeptics to say that all versions of truth are equal. Those among them who retain truth, however, relativize it and deprive it of specific and/or universal content. They say it is equivalent to "self-understanding," or they argue that truth varies according to place and historical context. They state that conflicting truths are not a problem because each one can be true in a different world (Goodman 1984: 30–35). Each person may have his or her own version of truth (Ferry and Renaut 1985: 287). Finally, they develop an anti-theoretical form of truth as theory with a substantive focus on daily life and on local narrative.

The affirmatives, like the skeptics, understand truth's dependence on language to be a serious restriction, but they take a middle-of-the-road position rather than defend an extreme linguistic relativism. The affirmatives argue that there can be a certain consensus about words or concepts, as is the case for professional social scientists. Meaning is still erratic in the sense that it is always acquired, shaped, or invented by professional or social interaction: the community dictates the terms but not in an absolutely arbitrary fashion (Smith 1988: 105). The affirmatives argue that a community of knowledge may establish a consensus of language and values, making it possible to communicate certain truths that, though they are not universal, hold for that community at a specific place and time (Fish 1987).[3] But they still conclude in the end that "no nondiscourse-dependent or transcendental rules [truths] exist. . . . What we call the mind or reason is only an effect of discourse" (Flax 1990: 35–36).

2. Skeptical Post-Modernist Objections to Modern Theory

The skeptical post-modernists reject modern theory and recognize a situation where a multitude of theories exists and none can claim superiority over any other. They present a broad and thoroughgoing substantive and methodological critique of modern theory. Theory building, as with truth seeking, is said to be characteristic of Marxists, neo-conservatives, positivists, structuralists because all have a "totalizing, logocentric project," a meta-narrative, and each emphasizes the social whole in the form of theory over the individual parts (Giddens 1984; Sloterdijk 1987). Post-modernism, however, denies that it has any such global project. It looks to "différance,"[4] to the uniqueness of the parts, rather than to the unity of the theoretical whole.

The skeptics' anti-foundational, anti-enframing predispositions guide their critique of theory (Vattimo 1988), as do their views of language. These post-modernists contend that modern theory assumes an epistemological reality and that no such reality exists (Baudrillard 1986: 141). Theory is assumed to operate without variation in every context, and this too is dubious in an ever changing post-modern world. The data and formal laws on which theory depend are not independent and objective; they are at best contextually relative and at worst totally arbitrary and constructed (Fish 1987: 1781). Theory must operate within the confines of language, as is the case with all truth claims, and this is a source of its major weakness because language is "always already" everywhere. Language categories and socially defined meaning are inescapable; they also make theory impossible.

The skeptics' broad and wide-ranging critique of modern theory includes all the following complaints. Theory conceals, distorts, and obfuscates (Nelson 1987: 18); it is "alienated, disparate, dissonant" (Der Derian 1989a: 6); it means to "exclude, order, and control rival powers" (Seidman 1989: 636); it is ideological and rhetorical, although claiming to be scientific (modern science is only a "cultural artifact") (Harman, 1988: 121). It is overbearing, seeking "stable ground" and aiming to "anchor a sover-

---

[3] The question remains as to how any criticism develops at all if the community norms are so powerful.
[4] Defined in the glossary.

eign voice" (Ashley 1989a). Theory, said to legitimate a monopoly of power, is thus considered little more than an "authoritarian weapon" by most skeptics (Kellner 1987: 6). Modern theory cannot abide the "radical undecidability" of opposing points of view. It needs to choose. It has no "respect for paradox," defined as an opposition in which it is never possible to choose one opposition over the other (Ashley 1989a: 271–73, 278). Finally, modern theory, the skeptics argue, fails to fulfill the very goals it sets for itself. It does not provide direction; it is not the basis for praxis or action because it is rather an ad hoc justification, a generalization of previous practice (Fish 1987: 1781–97).

In his essay, "Resistance to Theory," Paul de Man suggests that modern theory interferes with or "resists" the revolutionary aspects of post-modern reading. It works against the multiple interpretations post-modernists stress by seeking to specify a single interpretation, a theory for a particular text. But at the same time, he argues, theory "is itself its own resistance," and it inevitably ends up undoing itself. This means that texts work against the theories applied to them. A close reading reveals the rhetorical aspects of the text, a resistance to theory, and an exception to every assumed definitive theoretical interpretation. In the last instance, no theory is left standing. "Nothing can overcome the resistance to theory since theory is itself resistance" (De Man 1986: 19).

In general the skeptics have no aspiration, or perhaps, even capacity, to construct new theory in the modern sense of the word, as grounded on reasoned argument or observation and experience. They do not attempt to formulate a "theory" of the post-modern. Any such project would be contradictory because it would require modern reason and rational thinking, and the skeptics object to both (see Chapter 7). Instead of employing the word "theory," therefore, many skeptics substitute other terms such as "instantaneous lightning-flashes of paradoxical illumination" (Harland 1987: 107). Theory is referred to as "lightheaded" or an "invitation to discussion" (Sheridan 1980: 213–14). Sloterdijk (1987) offers the "politics and pleasures of the body" and the "right to happiness" as alternatives to social theory. If post-modern theory can be said to exist at all, for the skeptics it is a form of theory that relinquishes any special consideration (Der Derian 1988b: 9; Dear 1986: 379). Feeling no need to be logical, to reconcile oppositions, to test, or to choose between theories, it accepts inconsistency and contradiction (Ashley 1989a: 271–80).

3. Affirmative Post-Modernists De-center Theory and Substitute Everyday Life and Local Narrative

Although most skeptical post-modernists renounce the pursuit of absolute truth and many call for eliminating theory altogether, the affirmatives are not so adamant. They may reject the "innocence of theory" (Henriques et al. 1984: 12). They generally deny the truth claims of theory and annul its privileged status. They diminish its role and reduce its stature, but in the end many of them retain it by transforming it into ordinary, pedestrian "talk." They argue that although they aim to end the intellectual hegemony implicit in grand theory, this need not mean all theories are equal (Dear 1988).

Post-modern theory, for the affirmatives, is unsystematic, heterological, de-centered, ever changing, and local. Nonrepresentational, it is personal in character and community-specific in focus. Their decentered theory is said to be valuable for its own sake and never to claim special authority for itself.[5] It does not require the object-subject distinction of modern social science. It is "true" only in terms of its own discourse.

Some affirmative post-modernists seek to substitute for modern theory an anti-theoretical focus on the text (event) of daily (everyday) life, on local knowledge, on detail, on the contingent, on personal testimony, on direct experience of individuals and communities.[6] What they produce may reflect a concrete empirical reality, but it is an anti-positivist, anecdotal empiricism that savors detail and reserves a special place for what is unique in each and every life.[7] It has no need for modern history, and its subject, immersed in the everyday, has no autonomous ego. The affirmatives understand everyday life to be intuitive, based on feelings, nearly spiritual in content, an open admission to frivolity. Daily life constitutes an almost existentialist, deep understanding of everyday events, the "quotidien" (Barth 1980: 68). Because this "ordinary life of ordinary people" (Him-

---

[5] The problem, of course, is that in a contradictory fashion many affirmatives do attribute a privileged place to their own theories; Henriques et al. provide one example. This is discussed in Chapters 8 and 9.

[6] There are many paradigms of everyday life, and this concept is not the exclusive property of post-modernism. It is a popular approach for the neo-Marxists such as Henri Lefebvre (1988: 77–87). He abandons orthodox Marxism but integrates an everyday life point of view into a general anti-capitalist perspective. The everyday becomes a "mode of production," a "modality of administering society"; this "lived experience" is closely associated with capitalism. While generally "ambiguous and contradictory," it is also "the basis of exploitation and of domination." But it can be changed if a progressive project is applied to it. Heller also emphasizes an everyday life approach to social phenomena (Heller 1986: 150–63; 1990, chap. 2). From her consideration of everyday life it is apparent that she is no post-modernist, though her sympathy for everyday life may inspire some post-modernists. For Heller everyday life and everyday knowledge are pragmatic, concrete, factual, and cognitive as well as emotional. The same is true of *The History of Private Life*, which focuses on everyday life, a multi-volume series of books published by Belknap and Harvard University Press over the last several years.

[7] Post-modernism's anti-theoretical focus on daily life is not the only possible perspective on everyday experience. It is equally possible to seek to generalize from daily life, to draw theoretical conclusions at the micro-level. In this form the daily life focus, empiricist in character, would emphasize concrete reality. In this case what the researcher feels and perceives is offered as a basis of generalizable statements with broader application being the goal.

melfarb 1989a: 663–65) is so richly descriptive, it represents a revolt against Grand Theory, especially inductive theory that attempts to generalize (Fokkema 1984: 421). What goes on in the bedroom and bathroom takes on as much historical importance as what takes place on the battlefield and in government boardrooms. The modern is said to undervalue everyday experience as the post-modernists understand it. The mass media talks about what is remote from daily life. It ignores the impact of public events on everyday life and personal interest.[8]

Critics argue that an everyday life focus is only descriptive and can be neither reconstructive (Heller 1986: 156) nor substantive (Himmelfarb 1989a). This is likely to be the case for the skeptical post-modernists.[9] But the affirmatives' refusal to give up a political project means they assume that an everyday life focus permits just such reconstruction. Many affirmative post-modernists are activists who associate their focus on daily life with social change. Their aim is not only "to interpret daily life but to also transform it" (Huyssen 1986: 157–58).

As substitutes for truth and theory, the affirmatives also emphasize certain kinds of narratives, small narratives, community-based narratives, rather than grand narratives. They applaud traditional narratives that speak, for example, as folk wisdom, myth, popular "stories," legends, fragmented creative snippets of wisdom, and "petite histoire" (little stories). Traditional narratives focus on the local, assert neither truth nor totalizing theory, and propose no broad theoretical generalizations or ultimate truths (Rorty 1979). They are offered as only one interpretation among many (White 1978: 57). Traditional human narratives accept error, inconsistency, and relativism. These liberating narratives tell "the collective story of the disempowered . . . , placing their lives within the context of larger social and historical forces" (Richardson 1988: 204).[10] They present a common story that unifies people and promotes a social bond among individuals in their everyday life (Miller 1990). They explain the past to the present; they speak of fragments rather than unity.

---

[8] For some post-modernists this personal, private, subjective daily life experience that offers only a personal view, without any assertions about truth or theory, is an alternative to public experience. (Chapter 6 examines the links between post-modernism and the public sphere.) Left-wing critics of post-modernism argue that separating public problems and daily life leads to an acceptance of the status quo, of injustice and inequality.

[9] Heller argues that reconstituting everyday life means employing the standpoint of the subject as a participant within everyday life; because post-modernism abandons the subject, no such re-constitution is feasible (Heller 1986: 158). Of course, this is not a problem for the affirmative post-modernists who call for the return of the subject. Heller, however, does not consider this distinction between post-modernists.

[10] Skeptical post-modernism erases the subject and is anti-humanist. It is not surprising that the skeptics are excluded from this search, with the help of traditional narratives, for how the modern world disempowers people. To do so would raise problems for the skeptics because it might restore the subject and object and be humanist in content.

Post-modernists reject modernism's "Grand" narrative (Hassan 1987a: 91), meta(master)narratives (Lyotard 1984), and narratives that claim to be scientific and objective, that serve to legitimate modernity and assume justice, truth, theory, hegemony. These modern meta-narratives are the same narratives the skeptics reject as logocentric, linear, totalizing; these modern narrators speak with authority (such as Marx, Engels, Lenin, Jesus, Luther, and Mohammed) in "an all-knowing voice from afar and above, stripped of all human subjectivity or fallibility" (Richardson 1988: 203). Or as a pretense, truth and objectivity are offered directly by the narrative (in the case of modern science) without a human narrator. In this case, post-modernists contend, the narrator, the "camouflaged first person [I, me, we]," is "hiding in the bramble of the passive voice" (Richardson 1988: 203). Lyotard argues that the modern narrative is fraudulent in claiming to be superior to traditional narrative. It is, he contends, just like traditional narrative, that is, subjective, relative, and interpretative (Lyotard 1984: 26).[11]

Post-modernism rejects grand narratives because they all claim a beginning, an end, and a definitive theory, and this is impossible and pointless in a post-modern world (Taylor 1984: 62–69, 153). As I explained in Chapter 4, post-modernists reject the idea of history with a starting point, a normal progression, and a conclusion (that is, a linear story) (Taylor 1984: 62–69, 153), especially if these elements involve representation and/ or causality. Post-modernists criticize modern narrative as "representation that arrests ambiguity and controls the proliferation of meaning by imposing a standard and standpoint of interpretation that is taken to be fixed and independent of the time it represents" (Ashley 1989a: 263).

Replacing theory with everyday life and mini-narratives is not without contradictions. Substituting local memories, community truths, raising up what were previously "disqualified modes of knowledge" may well amount to substituting one version of truth for that which is no longer acceptable (universal truth), and this makes for inconsistency if one is complaining about truth claims in general (Habermas 1987a: 279–81).

4. Some Examples from Women's Studies, Public Administration, Sociology, Anthropology, Political Science, and Psychology

If social science is to adopt a post-modern point of view it must adapt to a situation where the goal of seeking truth is abandoned, where the possibility of modern truth and theory no longer exist. Here the affirmatives are

[11] Lyotard, a skeptical post-modernist, does not, as do so many affirmatives, advocate traditional narratives as a substitute for truth.

more successful and less threatening than the skeptics. Affirmative post-modern social scientists seek to develop a truth-free and theory-free understanding of their disciplines. Skeptics undermine the very basis for a social science. Some examples illustrate this.

The field of women's studies confronts the dilemma posed to any modern social science discipline by post-modern versions of truth and theory. Feminists disagree with modern Enlightenment versions of truth because they are assumed to be grounded in a male point of view—competitive and rational instead of emotional, caring, and intuitive (van Vucht Tijssen 1990: 148, 156). These feminists who reject theory as "patriarchal and oppressive" gather support from those post-modernists who deny the possibility of theory (Weedon 1987: 9). A post-modern critique of modern social science also initially appeals to some feminists (Nicholson 1990: 5). It is not surprising then that many feminists embrace post-modern philosophy: "Feminist theorists, like other postmodernists, should encourage us to tolerate, invite, and interpret ambivalence, ambiguity, and multiplicity, as well as to expose the roots of our needs for imposing order and structure no matter how arbitrary and oppressive these may be" (Flax 1990: 183).

But the post-modern view may not be any more acceptable to feminists than the male-dominated modern. Skeptical post-modernists assume all versions of truth are equal, and they contend that a feminist perspective is as arbitrary as any other. Feminists necessarily argue for the superiority of their own point of view (Di Stefano 1990). Feminists who are suspicious of the post-modern approach suggest that women need an epistemology where "knowledge is possible," where in their search to understand the world, their own vision is accepted as "valid" (Harding 1990). If, as the skeptical post-modernists argue, there is no truth, no objective means to distinguish between right and wrong views, then only power remains for deciding whose perspective will prevail; indeed, women are among the groups that, historically, have had very little power.

Another example of a confrontation between modern and post-modern versions of truth and theory arises in an applied area of the social sciences, post-modern public administration. The new post-modern form of this discipline does not provide "how to do it" information because there is no clear conceptual scheme, no single right answer or best approach, if truth and theory are abolished. The field of post-modern public administration lives with the conditions of tension and change and treats as suspect those in public agencies who have a "mission" or "mandate" that claims to represent truth. Post-modernists see such advocates as self-serving bureaucrats with "obsolete programs" because "the modern is obsolete" (Caldwell 1975: 569). Tension, resulting from this conflict between the modern and post-modern, leads to a division everywhere in the field: between government and public, within the administrative structure of government, and within the personality of each individual manager. For post-modern public administration there is no longer any "right" policy or superior guiding wisdom, no remaining shared assumptions because of the impossibility of modern truth or theory. How, then, is the post-modern administrator to deal with the urgent environmental and economic crises that require the immediate attention of governmental agencies?

The new post-modern public administration aims for "foresight, initiative, flexibility, sensitivity and new forms of knowledge" that are not truth claims, not technological or procedural so much as "interactive and synergistic" (Caldwell 1975). Supporters of this concept of administration assert that it is not nihilistic, that it is not a lazy attitude of contentment with ignorance; rather, they argue, it is a search for new forms of knowledge and new roles for administration in a post-modern world without truth. The post-modern administrator will be neither a technician nor a generalist. S/he will rather conceptualize and present policy alternatives. This requires competence and an ability to share information (not defined as knowledge) with the broader public.

Doubts about truth and theory lead post-modern sociologists to move in the same direction. Sociological theory, if it exists, may be "interesting": it may define problems and identify certain arguments, but it is neither "rational or true." Post-modern sociologists are not "enforcers of intellectual discipline and order" (Seidman 1989: 636). They survive not as truth givers ("legislators") so much as "interpreters," perhaps as those who arbitrate between communities of knowledge, each of which offers "truths" that are central to their own respective group but have no weight or special status in other arenas (Bauman 1987). These sociologists have no need for universal truth or final interpretations. They facilitate communication rather than decide which community reproduced the "appropriate meaning." The role of the sociologist is that "of translating statements, made within one communally based tradition, so that they can be understood within the system of knowledge based on another tradition" (Bauman 1987: 5).

Post-modern anthropologists disclaim all modern anthropological truth and theory. Truth in anthropology, considered mere invention, is constantly being re-invented. Post-modernists contend that modern anthropology creates the very phenomena it seeks to study and cannot therefore be involved in discovering truth. One post-modern anthropologist cites the example of the Maori of New Zealand. Early anthropologists studying the origins of these people offered histories, sometimes constructed on the basis of dubious documents, that have subsequently been woven into the Maori myths so thoroughly that today the distinction between truth and invention as concerns their origins disappears altogether. This development is said to be appropriate because "invention is an ordinary event in the development of all discourse, which therefore never rests on a permanent foundation. . . . 'Traditional culture' is increasingly recognized to be more an invention constructed for contemporary purposes than a stable heritage handed on from the past" (Hanson 1989: 890, 899).

When post-modern anthropologists give up truth and theory they simultaneously give up authority and surrender responsibility. The "monological authority" of the ethnographer who sets out to study an exotic people in a far away land is no longer defensible because the goal of such activity, the formulation of theory and truth, is no longer legitimate. The truth of an anthropological text then depends not on the "willed intentions of an originating author," but rather on the "creative activity of a reader" (Clifford 1988: 520).

Post-modern anthropology cannot offer truth, but it is not without content. It is interpretative, "experiential, dialogical, polyphonic." It is receptivity, dialogue, listening to and talking with the other. It reveals "paradox, myth, and enigma, and it persuades by showing, reminding, hinting, and evoking" rather than by constructing theories and approximating truth (Tyler 1984: 329). All that can be offered in post-modern anthropology is narrative, fragmented fantasies, one person's stories. Anthropology is in this view "persuasive fiction" (Strathern 1987) or poetry (Tyler 1984).[12]

In these examples from public administration, sociology, and anthropology we see that the disciplines in question remain intact, despite revisions initiated by affirmative post-modernists and generated by the absence of truth. Such continuity is less apparent when the skeptical post-modernists determine the agenda for redefining the role of truth in the social sciences. For example, the skeptics question the viability of political science as a field when they reduce political events to mere linguistic description. "Political language is political reality" for skeptical post-modern political scientists, and there is no other reality "as far as the meaning of events and actors and spectators is concerned" (Edelman 1988: 104). If language is always strategy, rationalization, construction, then truth is impossible (Edelman 1988: chap. 6).

Post-modern challenges surrounding truth and theory are not always easy to accommodate in any of the truth-dependent social science fields. For example, from a conventional point of view psychological analysis or therapy implies that there can be no cure if there is no truth (Kristeva 1986). Why bother with the struggle for understanding if there is no difference between consciousness and unconsciousness, manifest and latent, self-deception and self-awareness? If therapists in the field of psychology were to abandon any truth claims, would they not have to admit that all

---

[12] With respect to economics McCloskey (1990: 36, 162) makes a similar argument that he considers merely a "story," a form of "literature," rich rhetoric.

insight was of equal value? Would such an admission not undermine the very activity of therapy itself? Such worries do not discourage post-modern probes in the field of psychology. The question is now being asked, "How much, if any of the patient's dream text does the reader-analyst write in the process of clinical interpretation?" (Kugler 1988: 64).

Modern psychology has long emphasized that what the client in therapy told the therapist was only a narrative, a story, not a real representation of actual experience (Howard 1991). Post-modernists agree. But while the modern therapist's role might be to help the client sort things out, get below the surface, and achieve a more adequate understanding of reality, the post-modern therapist has no such intent. There is no true reality out there to discover. Therefore, the post-modern therapist merely "disrupts the frame of reference" and "manipulates meanings" by referring to marginalized subtexts, to alternative interpretations; in so doing the therapist "changes the client's meanings" (Hare-Mustin and Marecek 1988: 460–61). Modern versions of truth get lost along the way, and this threatens any version of psychology, psychoanalysis, or therapy that assumes reality and the superior truth value of some interpretations (those of the analyst) over others (those of the patient).

5. Consequences of Post-Modern Views of Theory and Truth for the Social Sciences

The consequences of the post-modern view of truth and theory are enormous. Rigid truth claims are unfashionable in the social sciences today, but the need for theory is central. Social scientists of every orientation find it extremely difficult to give up theory as the skeptics require. A world without theory means an absolute equality of all discourse, an end to foundational claims. The entire intellectual climate of the social sciences would be transformed. Truth would be replaced by new forms of post-modern "clarity," irony with regard to our own disbelief, recognition of our individual "will to power," discovery of "strength through moderation" and ultimately a "transvaluation of all values" (Hassan 1987: 197).[13]

One possible outcome of the absence of universal theory is overload. Here it is not only a question of no theory but also an instance of too many theories that are altogether equal. In a situation where there is no possibility of employing specific criteria to arbitrate between texts, among theo-

[13] The New Age post-modern current (discussed in Chapter 8) speaks of a movement for truth through global unity, worldwide peace around the planet, "transformational values," guided by a "spiritual aura" (Bordewich 1988). All this is would be difficult to integrate into modern social science.

ries, as concerns relative truth claims, there is no way of reducing their numbers, selecting some for greater attention, and ignoring those obviously irrelevant or fraudulent.

Critics argue that post-modernism erases the difference between truth and error (or between theory and nonsense) and that this opens the door to nihilism. "Since there is no truth, there is no error either, and all beliefs are equal" (Scholes 1989: 56). Vattimo, a skeptical post-modernist, acknowledges the validity of this complaint and argues that nihilism is a respected and viable philosophical tradition (1988). But most skeptics claim that when they recognize the impossibility of truth they are not endorsing nihilism. They argue, rather, that the absence of truth is a positive, liberating activity inasmuch as it accepts "complexity and complication" (Hoy 1989: 45). Derrida contends that the absence of any possibility of truth claims makes not for nihilism; rather, it makes totalitarianism impossible, he argues, because totalitarianism depends so completely on its own version of truth (Schwartz 1990: 10), and post-modernism undercuts it by negating the possibility of truth. Post-modern social scientists similarly argue that post-modernism mediates against totalitarianism because by abandoning truth claims it affirms the gentler practices of "listening, questioning, and speaking" (Ashley and Walker 1990a: 395).

The post-modern view—there is no truth, and all is construction—is itself the ultimate contradiction. By making this statement post-modernists assume a position of privilege. They assert as true their own view that "there is no truth." In so doing they affirm the possibility of truth itself. Few post-modernists escape this dilemma, but those who try (Derrida and Ashley are examples) relativize everything, including their own statements. They say even their own views are not privileged. They warn their readers that the views they express are only their own and not superior to the opinions of others. But even this relativist position, once stated positively, implicitly assumes truth. It assumes truth in the statement that what they are saying is not more veracious than any other position. There is simply no logical escape from this contradiction except to remain silent.

Modern social science seeks to produce objective theory that can be challenged on the basis of data. Theory is data dependent, and data has priority over theory in the sense that if data show the theory to be wrong, then the theory must be abandoned, given that the rules of method have been respected. Data and evidence are the basis for arbitrating between two competing theories. They may eventually both be found wrong; but both cannot be right. All this, the post-modernists argue, is mere propaganda because either theory does not exist or, if it does, then data are subordinate to theory (Gergen 1987: 2). Every fact is itself theory laden, a construction without meaning independent of language, intuitive interpretation, and context. Facts are defined, even invented, by the community and have no

meaning outside that collectivity (Smith 1988: 105). Post-modernists reduce social science knowledge to the status of stories.

A note of caution is in order before we proceed. The whole discussion
between post-modernists and a stereotyped positivist version of modern
social science overlooks points of agreement between the two. Many modern social scientists would agree with the post-modernists about the complexity of the social world. They would be the first to admit that although
truth is a goal in social science, it is admittedly never attained. But they
would disagree with the skeptical post-modernists who assert that this
complexity is so absolute as to render all "truths," no matter how absurd,
equal.

Post-modernism's questioning of truth and theory is only one dimension of its larger challenge to modern social science. The dispute between
the two is all encompassing, but it is especially severe as concerns methodology. A discussion of this topic is reserved for Chapter 7. First, we
consider a related topic, representation.

6

REPUDIATING REPRESENTATION

People . . . must know how to resist a diversity of
representational practices that would traverse them, claim their
time, control their space and their bodies, impose limitations
on what can be said and done, and decide their being.
(Ashley and Walker 1990a: 261)

It is as if everyone voted by chance, or monkeys voted. . . . At
this point it makes no difference at all what the parties in
power are expressing historically and socially. It is necessary
even that they represent nothing: the fascination of the game,
the polls, the formal and statistical compulsion of the game is
all the greater.
(Baudrillard 1983c: 132)

MOST POST-MODERNISTS are anti-representational. They
consider representation central to modernity, its social organization, its political structure, its underlying foundations and
philosophy.[1] Modern representation certainly stakes out its territory in the
broadest of terms. It is *delegation*; one individual represents another in par-
liament. It is *resemblance*; a painting represents on the canvas what the
painter observes. It is *replication*; the photograph (image) represents the
person photographed (object). It is *repetition*; a writer puts on paper the
word (language) that represents his/her idea or thought (meaning). It is
substitution; a lawyer represents a client in court. It is *duplication*; a photo-
copy represents the original. Representation in its diverse forms is central
to every field in the social sciences, and perhaps for this reason the battle
between modernism and post-modernism rages savagely on this terrain
(Shapiro 1988).

In this chapter the post-modern case against modern representation in
language, politics, epistemology, and methodology is considered. We see
that post-modernists trace core assumptions, whatever form they may take,
across all their various conceptual referents. And this is fair inasmuch as

---

[1] Some who are quite sympathetic to post-modernism, however, are unwilling to reject
representation and this is discussed below. Others find the entire post-modern critique of
representation confused and the link between it and anti-representation unclear or unnecessary (Arac 1986: xx–xxi).

representation, whether it refers to "playful fantasy" or "serious reality," shares structural similarities (Mitchell 1990: 12). Common to the post-modern critique of representation in every field is the view that it involves re-presenting one thing, person, place, or time as (or in) another thing, person, place, or time; it is assumed that the transference is made without loss of content or violation of intention. I point out the implications of the post-modern critique of representation for democracy and the theory of the public sphere. Finally, I consider some responses to post-modern anti-representationalism in the various social science fields.

The post-modern critique of representation, especially that of the skeptical post-modernists, has been inspired, historically and philosophically, by Nietzsche, Wittgenstein, Heidegger (see Olkowski 1988), Barthes, and Foucault. Apparent in it is Nietzsche's pessimism about democratic representation in politics and epistemological objectivity. Nietzsche (1954, 1967, 1969) opposed democratic representation because it allowed the weakest elements (numerically preponderant) in the society to form a majority and dominate the "strong and exceptional." This is because the "strong and exceptional" by definition are bound to be a minority. In a similar fashion Wittgenstein emphasized linguistic relativism (the irreducible pluralism of language) and the impossibility of representing any "reality" with language. Heidegger (1962, 1972, 1973, 1977) opposed democratic individualism, rationalism, advanced technology, the managerial society, capitalism, voluntarism—all of which have come to be synonymous with Western representational democracy. Barthes (1975: 33, 56) reasoned that words are only symbolic representations with no direct relation to the world. Foucault's contribution is more complex. He argued that between about 1650 and 1800 (classical period) representation was clear, authentic, straightforward; "representation was a universal, neutral, conscious, 'objective' mode of thought" (Sheridan 1980: 82). But when wo/man, as subject, appeared at the end of the eighteenth century, representation became "opaque" (Foucault 1970: 310). Because wo/man was the subject and object of her/his own knowledge, representation became more complicated. It became secondary and derivative even if not recognized as such (Foucault 1970: 313, 361). Foucault concluded that, when the object and subject of representation are closely linked rather than separate and autonomous, simple, natural representation is no longer possible (1970: 10), and thus the post-modern world is without genuine representation.

Most affirmative post-modernists are as hostile to modern political representation as the skeptics, but some call for new forms of representation (see Mouffe 1988, for example). This is the case with the affirmatives who support new post-modern social movements (discussed in Chapter 8) or those who have ties to oppressed groups that are still struggling to achieve adequate representation. To oppressed minorities and women, representation is not easily dismissed because it is essential to their demands for equality (Arac 1986: xxi). The affirmatives do not talk so much about doing away with representation as they do about the need for more and better forms of representation. For example, some call for substituting the "politics of presentation, placement, sublimation and allusion, revelation, symbolism, everyday life, and related alternatives" for modern representation (Nelson 1987: 10). Or they may be more concrete, as is the case with Richard Falk who tells us modern representation is "territorial in relation to sovereign states and statist in relation to world political institutions." But today, he continues, "territorial allocations of political authority" are no longer efficient, equitable, or accurate. New "critical behavioral patterns are non-territorial in their locus of effects, the state is porous, and the burden of current practice falls on the future." Falk proposes two specific and concrete representational improvements designed to reflect post-modern reality: first, a new legislative chamber, the "House of Overseas Delegates" (named by election and appointment), should be added to the United States Congress to provide representation for those countries effected by decisions emanating from the United States but who have no voice in those decisions; second, he suggests that the United Nations add "a third chamber constituted by representatives of the peoples of the world and of the nongovernmental sector of human affairs" (Falk 1989: 29).

1. The Post-Modern Critique of Representation

The crisis of representation crosscuts post-modernism in every field from art to psychology, and in each case "the end of the Order of Representation" is heralded. Representative democracy is alienating; representative art is boring; representative literature is desecrating, with its use of metaphor, figurative reference, deliberate manipulation of language (Elgin 1984: 925); representational history is deceptive; and so forth. What is really interesting cannot be represented: ideas, symbols, the universe, the absolute, God, the just, or whatever. Representation is alien to what post-modernists value: the romantic, emotions, feelings. According to the skeptical post-modernists, representation is politically, socially, culturally, linguistically, and epistemologically arbitrary. It signifies mastery. They argue that representation is dangerous and basically "bad" (Derrida 1982: 304; Arac 1986: xx). It signals distortion; it assumes unconscious rules governing relationships. It concretizes, finalizes, and excludes complexity. The affirmative post-modernists join the skeptics when they claim that modern representation is fraudulent, perverse, artificial, mechanical, deceptive, incomplete, misleading, insufficient, wholly inadequate for the post-modern age.

Post-modernists contend that representation depends on fallacious assumptions. Because ultimately all representation refers to other representations, nothing is ever authentic (Mitchell 1990: 16–17; Baudrillard 1981). Representation assumes the validity of a copy that is only a simulacrum, a copy of a copy, a copy for which there is no original. The fraudulent turns out to be as authentic and true as reality because the distinction between true and false fades in a post-modern world (Baudrillard 1983c). Post-modernists argue that there is no content to society apart from the rhetoric of representation (Ryan 1982: 574–75). Political rhetoric creates a world in the mind and a whole set of social relations that it is supposed to be "representing." In fact, it just conceals its own function of manipulation of what exists.

The post-modern call for an end to the order of representation is related to other post-modern concepts. The end of the author and the death of the subject perspectives of the skeptical post-modernists are in line with post-modernism's anti-representationalism. The author (subject) needs to represent the invented characters of a novel or the actors in a play (Touraine 1988a: 151–53). Eliminate these, as the skeptical post-modernists suggests (Chapters 2 and 3), and one can quite easily do without representation. Representation goes along with humanism in politics, giving voice to the largest number of people possible, and skeptical post-modernists reject it. Theory is impossible without representation in the sense that theory tries to sketch out, map (represent), reality. These post-modernists argue that in the absence of truth one must welcome multiple interpretations, whereas representation assumes something out there is true or valid enough to be re-presented. Modern representation assumes "meaning or truth preceded and determined the representations that communicated it." Post-modernists argue it is the other way around; representations create the "truth" they supposedly reflect (Ryan 1988: 560).

Representation assumes a clear distinction between presence and absence, and skeptical post-modernism erases both. In Chapter 4 we saw how the post-modern view of time questions the idea that something or someone is ever entirely present or absent; post-modern conceptions of space consider representational maps wholly inadequate. Representation is the practice of taking one thing for another, and this assumes the identity of a concept with some undefinable, unspoken presence.[2] For example, "the

---

[2] Hanna Pitkin's (1967) consideration of representation anticipates much of what is today considered post-modern. Her work, especially her definition of representation as the re-presentation of something not literally present, appears to have inspired post-modern political science.

representation of citizens . . . secures the presence of the people in their absence" (Norton 1988: 5).

The relationship of representation to language, symbols, and signs is another site of conflict, and the skeptical post-modernists pursue this point with energy. Representation takes for granted the referential status of words, images, meaning, and symbols; it assumes that each constitutes a fixed system of meaning and that everybody understands them more or less the same way. An anti-representational stance assumes the opposite: many diverse meanings are possible for any symbol, gesture, word, and these diversities are to be explored. Language has no direct relationship to the real world; it is, rather, only symbolic (Barthes 1975: 33, 56). Representation, then, is inadequate in all its various forms because images of the world are language dependent and cannot be exchanged between people with any degree of certainty. All representation is mediated by language that makes it "linguistically reflective" rather than reality related. Signs "no longer represent anything and no longer have their equivalent in reality" (Baudrillard 1983a: 19).

The affirmative post-modernists do not disagree with the skeptics' critique of modern representation. But they do employ modern representation in their own intellectual work. This implies an inconsistency. But, as I discuss shortly, the affirmatives also call for more adequate forms of political representation. The skeptics' critique of representation depends on linguistic indeterminacy, and this theme is less important to the affirmatives, perhaps because the affirmatives have a stake in communicating their own positive project to others (more about this in Chapter 8).

2. Representation in Methodology and Epistemology

Hostility to representation is linked to the post-modern preference for soft rather than positivist epistemology, to its aversion to objectivity, and to its insistence that difference is more important than sameness. Anti-representation leads post-modernists to criticize modern scientific epistemology for its materialist concept of reality, for its separation of subject and object, and for its emphasis on generalization. Most of what follows in this section reflects the skeptics' point of view, an opinion from which the affirmatives only occasionally dissent.

As shown in Chapter 7, section 2, post-modern methodological alternatives of deconstruction and intuitive interpretation make no claim to representation. One main goal of deconstruction is to lay out the deficiency of representational claims (Hoy 1985a: 44). Representation is epistemologically objectionable because it assumes the ability to reproduce and duplicate external reality. Objects are supposed to refer directly to things outside themselves that can be represented. In other words, representation implies that things exist independently in a real world, and the post-modernists contend the real no longer exits. Attempting to represent an exterior world also affirms reality as knowledge, as universal, as truth, and post-modernists dispute the possibility of all these (Megill 1985: 94–95; Nelson 1987: 17).

Post-modernists argue that representation likewise assumes that an "individual's information processing procedures" can in fact represent "external reality" (Henriques et al. 1984: 98). An "external object of nature is conveyed to the inner subject or mind through the agency of 'representatives' of sense or 'ideas' " (Redner 1987: 674). Post-modernists doubt this, and they seek a more subjective, non-representational conception of reality. They abandon any attempt to represent the object of study "as it really is," independent of the process of inquiry. Post-modernists argue that representation implies objectivity, that is, an observer independent from the thing or person being represented (Baudrillard 1983a: 20–22). Within the framework of representation there is a separate subject and object; the subject as researcher seeks to represent and the object of inquiry is represented. Because of its claim of objectivity, representation leads to a "compulsion to judge accuracy or correctness" (Rosmarin 1985: 87), and post-modernists reject such judgment as logocentric, without any basis.

Post-modernists believe that representation encourages generalization, and in so doing it focuses on identity and fails to appreciate the importance of difference. Representation takes a "resemblance between things" and ascribes "complete congruence, denying difference" (Judovitz 1988: 68, 70–71). It emphasizes the sameness of the original and the represented. It assumes homogeneity, implying equivalence and identity of interest.

Post-modernists argue representation is always indeterminate because the definition of what is represented must necessarily be constituted on the basis of the difference between what is being represented and everything else (Baudrillard 1981, 1983c). When Derrida notes that "différance is also the element of the same" (Derrida 1981: 9), he is suggesting that "meaning can never come to rest on an absolute presence, its determinate specification is deferred, from one substitutive linguistic interpretation to another, in a movement without end" (Abrams 1981: 39). Difference, of course, can never be established because definition is forever postponed.

The post-modernists then question the possibility of ever authentically representing anything. They suggest focusing not on the generalizable, the unified, what is common to the modern world, but rather on all that difference implies, what can never be adequately represented. This calls for a nonrepresentational methodology or none at all.

3. Post-Modernism, Democracy, and Representation

Questions related to politics and post-modernism are the subject of Chapter 8, but democracy is so closely identified with the concept of representation that the relationship of the two demands immediate consideration. Post-modern anti-representationalism takes two forms: the first, advanced by the skeptical post-modernists is pessimistic and anti-democratic.[3] Many characterize it as nihilist, negative, and despairing. The other current, stressed by the affirmatives, is more optimistic and pro-democratic. The affirmatives argue for the positive reconstruction or replacement of representation; or they abandon modern political representation for more direct versions of democracy.

Almost all modern political systems make some attempt to be representational. Those assumed to be represented vary from the "people" to the "proletariat."[4] Specially designated individuals, assemblies, parties, workplace units, or whatever are authorized to represent, to speak for others, to re-present their views in the public sphere. If, as most post-modernists contend, this device for representing a large number of individuals in mass society is unacceptable, an aberration, then a crisis of representation results. The crisis of democracy may follow closely.

The skeptical post-modernists understand political representation to be a symbol of modern Western democracy, and they reject both.[5] Modern representation is said to distort political action and discourse because it is so easily manipulated. First, the mass media, the "consciousness industry," is said to "upset choice" and to encourage candidates for public office to give only a superficial consideration to political issues, thereby rendering

[3] Post-modernists are not the only ones who propose that political representation is a fiction. E. Morgan (1988) presents what reviewers call an "elitist" view from the right; he argues that representation, resting on the invention of popular sovereignty, is pure fiction. Few post-modernists would disagree. But this alone does not make post-modernists conservative (see Chapter 8).

[4] If democracy means simply that "the people rule," then the link to representation is tenuous. Many totalitarian governments claim to be both democratic and representative in the sense that they rule in the "interest" of all the people.

[5] Post-modernists do not naively attribute representational infractions to any single political system, but rather they target all systems of modern rule because they all involve the domination of the weak by the strong. Representation may be the "central core of bourgeois ideology," but socialists and communists also appeal to representation as a vehicle of legitimation (Redner 1987: 675). In a representative democracy people authorize representatives to re-present their needs, demands, and interests in the decision-making process (à la Hobbes and Locke). The state is assumed to "represent" the people as John Stuart Mill tells us. But Lenin argued along the same lines that the vanguard political party "represents" the fundamental interests of the proletariat because it embodies the true proletarian consciousness (Lenin 1905: 18–19; 1917: 403–4). Ke (1990) compares liberal and socialist representation and finds they differ as to a "formalist" or "substantive" focus.

representation inauthentic (Baudrillard 1983a). Politics has become popular theater and media image, rather than the public discussion of political policies. Second, bureaucracy, administration, and management are faulted as substitutes for genuine representation in their takeover of political legislation. Policy making substitutes for political decision, and committee deliberation replaces open, public debate (Redner 1987: 674, 677). As a result, people no longer feel they "belong to the order of representation." They have ceased to "speak," to "express themselves." The masses are surveyed, polled, tested, but not to encourage the interactive representation that was assumed in the past when social meaning flowed "between one poll and another." All that is left, today, is the silent majority living in the absence of viable representation (Baudrillard 1983a).

The skeptical post-modernists argue that democracy assumes representation, and because representation fails, so too does democracy.[6] They conclude that democracy is mere mass assemblage and dissent is no longer possible. Representation enforces consensus, and democracy-as-majority-rule dictates to the minority and to those who disagree.

Skeptical post-modernists have been thoroughly criticized for their anti-representational and anti-democratic views even by those who share their critique of modernity (Cahoone 1988: 228). If post-modernists seek to substitute "creation" for representation in the arts (Graff 1979: 23), then in politics they substitute narcissistic, hedonistic, individual, anarchistic forms of political expression for the more pragmatic, parliamentary forms of mobilization required by representative democracy. Skeptical post-modernists are criticized for their failure to support participatory forms of government and decision making. Certainly democracy has its weaknesses, but to do away with representative democracy, as some skeptics propose, is more likely to lead to authoritarianism than anything else. The skeptical post-modern anti-representational views are attributed to the post-modern individual's overdeveloped, "overprotected" sense of self. S/he cannot accept that s/he might be "represented" by anyone else. Lipovetsky, along these lines, contends that the post-modern personality is fundamentally anti-democratic (1983: 141–43).

Affirmative post-modernists criticize representative democracy as inadequate and unauthentic, as "inferior and derivative," and as legitimating repressive regimes. But they favor "political self-determination and freedom" (Redner 1987: 676); thus, when they speak about the absence or the demise of democracy they do so with regret. Many of them favor more

---

[6] Anti-democratic sentiments today are not limited to post-modernists. Celebrations of the bicentennial of the French Revolution a few years ago saw the simultaneous publication of many major works on that topic and revealed profound pessimism concerning democracy. The authoritarian, even totalitarian, potential of democratic social movements was a central concern (see, for example, Furet and Ozouf 1988).

direct forms of democracy (Walker 1988a). They call for a "deepening of democracy" (Walker 1988b: 116), for greater and more meaningful, authentic self-government in which broad democratic participation is possible and meaningful. Democracy needs to come to mean "empowerment" (Walker 1988b: 140).

The affirmative post-modernists are anti-representational, and their demand for direct, authentic democracy is consistent with their other positions. Calling for the end of author(ity) and positing multiple interpretations, in a sense, can be viewed as authentically democratic. Affirmative post-modernists deny that anyone can have a monopoly of truth, whereas modern versions of representative democracy assure a monopoly of truth to the electoral victor. Affirmative post-modernists are anti-elitist, in the sense of doing away with the expert role in judging art, music, and literature. They demand popular control, unmediated by the state, over national and social resources (Aronowitz 1988a: 48). They advocate direct democracy as local autonomy where every citizen can participate in political discussions because this fosters the development of subgroup identity,[7] and with it post-modern social movements flourish (see Chapter 8).

Affirmative post-modernists emphasize free choice, openness, tolerance (Nelson 1987: 10), liberty, personalism, and some forms of individualism (Lipovetsky 1983). They interpret these to be compatible with post-modern versions of democracy that might include cooperatives and collective social forms (Lipovetsky 1983). Skeptical post-modernists would agree if these collectives do not infringe on the liberty of the individual (Corlett 1989; Harvey 1989: 351) and, thus, do not deprive the post-modern individual of his or her autonomy.

4. Representation, the Decline of the Public Sphere, and Post-Modernism

Public-sphere theory, the view that a public sphere independent of the private sphere is essential for a healthy polity, is of interest to post-modernists because it does *not* require representation and because it too is critical of modern representative democracy. Post-modern reactions to the theory of the public sphere vary, however, revealing important internal differences about political representation and democracy. Some affirmative post-modernists argue for the revival of a public sphere distinct from the private sphere; they hope that this will make for authentic post-modern democracy. As we shall see, the skeptics disagree.

We begin with a description of public-sphere theory as formulated by

[7] Conservatives see the overdevelopment of subgroup identity on the basis of race, religion, or nationalism as a source of danger to representative democracy (Himmelfarb 1989b: 25).

Habermas (1974, 1989b) because this version of the theory is most frequently of interest to post-modernists.[8] Next I present post-modern reactions to the public-sphere theory.

Historically a public sphere of interactive discourse, separate from the private sphere, assumes *not* representation, but only an interested, educated, articulate citizenry that looks beyond personal self-interest and private issues and emphasizes the common good. The existence of a healthy public sphere in a democracy means decisions are the result of rational-critical debate, intersubjective communication, preferably of a face-to-face character that takes place in an open forum where it can be publicly reviewed. The public sphere assumes that political authority will be judged on the basis of rational criticism (Habermas 1989b).

It is not essential that every citizen participate or that s/he even be represented in the public sphere, but it is essential that all those interested in topics of public concern be able to take part in a general conversation, that the broadest range of opinion on a topic be publicly aired, and that the rules of evidence and argument be consciously applied. This activity seeks a judicious, wise, thoughtful agreement about society's needs and the best policy for a nation. The concept of the public sphere assumes that public dialogue and public deliberation, freely engaged among private individuals, can achieve an approximation of truth through an exchange of ideas (Habermas 1974: 55). The result is reconciliation of differing views—if not consensus, at least general agreement.

But today, public-sphere theorists argue, the public sphere as an independent arena of discussion, distinct from the state, is threatened (Agger 1990: 29). The distinction between public and private is said to be disintegrating. If the public and private are fused, then the public sphere ceases to function, and an impartial assessment of the state sphere is no longer possible. Those institutions that made rational discussion possible in the past and guaranteed the integrity of the public sphere (freedom of speech, assembly, and communication) today undermine it.[9] The failure of repre-

---

[8] Habermas himself admits that it is an ideal, never realized, concept (1989b). See Calhoun (forthcoming c) for a summary of Habermas's book *The Structural Transformation of the Public Sphere*.

[9] For example, the role of the mass media is no longer either to communicate information about political matters to the public or to facilitate activity in the public sphere. It rather deforms public debate and transforms politics into theater and entertainment (Habermas 1978). It obliterates the distinction between private and public (Kellner 1989b; Baudrillard 1983c) as people internalize the mass message, and it becomes reality for them. The questions considered appropriate for public discussion are more limited, and the "threshold of opinions considered subversive" grows because the media defines political issues as matters of emotion and image (Bauman 1986–87: 90). Today the mass media function to guarantee only participation and integration, not the functioning of a healthy public sphere separate from the private sphere.

sentation as it has developed in modern democracies is held responsible, in good measure, for the decline of the public sphere.

Habermas argues that modern representation has been antithetical to the survival of a healthy public sphere for several reasons. Modern legislatures and parliaments are not forums for differing opinions, for criticism and debate, because the modern representative is instruction-bound. S/he merely re-presents and defends preconceived opinion that reflects the collective self-interest of those who either elected him or her or financed the winning electoral campaign. The role of the representative today is to set forth the demands of their constituency, be it the political party, a pressure group, labor unions, and so on.[10] Representation becomes the "translation of interests" (Habermas 1974: 55). The legislature is transformed into a theater, offering platforms for presenting propaganda. No meaningful exchange occurs. No one changes his/her mind as a result of enlightened discussion of differing points of view.

What derives from modern representation is not the best reasoned approximation to truth, not rational consideration of issues, as promised by public-sphere theory. Rather a leveling out of collective self-interest results in the form of a compromise between competing organized interests. The basis for such accommodation is often secret, scarcely ever publicly reviewed. No one is responsible for the universal interest (Bauman 1987). Compromise replaces trust in reason (Habermas 1989b).[11]

The questions for post-modernists are whether the existence of an authentic public sphere would facilitate a post-modern form of politics without representation and whether this would be desirable. The affirmatives are distressed at the decline of the public sphere, but few relate this to the crisis of representation. Some take refuge in daily life experience, hoping that the private sphere will remain private even if the public sphere disintegrates. In this scenario the need for representation is diminished as each individual represents himself or herself in everyday life. Those affirmative

---

[10] Such representation, to the extent that it works, is imperfect: not all individuals are represented by groups to begin with, and those that are "are imperfectly represented" (Habermas 1974: 34–35).

[11] This author is of the opinion that there is, in fact, no inherent contradiction between representation and a vibrant public sphere. Historically in the West an independent public sphere flourished in instances where individuals represented themselves, at least for those sectors that had any chance of influencing decisions. If certain conditions are met, representation could certainly contribute to the growth of a public sphere today. Representatives would need to be able to follow their own consciences and look to the general interest to freely formulate and express reasoned arguments and explore policy consequences. The parliamentary or legislative body would have to function as a body of wise men and women whose role was to consider what was best for all the people. Delegates would present a wide range of differing opinion. Debates and discussion would need to be public rather than confidential and broadly diffused rather than restricted to a narrowly circumscribed group of citizens.

post-modernists involved in political projects are the most concerned about the need for a public sphere. They applaud the emphasis public-sphere theory places on authentic participation. They call for expanding the space for the public sphere into areas where modern representation is unnecessary. Thus all citizens can be personally involved in critical debate in the public sphere (Harvey 1989: 351). This can be accomplished by increasing the locations where decisions are made at the community level. Some affirmatives link the call for new forms of democracy to a renewal of a "public space," independent of political party and state, as an expression of everyday life. But they caution this is possible only if the whole society assumes responsibility for issues, demands, and conflicts (Melucci 1990: 6). Would some form of representation be required to assure the success of this project? Agger (1990) implies as much when he calls for a public sphere that is open to all through the "public voice." The public voice encourages a representation of voices. It resists elite culture and encourages writers and intellectuals both to communicate their ideas in "a new voice," in jargon-free language that enjoins a broader base, and to bolster its participation in the production of a democratic public sphere.[12]

Neo-Marxists, some of whom are close to affirmative post-modernists (see Chapter 8), call for the creation of autonomous public spaces where intersubjective communication is still feasible. These spaces, they argue, should not be controlled by profit, the marketplace, and they should not function to legitimate the state (Habermas 1987a).

The skeptical post-modernists have more reservations about public-sphere theory.[13] They doubt that the public sphere can be revived in a post-modern era, and even if this were possible, they are suspicious about its democratic aspirations that they consider a facade. They argue that the public sphere is part of modern oppression because discussion in the public sphere depends on "force." Such discussion is a form of "struggle," and the stronger argument always carries the day. Opinions must be surrendered to the one "determined" to be the "better." Public-sphere theory incorporates Enlightenment thinking, they charge, because it assumes that false arguments are the result of error, bad faith, faulty logic. In the end discourse in the public sphere assumes one person is the "winner" and the rest "losers." Public-sphere rhetoric is charged with disguising or ignoring the

---

[12] "Democratizing expert language reinvents languages, overcoming the distinction between quotidian discourse and a more rarefied code heretofore monopolized by jealous professionals." Agger's hope is that such an activity could "empower these dulled readers to become writers—public figures—themselves" (Agger 1990: 215, 219). Agger is not, however, naive about the possibility of this project. As he points out, the political economy of publishing dissuades intellectuals from writing texts relevant for the public sphere (1990).

[13] Marxists and feminists also criticize the concept of the public sphere. For the Marxists it is too bourgeois, and it forgets inequality. For the feminists it is an entirely masculine concept (Fraser 1989: 117–19, 165–69).

competition that leads to the repression and annihilation of one side. Finally, the skeptics criticize the public-sphere assumption that even losers are winners because the losers agreed to the rules and through their loss confirm the community.

Thus, skeptical post-modernists reject the "dialogue idea" of the public sphere as "foolish idealism" (Sloterdijk 1984: 199). Such dialogue involves an independent acting modern subject concerned with political issues. The skeptics doubt the viability of the modern subject so necessary to the public sphere. The skeptics emphasize subjective private experience as ultimate reality and the public space as an artificial construction (Barth 1980: 69). Their post-modern individual pulls back from public discourse into the private personal sphere by choice or because of a lack of confidence in public governmental institutions and in the social welfare system. There is a general "privatization of individual concerns" (Bauman 1987). In a post-modern age everybody has his/her own truth, based on each individual's personal experience. All that remains is individual opinion, nameless, alienating, anonymous, mass politics that serves to isolate the citizen. Collectives no longer mediate between individual and state. People are detached; they watch TV rather than read out loud or interact with friends and family (Lash and Urry 1987: 297).[14]

Finally, the skeptics criticize public-sphere theory because it assumes the possibility of effective intersubjective communication. The transmission of public information to citizens and group discussion of public issues would be hopeless without successful communication. Because the skeptics emphasize the relative and subjective character of language and symbols they reject these assumptions that are so essential to public sphere theory. In addition, public-sphere theory places great emphasis on rationality and reason, and the skeptical post-modernists are suspicious of both.

Critics of post-modernism argue that despite general agreement about representation, post-modernists and public-sphere advocates are inherently in conflict. The public space is impossible in a world peopled by narcissistic post-modern individuals for whom an escalation of expectations means one is less likely to abide by the "rules of public discourse" and more likely to worry about how to get the most for oneself despite the "rules" (Sennet 1977: 334–36). If a public sphere is to survive and thrive, individ-

---

[14] Some on the left are hopeful that the very trends that make for a post-modern society might bring about the return of the public sphere. Increased mass media consumption could increase exposure to issues of public debate. It could both increase a citizen's knowledge of the public's power and enhance political efficacy. It could encourage universalism by breaking down individual particularistic identities (Lash and Urry 1987: 297). Some even see hopeful, democratic signs in the populism of post-modernism itself. It is, they say, democratic in its support of the multiplication of local TV and radio stations, regional news, expanded telephone and FAX services and the expansion of new forms of personal expression (e.g., new subgroup formations, computer bulletin board services) (Lipovetsky 1983).

uals will be given greater choice; they must accept greater responsibility, something the narcissistic post-modern individual avoids.

It has even been suggested that the fusion of the public and private sectors or their mutual collapse is cause for the rise of post-modernism. As system responsibility is reduced, as values are increasingly considered relative, as consumerism expands, people invest more in the private sphere. The individual is disaffected by the disappearance of the public sphere, and s/he turns inward, away from the public and toward everyday life concerns. But the private too is disappearing as an entity, and all that remains, say the skeptical post-modernists, is emptiness. In this environment, given this climate of opinion, post-modernism flourishes.

5. Implications of Post-Modern Anti-Representationalism for the Social Sciences and Some Examples

The post-modern call for an End of the Order of Representation poses both methodological and substantive problems for all the social sciences. Difficulties in both mapping social relations and doing comparative analysis result. Examples from sociology, anthropology, and political science are presented.

To the extent that social scientists attempt to "map" the social world in the sense of representing it, their efforts are questioned by the skeptical post-modernists, for whom any effort at constructing such maps will surely fail. Without the possibility of such representational mapping, the skeptics are, conspiciously, unable to either describe the social world or formulate theories about it because both processes assume representation. The affirmatives are willing to acknowledge that representation as mapping in the social sciences is likely to be imperfect (Jameson 1984a, 1988), but they still believe the effort to represent the social world is worthwhile. This position allows the affirmative post-modernists to continue doing social science, to engage in the representationally dependent activities of description, explanation, and theory construction even though in more modest forms.

Dismissing the possibility of representation undermines modern social science methods in general, but its questioning of comparative analysis is especially thoroughgoing. The very act of comparing, in an effort to uncover similarities and differences, is a meaningless activity because post-modern epistemology holds it impossible ever to define adequately the elements to be contrasted or likened. The skeptical post-modernists' reservations about the possibility of generalizing and their emphasis on difference, discussed above in Section 2, form the basis of rejecting the comparative method. If, as they conclude, everything is unique (Latour 1988: 179–81), then the comparative method is invalid in its attempts to search for and explain similarities and differences while holding certain dimensions constant (assuming a degree of sameness in other variables).[15] The affirmative post-modernists, as well, question the linguistic representation upon which any comparative statements are necessarily based. They also argue that comparative analysis makes assumptions about presence or absence, and this too is a contentious matter.

The field of anthropology has been especially sensitive to the post-modern call for an end to the order or representation. Some anthropologists reduce the whole of the post-modern challenge to this crisis of representation. Thus, there is a broad questioning in the field of anthropology as to the "uncertainty about adequate means for describing social reality" (Marcus and Fischer 1986: 8). The problem is fundamental in such a field, where so much depends on accurate description, on some degree of correspondence between what the scholar finds and what is "really out there." In anthropology this means there is doubt about whether it is even possible to describe (represent) other cultures and formulate theories about them (Rabinow 1986). But it also involves knowing what questions are appropriate for an ethnographer to ask about another culture.[16] As a result of the internal turmoil provoked by post-modern anti-representational views in anthropology, changes are occurring in how anthropologists and ethnographers write about other societies. For example, some post-modernists in these fields avoid the word "represent" altogether; they contend their goal is merely to "evoke." Evoking is preferable to representing because it is assumed to free one of objects, facts, descriptions, generalizations, experiments, and truth (Tyler 1986: 129–30). This solution may not satisfy all anthropologists because it implies a clear relinquishing of professional authority (Marcus and Fischer 1986: 8).

Sociology too has experienced a period of post-modern floundering, an identity crisis over the problems of representation.[17] "Totalizing vision is replaced by concerns with contextuality, exceptions, indeterminants," and meaning in general (Richardson 1988: 200). Some post-modern sociologists resolve the crisis of representation by abandoning the activity of the-

[15] Richardson discusses the dilemma involved in comparing. He attempted to write in the post-modern narrative voice in order to underline the uniqueness of each case studied and to avoid representational assumptions; but he was simply unable to talk about any collective story (1988: 205).

[16] Questions about questions as such are said to be "essentializing because they emerge from the very models they set out to interrogate" (Bove 1990: 53).

[17] The crisis of representation in sociology was heralded early in France by Pierre Bourdieu, who can hardly be regarded as a post-modernist. He employed Derrida's epistemology, concepts, and vocabulary in his work long before North American social scientists took much notice of it (Bourdieu 1984 is an example). At the same time that Bourdieu indulges and savors the dilemma of representation, as formulated by the French post-modern literary community, he nevertheless retains his critical positivist survey research methodology and an ideological commitment to the meta-narrative of Marxism (1984: 482–84).

ory construction altogether because it depends on the now dubious ability to re-present (Seidman 1989). Post-modern anti-representation leads others to reduce the claims they make for their scholarly research, transforming sociological activity into "storytelling" (constructing mini-narratives) rather than inquiry. It becomes "allegorical" or literary rather than scientific (Richardson 1988: 200–204). This strategy has certain advantages: One cannot be criticized by post-modernists if one simply refuses to make any knowledge claims, one cannot be denounced by one's modern colleagues for not being "scientific" if one erases the distinction between science and literature (Clifford and Marcus 1986: 4).

Another strategy suggested by some post-modern sociologists and anthropologists involves erasing the barrier between the representing subject and the represented object of inquiry. They propose to go "among the people" and simply let them "speak for themselves" (Pratt 1986: 32). This strategy is designed to end the "illusion of objectivity" and reduce the need to represent. This may not resolve the crisis of representation so much as shift the burden of representing from the researcher to "the people."

Post-modern anti-representation orients the ideological content of political science inquiry as concerns democracy though not in a singular, unilateral direction.[18] As formulated by the skeptics, post-modern anti-representationalism undermines confidence in democracy, erases any normative preference for representative democracy, questions the struggle for reforms concerning equality of representation, and discourages experimentation with new forms of democracy. It almost precludes any defense of modern Western forms of representational democracy as they are known today. The affirmatives who turn to public-sphere theory face equally serious problems. The requirements of critical debate and discussion in the public sphere are so obviously demanding that only a small portion of the population can meet them. Public-sphere theory gets around the shortcomings of representation, but it is vulnerable to the charge of elitism.

Post-modern anti-representationalism in political science raises the problem of relevance. Extreme skeptical post-modern political theorists call for the end of the "Order of Representation," and this includes representative democracy. Their cynicism with respect to democracy appears ill-timed in light of recent world events. Many former socialist and communist countries have recently opted for representative democracy. Certainly modern Western democracy has its weaknesses and inadequacies, but to denounce it as thoroughly as do some skeptical post-modern political theorists appears a bit naive. Some affirmative post-modern political scientists

---

[18] In political science the post-modern anti-representational influence is evident in the writings of a whole new generation of political theorists (William Connolly is an example), and it has been instrumental in reorienting the scholarly product of some of those whose political theory careers began in the 1960s such as Murray Edelman, Michael Shapiro, and Henry Kariel.

call for direct democracy, but they are fuzzy on the details and means by which this can be successfully applied in large societies. Many post-modern political scientists, as a result of "real world events," face what might be called a crisis of credibility, yet to be resolved and in need of immediate attention.

7

EPISTEMOLOGY AND METHODOLOGY:

POST-MODERN ALTERNATIVES

"I behaved stubbornly, pursuing a semblance of order, I
should have known well that there is no order in the universe."

"But in imagining an erroneous order you still found
something. . . ."
(Eco 1980: 599)

I N THIS CHAPTER I consider post-modern views of what are generally called "foundational" matters and outline the consequences of
these conceptions for the social sciences. Post-modern answers to
questions of how we know what we know, how we go about producing
knowledge, and what constitutes knowledge itself are very different from
those of the most conventional versions of modern social science. The
skeptical post-modernists reject modern views of science, epistemology,
and methodology. They have little faith in reason, and they disavow conventional criteria for evaluating knowledge. The affirmatives do not reject
modern perspectives on these topics quite so vehemently, but they do propose drastic revisions to all of them. Here I present an example of post-
modern deconstruction of the foundations of legal studies and consider the
impossibility of post-modern planning without reason and rationality.

1. Epistemology: Modern and Post-Modern

As inspired by the natural sciences, modern social science seeks to function
on the basis of epistemological hypothesis and counterhypothesis, by assuming an independent reality and requiring theory be tested. By contrast,
the affirmative post-modernists organize knowledge around personal, intuitive, and epistemological concern. They are often inspired hermeneutics.[1] The skeptical post-modernists practice "epistemological impossibilism" or "a pervasive sense of radical, unsurpassable uncertainty, a sort of
epistemological nihilism" (Calinescu 1987: 305).

---

[1] Epistemology has to do with the nature, validity, and limits of inquiry. Here it also includes ontological dimensions such as the nature of reality.

a. A Theory of Reality, Non-Reality, Un-Reality

While modern social science strives to discover and depict what it calls external reality, post-modernists hold that there are no adequate means for representing it. Modern social science has been less secure and more circumspect about "external reality" of late, and some of its philosophers even imply that it can be understood only within paradigmatic assumptions subject to change from time to time (Kuhn 1970). All post-modernists deny any view of reality that assumes the independence of individual mental processes and intersubjective communication. Many skeptical post-modernists even refuse to enter the discussion on the nature of reality; they either doubt that a conception of reality need exist at all (Fokkema 1984: 45) or argue that if it does it is "the consequence rather than the cause of scientific activity" (Latour and Woolgar 1979: 153, 183, 236; 1988: 159). "It must be clear that it is our business not to supply reality but to invent allusions to the conceivable which cannot be presented" (Lyotard 1984: 81). The very notion of reality construction implies that some versions are "valid and others not" (Edelman 1988: 6).

Baudrillard offers a good example of a skeptical post-modernist view of reality when he argues in his travel log of *America* (1989a) that there is no real world: Disneyland is authentic because it does not purport to be real; everything outside Disneyland, what is reputed to be real, is exclusively images, "simulacra." For the skeptics post-modern signs are not representative of reality; rather they produce reality (Ryan 1988: 565–66). They work "creatively and anarchically and irresponsibly." The post-modern sign subverts the modern and overcomes the "controlled system of meaning," by extension "the socially controlled system of every kind" (Harland 1987: 124).

The affirmatives and a few skeptical post-modernists agree with a *constructivist* theory of reality. They dismiss the distinction between mental states and the outside world as pure illusion. "To the extent that the mind furnishes the categories of understanding, there are no real world objects of study other than those inherent within the mental makeup of persons" (Gergen 1986: 141). The physical world is the dream. When one " 'awakens' from the 'dream' of the physical world," one realizes that the dreamer is "the cause of the events and the relationships. The out-of-consciousness collective/universal mind is the creator of the world the individual mind experiences." We spend most of our lives in this "reality dream." There is no reality to any event apart from the meanings attributed by those who perceive them (Edelman 1988: 2). Humans are "cocreators [with god] of the universe" (Harman 1988: 125–26).

A *contextualist* theory of reality is also of interest to these post-modernists. Modern ethnomethodologists inspired this view, but post-modernists such as Stanley Fish (1989: 34) have elevated it to a position of importance by arguing that all knowledge claims (all facts, truth, and validity) are "intelligible and debatable" only within their context, paradigm, or "community." They are merely the result of agreement among professional communities. Reality is the result of the social processes accepted as normal in a specific context.[2]

Skeptical post-modernists also advance a theory of reality: they see it as *linguistic convention* (Eagleton 1983: 105; 1985). If language itself is relative and even arbitrary, and if language is the only reality we know, then reality is, at most, a linguistic habit (Murphy 1988: 179; Flax 1990: 35). "There are no independently identifiable, real-world referents to which the language of social description is cemented" (Gergen 1986: 143). Even natural science in a post-modern era "is a discursive field with presuppositions that are themselves problematic" (Aronowitz 1988b: 432). It is merely a universe of discourse, a rhetoric based on action that is itself only discourse (Latour 1987). This discourse takes the form of a power game (Seidman 1990), a struggle, a war with verbal negotiation, pressure, lobbying, and other elements designed to gain support, to "enroll," to mobilize resources, that in the end assures an intellectual monopoly for the "product" (Latour 1988: 182–84). No external reality actually exists as the ultimate "arbitrator" (Latour 1987: 37).

The affirmative post-modernists, preferring the contextual and constructive versions of reality that are more consistent with their epistemological conceptions, disagree with this strict linguistic relativism. Social science must be more than just "a linguistic habit" if it is to be worth the effort (Griffin 1988a: 20–30). Post-modern social science requires a theory of reality that is enabling, that permits content, even though it is "soft," provisional and emotional, some would say philosophically idealist, relative, and subjective, rather than positivist or philosophically materialist or objective (Redner 1987: 676; Lambropoulos 1986: 50; Bauman 1987: 4; Hare-Mustin and Marecek 1988: 455–56; Harland 1987: 177).

Post-modern views of reality are reproached for some of the same shortcomings as idealist philosophical conceptions of reality. Critics argue that debate over issues such as the existence of an independent reality are of interest only to post-modernists (and other intellectuals) who, insulated from reality, never personally experience the violence, terror, and degradation prevalent in modern society. They point to the brutal presence of an "obviously existing reality" that solidifies around poverty, starvation, AIDS, drugs, and gang warfare. Only if one's daily life, daily "lived" real-

---

[2] The skeptics deny any role for context in interpretation, and the result is absolute indeterminacy. Their preferred method, deconstruction (evaluated below in this chapter), assumes context is irrelevant (Himmelfarb 1989b: 665).

ity, is not harsh and unpleasant could one conceive of reality as entirely a mental construction.[3]

b. Modern Prediction and Causality or Post-Modern Intertextuality

Intertextuality is a common post-modern substitute for modern social science's causal explanation. Modern social science has assumed causality and prediction were essential to explanation (Feigl 1953a: 11);[4] post-modernists consider both uninteresting because, they argue, the requirements of temporal priority and independent, external reality assumed by these concepts are dubious (Edelman 1988: 2). Absolutely interactive intertextuality implies a strong denial of the possibility of direct causality because in a world where everything is related in an absolute interactive way, temporal priority, required by causality, is nearly impossible to establish.

The post-modern world is said to be "intertextual," and this means, for the skeptical post-modernists, that everything one studies is related to everything else (Latour 1988: 163).[5] For the skeptics the world is so complicated, chaotic, and intertwined that it would be impossible to untangle the threads that connect all these interactions or offer any definitive pronouncement about the direction or magnitude of the forces that pulse and

[3] Shapiro (1989a: 20) offers an example of how a post-modern view of reality, taken to the extreme, yields the ridiculous. He seems to say that because there is such great distance between "experience and knowledge" in modernity, we necessarily depend on "knowledge agents" to link the two. As a result the "persons interested in relating their fears to situations of danger have to become consumers of representations from institutions that have the legitimacy to produce interpretations of danger." Therefore, he continues, fear is known only indirectly, and it is not authentic; fear itself is "contentious" because it is only representational. But, of course, those who live with a constant exposure to danger—the threats of being mugged, raped, caught in the cross fire of gang warfare and shot—do not have the luxury of considering fear "contentious," nor do they need to have their fears mediated by "knowledge agents" if they experience such things in their neighborhood on a daily basis.

[4] Modern science, which has so influenced modern social science inquiry, is premised on a predictable, determined world that can be understood as a system of causal relations. Independent variables are assumed to predict dependent variables within certain known statistical limits (Hoover 1980: 76–78; Nachmias and Nachmias 1976: chap. 11). Those who work within this model admit that full knowledge of all causal variables is impossible, so they endeavor to isolate temporarily the most important variables and to make a general assessment of how specific phenomena are related. Causal links, usually based on the temporal priority of the independent variable, are indicated. This procedure is said to be sufficient in most cases because only a few variables account for the greatest proportion of the total variation in any outcome (Grunbaum 1953; Hoover 1980: chap. 4).

[5] Pavic's work of fiction entitled *Dictionary of the Khazars* is a striking example of an "intertextual" novel (1988). Everything is related to everything else across time (centuries) and despite impossible geographical impediments. The ultimate "proof" of its post-modern intertextuality is that, as he boasts, the reader can open his novel and begin reading it equally well at any point. Post-modern literature assumes that everything is interconnected so it makes no difference where one starts or finishes a post-modern reading (Barthes 1975).

shiver about us. "A butterfly stirring the air today in Peking can transform storm systems next month in New York" (Gleick 1987: 8).[6] Every text (event) is related to every other text (event), as was explained in Chapter 2. In the extreme, for the skeptical post-modernists, no explanation is possible because either everything appears random (Fokkema 1984: 45) or everything is so tightly intertextually related (Latour 1987) that no order can be discerned.

Skeptical post-modernists deny the causality implicit in the materialist philosophical view. So, for example, they reject the argument that "once the machine works people will be convinced." They dispute left-wing causal explanations organized around the concept of class struggle including the view that modern social science serves the bourgeoisie (capitalists) and oppresses the working class. But they are equally adamant in rejecting the idealist contention that "the machine will work when all the relevant people are convinced" (Latour 1987). The causality implied by the view that social science is a human construction is balanced by the contention that social science constructs human beings. For example, employing social science research techniques necessarily requires conforming to their "rules" of science, and thus one is, in turn, "constructed" by the research enterprise (Latour 1987). Books "write" their authors to the extent that writers must conform to the political economy of publishing (Agger 1990: 218). Even scientific procedures such as pasteurization are said to have re-created social and intellectual life when bacteria, microbes, became social actors outside the laboratory and moved into society (Latour 1988: chap. 2).

The affirmative post-modernists add teleological explanation to a weak form of intertextuality. They are more likely than the skeptical post-modernists to see intertextuality as relational rather than entirely chaotic. Teleological explanation is intended to reintroduce unconscious processes back into social science (Harman 1988: 123). For these post-modernists, explanation takes complex forms of purposeful goal-oriented human outcomes, directed toward a telos permitting consideration of unconscious processes ("deep intuition"), more holistic than those of modern social science (Griffin 1988a: 20–30; Harman 1988).

Post-modern methodological assumptions are alien to those forms of modern social science that assume prediction and precise probability statements. Thus, if post-modernists ever look to modern social science for methodological inspiration, they necessarily seek out approaches such as systems analysis or structural analysis where intertextuality is the rule and

[6] Such observations are viewed by skeptical post-modernists as indicating the impossibility of comprehending complexity, whereas for modern scientists they pose a challenge that can be met through the formulation of appropriate (chaos) theory (Gleick 1987: 3–8, 30, 56, 118, 153, 211, 240, 299, 300; Holden 1986; Prigogine and Stengers 1984).

predictive models are secondary.[7] But post-modernists are not limited to borrowing from modern social science. As discussed below, both their reading of interpretation and their conception/invention of deconstruction give a large place to intertextuality.

c. Relativism versus Objectivity—the Role of Values and the Normative in Inquiry

A range of views concerning values and normative questions occurs within modern social science. It is often assumed that values should not bias inquiry, that research should be impartial and investigators detached. At the same time the impossibility of setting aside all normative values is acknowledged; hence researchers must make them explicit in the hope that this will alert readers to their existence.

Post-modernists agree that values, normative questions, feelings, and emotions are all part of human intellectual production. The skeptical post-modernists stipulate that no particular value system can be assumed superior to another. For some skeptics these ethical choices cannot even be treated as the normative choices of a moral person; they are simply a linguistic category, a construct (De Man 1979: 19, 206). The skeptics do not eliminate values from inquiry; rather, they consider all values more or less equal. Thus no special privilege can be attributed to any particular point of view.

The affirmative post-modernists argue that a plurality of legitimate value systems does not necessarily imply ethical relativism. Dissimilar sets of values exist, and it is perfectly legitimate to argue about which is preferable, given the alternatives. As the affirmatives see it, facts, meanings, and values cannot be considered independent of one another. This vision of post-modern social science, of course, leaves unanswered the questions concerning which specific values are to be fused with social science because the affirmatives disagree among themselves on the values they prefer.

While modern social science strives for objectivity and shuns relativism, post-modernists are anti-objectivist, and some embrace relativism.[8] The affirmatives call for the "return of the human mind" into the epistemological register (Aronowitz 1988b: 535). The skeptics argue that to abandon objectivity is itself a sign of maturity and tolerance (Edelman 1988: 5). If

---

[7] Some affirmative post-modernists do, in fact, employ systems analysis (see Capra 1982).

[8] Certain post-modernists, especially continental Europeans, are quite comfortable about being identified as relativist (or idealist). But North Americans and British post-modernists prefer to distance themselves from relativism, at least in its more extreme forms (Dear 1988: 11). Post-modernists avoid these and other similar terms for another reason: they are often presented as definitional dichotomies that, post-modernists argue, automatically imply hierarchy and the superiority of one element of each pair.

reality is a linguistic convention, then meaning and knowledge can only be relative (Wortman 1987: 171). Some go so far as to contend that post-modernism itself is "the consolidation of relativism" (Heller 1987: 177). In the field of anthropology, for example, post-modernists argue that relativism is a welcome relief (Marcus and Fischer 1986: 32) because it recognizes that in their field "no cultural tradition can analytically encompass the discourse of another cultural tradition" (Tyler 1984: 328).

As was the case with norms and values, the affirmatives are uncomfortable with either extreme of objectivity or relativism. Consequently, and often in search of compromise, some of them adopt an inherently contradictory position. Feminist and ecological post-modernists, for example, are ambivalent about post-modern relativism and anti-objectivism, especially when discussion turns to their own particular group. Feminists applaud post-modernism's criticism of modern social science and its denial of a privileged status for male opinion. But they denounce post-modernism for not giving special authority to women's voices; they argue that, in the cases of "rape, domestic violence, and sexual harassment," there is a difference between fact and "figuration." The victim's account of these experiences is "not simply an arbitrary imposition of a purely fictive meaning on an otherwise meaningless reality," and they warn post-modernists against the "total repudiation of either external reality . . . or rational judgment" (Hawkesworth 1989: 555). Post-modern feminists face a possible inconsistency between embracing a relativist form of post-modern philosophy and combining it with a very real commitment to challenge an objective reality.

Post-modern organizational studies illustrate the consequences for the social sciences of this questioning of values and relativism; that is, it leads to critique rather than construction. Post-modernists in this field suggest that modern approaches "silence" all those who would challenge them by imposing unspoken assumptions on foundational questions and normative matters (Arrington and Francis 1989). They contend that their field is "indeterminate," rather than "scientific, or objective," and they call for a total and complete reconsideration of disciplinary "commitments" (Arrington and Francis 1989: 1).

Critics of post-modernism attack its relativism and also its value equivalency. These critics interpret the skeptics' views as defending moral neutrality. Post-modernists are "unable to provide grounds for their normative judgments which can serve as the basis for discourse with those who do not already share their orientation" (Calhoun forthcoming b: 44). Critics argue that if all norms and values are equal, as many post-modernists claim, then it is impossible to prioritize or compare values, to make choices between moral alternatives. It follows that post-modernism does nothing to prohibit "the ruthless pursuit of wealth and power" (Cantor 1989: 2368–

69). In addition, the very premise that moral choices are impossible, that no choice can be made between bipolar oppositions such as good and bad, seems absurd. It goes against common everyday lived experience. For example, most modern, Western legal systems assume (and psychologists concur) that a child normally attains the capacity to choose between right and wrong by age ten. Finally, critics argue, it is one thing to acknowledge relativism and subjectivity as inevitable, but quite another to cultivate them as virtues, as is the case with some skeptical post-modernists.

2. Modern Method or Post-Modernism's "Anything Goes"

Post-modernists are not inclined to use the word method, though they sometimes discuss "strategies" or "struggles" around truth and knowledge in terms that approximate methodology. However, in the absence of any adequate substitute for this word, there is little choice but to employ it over the probable objections of most post-modernists. By "methodology" I mean how one goes about studying whatever is of interest; it relates to the process of inquiry, but it does not tell us what to expect to find. Method, not assumed synonymous with the rules and procedures of modern science, is considered here to apply more broadly.

Some idea of method in the sense that it is used in modern social science helps provide a reference point for understanding the post-modernists' critique and the alternatives they offer for the "old, past, closed" conventional methods (Fraser 1984: 138; Agger 1989a: 10–12). Modern social science is guided by general rules of method that direct the conduct of research. Its most orthodox practitioners assume that there is but a single method, a self-correcting scientific method that is universal in its application across disciplines (Feigl 1953b: 382–84; Nachmias and Nachmias 1976). "The scientific method seeks to test thought against reality in a disciplined manner with each step in the process made explicit" (Hoover 1980: 36).[9]

---

[9] The classical model of modern science defined its project as grounded on evidence drawn from experiments and concrete experience, based on direct or indirect observation, confirmed by intersubjective agreement on what was observed (Feigl 1953a; Grunbaum 1953). These "conventions," which "might be described as the rules of the game of empirical science," were said to be justified by the fact that they "proved fruitful" (Popper 1959: 53–55). These scientific procedures were subjected to a whole range of challenges in the 1960s and 1970s (see Mokrzyski 1983: chaps. 2, 3, for a summary of those originating in history and culture). As a result, modern science became more modest: instead of trying to "prove" theories, it required hypotheses be formulated so as to permit falsification (Popper 1959). This did not really modify the basic system of categorizing, classifying, testing hypotheses against reality, interpreting results, and building theory (Hoover 1980: 35). It only made it more sophisticated. Concepts were still defined in real terms rather than nominal terms and linked to indicators that permit measured value to be assigned to the variables that represent them (Bier-

a. Post-Modern Methods: Deconstruction and Intuitive Interpretation

Many post-modernists contend there are no methods, no rules of procedure to which they must conform, only the anti-rules, the "skeptical" rigor
of their post-modernism (McClosky 1985: 20; Norris 1982: 57; Rorty
1979: 318). Only logocentric systems that claim to be externally valid, that
seek "transcendental truths," they argue, are preoccupied by method (Fish
1987). By rejecting these rules, post-modernists declare that, as far as
method is concerned, "anything goes" (Heller 1987; Feyerabend 1975).

Post-modernism is oriented toward methods that apply to a broad range
of phenomena, focus on the margins, highlight uniqueness, concentrate on
the enigmatic, and appreciate the unrepeatable. All its methods relinquish
any attempt to create new knowledge in the modern sense of the word.
Post-modern social science presumes methods that multiply paradox, inventing ever more elaborate repertoires of questions, each of which encourages an infinity of answers, rather than methods that settle on solutions.

Post-modern methodology is post-positivist or anti-positivist (Fraser
1984: 138).[10] As substitutes for the "scientific method," the affirmatives
look to feelings (Hirschman 1987), personal experience, empathy, emotion, intuition, subjective judgment, imagination, as well as diverse forms
of creativity and play (Todorov 1984). But the actual content of these
terms and their methodological significance are relatively vague and difficult to communicate to others. The skeptical post-modernists might deny
most of these as substitutes for method because, they argue, we can never

---

stedt 1959). Data were evaluated for statistical representativeness, bias, and general fairness
and interpreted with the aid of reason and logic (Hempel 1988: 8). Results at every stage of
the research were subject to confirmation by other observers. When data repeatedly contra-
dicted a theory, the theory was either abandoned or it withered away gradually with the
proliferation of competing theories or "research-programmes" (Lakatos 1970). Only after a
more "relaxed empiricist perspective" developed within modern science was it acknowledged
that there would be instances when "a comprehensive theory is not abandoned for conflicting
with a few recalcitrant observation reports—especially when no better theory is in sight"
(Hempel 1988: 23, 26). Modern science still holds that if erroneous theory is mistakenly
accepted, it will eventually be uncovered and corrected through replication and further research (Hoover 1980: 36). The "fairness" of methodological procedures is still said to lend
credibility to results and guard against arbitrariness. The idea of progress remains, and this
implies the cumulation of research results, "better and better testable theories" (Popper 1959:
356). The knowledge produced by the scientific method is assumed superior to that resulting
from speculation, reflection, feelings, and intuition. Post-modernists would disagree (Graff
1979).

[10] Skeptical post-modernists question qualitative as well as quantitative methods. For example, they reject action research and participant observation because each requires an author
and often assumes agency (Touraine 1988).

really know anything, not even our own feelings and emotions (Schwartz 1990: 32).[11]

In its more concrete formal manifestations, post-modernism encompasses two methodological approaches: introspective, anti-objectivist interpretation and deconstruction.[12] The distinction between the two is not always clear, and some consider deconstruction "nothing other than interpretation" (Sarup 1989: 60). But deconstruction does emphasize negative critical capacity while interpretation expresses a positive point of view. Skeptical post-modernists employ it broadly to examine texts, and, because everything is a text, the uses of deconstruction are unlimited. Affirmative post-modernists generally favor interpretation over deconstruction if only because their various projects require construction rather than deconstruction.[13] The affirmatives also employ deconstruction to undercut privileged texts, but they are, at the same time, wary of it because their views are as vulnerable as anyone else's to being deconstructed.

Post-modern interpretation bears but slight resemblance to the more conventional social science forms of interpretation.[14] Modern social science understands interpretation to be the careful consideration of data with the goal of locating patterns. Meaning is not arbitrary, and some interpretations are assumed better than others. Modern social science allows for any number of nonconflicting interpretations; it also contends that when interpretations conflict all may be wrong, but ultimately only one can be accurate. The process of sorting out divergent interpretations may be slow and indirect, but it is unrelenting. Old theory may be swept away

[11] They would accept creativity and play inasmuch as these do not claim to substantiate knowledge.

[12] Some post-modernists resist defining deconstruction as a method, while others insist it is an anti-method (Norris 1982: 76–79). In any case, deconstruction and interpretation are as close to method as post-modernism comes, and it is not a distortion to refer to them as such (Dear 1986: 373; Norris 1982; Culler 1982).

[13] Deconstruction and post-modern interpretation are consistent with most aspects of post-modern epistemology. Deconstruction is avowedly, intentionally, and intensely subjectivist and anti-objectivist by design (Dear 1986: 372–73). It hesitates to dismiss any perspective as entirely without interest. It precludes universal knowledge or global theory because it is itself an anti-theoretical enterprise. It refuses to institute hierarchies of good and bad theories. Post-modern interpretation is intertextual rather than causal. Post-modern interpretation denies a correspondence theory of truth and suspects reason and rationality. Challenging representation (Chapter 6) is consistent with the view that any number of interpretations are equal because representation is impossible (Hoy 1985a: 53).

[14] Neither does it resemble hermeneutic interpretation, which is more subjective and less ambitious than modern social science's interpretation. Hermeneutic interpretation, unlike post-modern interpretation, seeks to probe the "silences," to uncover a deeper meaning, masked and hidden perhaps, but waiting to be discovered (Dreyfus and Rabinow 1983: 124; Madison 1988: 115). The skeptical post-modernists say there simply is no "meaning" to uncover. Hermeneutic interpretation accepts truth, universality, and a shared discourse (a community of understanding).

by a singularly impressive interpretation of a crucial experiment, but it is just as likely to be passively abandoned as a result of long-term conflict between a number of interpretations (Lakatos 1970). The character of interpretation within the boundaries of modern social science is closely defined: it seeks reconciliation and the unification of opposing truths, not the multiplication of scenarios.

Modern interpretation has been redefined, re-deployed with new post-modern meanings assigned. Post-modern interpretation is *introspective* and *anti-objectivist*, a form of individualized understanding. It is more vision than data observation. It disperses the modern identity and any clear distinction between self and other, fact and values. In the field of anthropology, for example, it gravitates toward "narrative" and centers on "listening to" and "talking with" the other (Tyler 1986: 139–41, 335). In psychology, theories of interpretation no longer "ground." They rather only "mediate" (Kugler 1988: 63).

Post-modernists recognize an infinite number of interpretations (meanings) of any text are possible because, for the skeptical post-modernists, one can never say what one intends with language, ultimately all textual meaning, all interpretation, is undecidable.[15] Because there is no final meaning for any particular sign, no notion of a unitary sense of a text, these post-modernists argue that no interpretation can be regarded as superior to any other (Latour 1988: 182–83).[16] In its world of plural constructions, diverse realities, an absence of certainty, and a multiplicity of readings, post-modernism refuses to privilege one statement over another; all interpretations are of equal interest (Miller 1972: 8; 1977: 447).

Some skeptical post-modernists, perhaps exaggerating to create an effect, charge that every interpretation is false (Miller 1981: 249); every understanding is a misunderstanding (Culler 1982: 176).[17] "Every reading of a text will always be to some extent a misreading, a version that selects certain details, meaning or structural features at the expense of other details which could just as well have figured in the critic's account" (Norris 1988: 129). What is actually written is not so important because a text (any event) does not constrain interpretation; interpretation, rather, models the text.

[15] The inspiration for absolute pluralism in interpretation can be traced to Nietzsche. Derrida's view of interpretation as play is grounded on "the Nietzschian affirmation, that is the joyous affirmation of the play of the world and of the innocence of becoming, the affirmation of a world of signs without fault, without truth, and without origin which is offered to an active interpretation" (Derrida 1978: 292).

[16] Foucault's "interpretive analytics" similarly assumes everything is interpretation; yet because all interpretation is arbitrary there can be no final interpretation (see Dreyfus and Rabinow 1983: 106, for an explanation of Foucault's concept).

[17] See Ellis for an explanation of the absurdity of this view (1989: chap. 4). He argues it is "neither a valid nor an invalid position but no position at all" (1989: 112).

Deconstruction involves demystifying a text, tearing it apart to reveal its internal, arbitrary hierarchies and its presuppositions. It lays out the flaws and the latent metaphysical structures of a text. A deconstructive reading of a text seeks to discover its ambivalence, blindness, logocentricity. It is "the careful teasing out of warring forces of signification within the text" (Johnson 1980: 5). Instead of sorting out the central arguments of a text, deconstruction examines the margins (Hoy 1985a: 44); but at the same time this effort penetrates to the very core of the text and examines what it represses and how it is caught in contradictions and inconsistencies. Deconstruction employs a text's "own stratagems against it, producing a force of dislocation that spreads itself throughout the entire system, fissuring it in every direction and thoroughly delimiting it" (Derrida 1978: 20). A deconstructive approach examines what is left out of a text, what is un-named, what is excluded, and what is concealed. But the goal is to do more than overturn oppositions, for this would permit new hierarchies to be reappropriated (Derrida 1981: 59). Deconstruction is not designed to merely unmask "error," for this would assume that truth exists (Vattimo 1988).[18] Deconstruction, rather, aims to transpose a text—transforming it, re-defining it—all the while simultaneously operating within the decon-structed text itself. Deconstruction attempts to undo, reverse, displace, and resituate the hierarchies involved in polar opposites such as object/subject, right/wrong, good/bad, pragmatic/principled (Culler 1982: 150).[19] Post-modernists refuse to "reconstruct" a text or to predicate an alternative view or reestablish a hegemonic vista (Fish 1989: 493). It discloses tensions but does not resolve them (Hartman 1988). Following Nietzsche, "decon-struction deconstructs itself, and at the same time creates another labyrin-thine fiction whose authority is undermined by its own creation" (Miller 1981: 261). The entire process of deconstruction is complex, and in the end, post-modernists argue, the text deconstructs itself (de Man 1986: 118).

As conceived and presented by post-modernists in the above terms, de-construction may appear to many modern social scientists, at first encoun-ter, to be an abstract process. It is, in fact, not so complicated once the basic underlying principles and strategies of the deconstructive method are

[18] If this is the case, then it is a mistake to assume, as does Henry Kariel (1988a), that deconstruction is merely critique, that it does little more than "enliven prevailing clichés by elaborately articulating them" in the social sciences at the moment.

[19] Here is an example of post-modern deconstruction of difference. The post-modernists emphasize difference when referring to individuals (see Chapter 6, section 2). They are less sympathetic to its application in the case of general (bipolar) categories. Such categories, they contend, imply not only hierarchy but judgment as to the superior, normative qualities of one bipolar term over the other. Derrida argues that while bipolar opposites appear "different" they are also the same (Derrida 1981: 9).

distilled. The results of any such endeavor might include the following guidelines:

— Find an exception to a generalization in the text and push it to the limit so that this generalization appears absurd; in other words, use the exception to undermine the principle.
— Interpret the arguments in a text being deconstructed in their most extreme form.
— Avoid absolute statements in deconstructing a text, but cultivate a sense of intellectual excitement by making statements that are both startling and sensational.
— Deny the legitimacy of all dichotomies because there are always a few exceptions to any generalization based on bipolar terms, and these can be used to undermine them.
— Nothing is to be accepted; nothing is to be rejected. It is extremely difficult to criticize a deconstructive argument if no clear viewpoint is expressed.
— Write so as to permit the greatest number of interpretations possible; ambiguity and ambivalence are not to be shunned but rather cultivated. Obscurity may "protect from serious scrutiny" (Ellis 1989: 148). The idea is "to create a text without finality or completion, one with which the reader can never be finished" (Wellberg 1985: 234).
— Employ new and unusual terminology in order that "familiar positions may not seem too familiar and otherwise obviously relevant scholarship may not seem so obviously relevant" (Ellis 1989: 142).
— "Never consent to a change of terminology and always insist that the wording of the deconstructive argument is sacrosanct." More familiar formulations undermine any sense that the deconstructive position is unique and distinctive (Ellis 1989: 145).

b. Problems with Post-Modern Methods

Skeptical post-modernists assert that deconstruction is itself immune to critique because it "cannot be described and stated as other positions can," because it is impossible to apply modern reason and logical analysis to it (Lyotard 1988b: xi). Deconstruction is said to have its own alternative logic that can never be made explicit (Ellis 1989: chap. 1).[20] For example, Ashley and Walker (1990a: 265–66) argue that any attempt to summarize post-modern texts in the field of international relations, to "say what they must mean would be to do violence to them." Nevertheless, despite efforts

[20] Ellis (1989) takes up this challenge and offers a most impressive and thoroughgoing critical assessment of deconstruction in the humanities, especially in the field of literary criticism.

to ward off criticism, some important problems with post-modern methods have been outlined.

Within a modern perspective some interpretations are almost always found more defensible than others. Even in instances of radical uncertainty, sufficient reasons can often be presented for preferring one interpretation over others (Graff 1990: 174). Texts (events) are part of the modern world, influenced by political, economic, and social forces, and in turn they have the potential to exert an impact on their environment. Interpretations are enmeshed in a network of influences and constraints.

The methodological relativism of post-modern interpretation is troubling to some post-modernists (Norris 1988: 188, is an example). Of course, it may be impossible to satisfy everyone as to the adequacy of certain interpretations, but it is not difficult to invent a trivial example of an interpretation so obviously false that there would be general agreement as to its insufficiency. For example, the *Declaration of Independence* and the *Communist Manifesto* are political texts that were both shaped by and in turn molded human affairs. Although open to many interpretations, certain interpretations are more appropriate than others: neither the *Declaration* nor the *Manifesto* tells us how to play baseball.

Post-modern efforts to answer concerns about methodological relativism are not reassuring. Some claim to transform this defect into a strength. If, as critics charge, post-modernism is "caught up in the infinite regress of deconstructionism, where nothing is better than anything else," these post-modernists respond: deconstruction also means that one is drawn into an "infinite expansion" where one is freed from "the intellectual myopia of hyper-determined research projects and their formulaic write-ups . . . , 'normal science' " (Richardson 1988: 200). Such a response is simply inadequate.

Despite argument to the contrary, post-modern methodological endeavors are not entirely without order or rigor (Scholes 1989: 834). And, indeed, the distillation of deconstructive principles outlined above suggests an underlying logic. As such, they are not immune to criticism. Deconstruction, for example, is as logocentric, in terms of its assumptions, as the systems of thought it attempts to unravel:

> If deconstruction "demystifies a text, tearing it apart to reveal its internal, arbitrary hierarchies, and its presuppositions," this implies that there really are internal arbitrary hierarchies and presuppositions—certain ones, and not others; observable; describable; subject to intersubjective demonstration. If deconstruction can "reveal" something, the something must be there to be revealed. And likewise post-modernists speak of how the texts being deconstructed are caught in "contradictions," "inconsistencies," things that are "left out" and "concealed." Either there are criteria of "consistency," etc., and

intersubjectively valid ways of ascertaining what is "left out," or such sentences are themselves merely "texts," the meaning of which is up for grabs.[21]

The post-modern claim that "anything goes" when it comes to methodology is an exaggeration.[22] Post-modern science, at least as constructed by the affirmative post-modernists, is not without methodological preferences though sometimes these are negative in tone, instructions precluding certain methods rather than positively requiring them (Rosenau 1992). For example, post-modernists criticize modern science for its quest for "identity, whether of structures or of subjects." They replace this with "the assertion of difference." In the name of difference, an "attack has been mounted on synthesis and generalization" (Soper 1986: 90). A very restricted view of "anything goes" results because it excludes "synthesis and generalization" among other things.

Some critics argue that stripped of some of its Derridean language of presentation, deconstruction seems boring, trivial, "homogeneous," and "monotonous." They claim that it makes "everything sound the same"; it says basically the same thing about all texts. By concentrating so exclusively on language, deconstruction neglects the broader significance of a text. It appears little concerned with the most important aspect of a text—what it means (Culler 1982: 220).

It has also been suggested that deconstruction may be no more and no less than a general case of critique. It warns "against being bamboozled by rhetorical devices." It suggests caution in attributing meaning. But none of this is new or exclusive to deconstruction (Donoghue 1989: 37). And if this is all there is to deconstruction, then it is not a uniquely post-modern tool. Modern science purports to do the same.

Critics also charge that deconstruction makes no positive methodological contribution. It is *destructive* (Habermas 1987a: 161); it does not *construct* knowledge. If, as skeptical post-modernists contend, all interpretations are equally interesting and the arbitrary character of language precludes judgment about the adequacy of any given interpretation, then all these interpretation-dependent social science fields are in jeopardy. The role of deconstruction in geography and anthropology is an example of what post-modernists in these fields themselves identify as "guerilla activity." Their post-modern activity is designed to show these fields to be "mere fictions." The post-modern revision from within aims openly to fragment these disciplines altogether, to make room for interpretive at-

[21] Harry C. Bredemeier, personal correspondence, Aug. 7, 1988.

[22] Latour carries the skeptical post-modern position to its logical conclusion, its most consistent form, by suggesting that even the statement "anything goes" must be abandoned because it implies a positive, affirmative view that, he argues, is impossible to defend (1988: 168–69).

tempts (Marcus and Fischer 1986: 26; Gregory and Walford 1989). Even those social science fields that do not emphasize their "scientific" character are seriously threatened. For example, psychoanalytic interpretation is qualitative rather than rigorously quantifiable, but it is pure myth without any methodological protection within a post-modern perspective (Kugler 1988). This complaint comes not just from the ranks of modern social science, but it is equally worrisome for the affirmative post-modernists who have their own project: to forge a new post-modern science (Rosenau, forthcoming a). Deconstruction denies privilege to any particular point of view, and yet the affirmative post-modernists claim the superiority of specific value perspectives and particular political positions such as feminism, environmentalism, peace, ecology, and religion (Griffin 1989). Some affirmative post-modernists argue that deconstruction must ultimately move to reconstruction and to "attempt to provide a new 'master narrative' " (Dear 1986: 376). It may not be possible if deconstructive logic is "not necessarily well adapted to productive, original thinking but rather to creating its illusion" (Ellis 1989: 144, chap. 6).

It is far from evident that replacing conventional social science methodology with post-modern methods of interpretation and deconstruction constitutes any improvement in the social sciences. If adopted without modification, post-modern methodology leaves social science with no basis for knowledge claims and no rationale for choosing between conflicting interpretations. The example below illustrates this case.

c. Applying Post-Modern Interpretation and Deconstruction: The Case of Legal Studies

The effects of deconstruction are evident from examples in a number of different fields where post-modern scholars have set about deconstructing the foundational assumptions of their respective disciplines, including international relations (Ashley 1989a, 1989b), organizational theory (Arrington and Francis 1989), and sociology (Seidman 1989, 1990; Agger 1989a). It has also had an impact on the more applied social sciences where, for example, the supposedly "objective" and "neutral" philosophy of entrepreneurship and organizational management, upon being deconstructed, is shown to elevate the interests of the "enterprise over those of everyone else." In the tradition of affirmative post-modernism, conventional management theory is deconstructed, and a new metatheory of post-modern management is developed with its goal of bringing "relief of unequivocally identifiable suffering" (Carter and Jackson 1987: 79–85).

Legal theory is an arena where post-modern views of epistemology and method have created one of the most serious intellectual crises, questioning the very legitimacy of judicial systems and the integrity of legal studies.

Historically law was assumed neutral, fair—an uncontroversial way to solve disputes in an impersonal, predictable, noncontroversial manner. Respect for the law indicated an advanced, stable civilization with a highly educated citizenry. Conventional legal philosophy assumed that adjudication could and should be factual, analytical, free of bias, neutral, objective, that it had determinate meaning, that legal statutes constituted a system of self-contained, codified rules in some way independent of arbitrary and compromising political, economic, and social factors (Norris 1988: chap. 1).

Post-modern interpretation and deconstruction turn these assumptions upside down; they argue that there is no definitive meaning in law and question the possibility of any truth claims based on reason in the field of law.[23] For the affirmative post-modernists, law is political, subjective, controversial, mere personal interpretation. The skeptics, going even further in the direction of radical indeterminacy, state that no interpretation of any law is ever really legitimate. Legal texts are said to be self-referential; their meaning, just as with literary texts, is simply indefinite, linguistically relative, subject to numerous interpretations, none of which is privileged.[24] Meaning is imposed, and every reading of a legal text is said to necessarily be a misreading.[25] All legal texts are also "undecidable" or "incoherent" because legal language, as with all language, either has no final meaning for post-modernists (Hoy 1985b: 166) or merely supplies a function of power relations (Foucault 1975).

As suggested in Chapter 4, post-modernists deny that origins, historical

[23] Many post-modernists are part of the critical legal studies movement (Norris 1988: 127). But they have important disagreements with other sectors of the critical legal studies movement, especially the Marxists.

[24] This discussion revolves around the law and literature debate. The outcome depends on how one views "literature" and how one defines "law." If as Davenport holds (1983, 1985) literature is scientific and interpretation objective, then one best interpretation of a literary text is possible. In this case the assimilation of law and literature would not be a challenge. But if, as is more commonly the case, literature is assumed subjective, if its "meaning cannot be extracted from literary texts but can only be put into them," then law, if it is merely literature, will also be seen as arbitrary (Posner 1988: 1–5). Posner argues against this. It is, he says, acceptable to set aside the intentions of an author in literature but not in law (1988: 28–29). Although it is of no great consequence to "merely assign some coherent and satisfying meaning when studying a literary text, it would have disastrous consequences to do so in the field of law. But post-modernists will not give jurists peace in any of this, and they assume literature as subjective and strongly deny any difference between the two types of texts" (Fish 1989: chap. 13; Minow 1987: 79). For more on this topic, see the "Symposium: Law and Literature" in *Texas Law Review* 60 (March 1982) and "Interpretation Symposium" in *Southern California Law Review* 58 (January 1985).

[25] If all readings (legal interpretations) are "misreadings," then it is pointless to debate whether it is best (1) to interpret laws according to the original author's intentions or (2) to reinterpret laws so that they remain relevant for the contemporary period.

or biographical, are accepted grounds for establishing meaning; thus, they refuse to interpret laws according to origins. They reject the view that there is but one true interpretation of the U.S. Constitution and that its framers set it down once and for all. Post-modernists also disagree with the afore-mentioned modern view that a text means what its author intends it to mean (Hirsch 1967; Michaels 1983: 344). A modern judge who writes a legal decision assumes that s/he is setting precedent for future decisions and that s/he is attributing meaning in a definitive sense. From a conventional, modern perspective, one need only understand the intention of this judicial author to determine meaning.[26] Post-modernists discard the author in law for the same reasons they attribute little importance to the literary author (see Chapter 2). They question the authority of the author and legal authority and suggest that judicial decisions are arbitrary.

The "intention versus interpretation" debate in the field of law has always been a source of controversy (Patterson 1990: 136–38), but the post-modern challenge is of a different order. Conventional legal theorists are so threatened by post-modern deconstruction (they would say mystification of the law) that they label post-modern critics "nihilists" (Fiss 1982; Norris 1988: 128; Pangle 1989; Hoy 1985b) because "if every lawyer and judge felt free to imprint his personal reading on any statue, chaos would threaten" (Posner 1988: 20).

The theory of the interpretive legal community—the view that legal judgment is simply consensus belief—is a compromise between traditional legal philosophy and skeptical post-modernism's absolute equality of interpretation. Ironically it ends up with few supporters in either camp, though it is of some interest to the affirmative post-modernists. It abandons truth as a goal and suggests that meaning is determined by the community (Fish 1980).[27] Legal opinion in this case is said to be a result of the shared language and shared reality of the legal community. As such, legal opinion can make no absolute truth claims because rules do not constrain community interpretation (Fish 1984: 1332). Legal philosophy is admittedly constructivist and rhetorical. When interpretative communities speak they cannot attribute definitive meaning.[28] One attempt to make this view more

---

[26] In literature the best interpretation is that closest to "the writer's mental world, the world of his empirical beliefs" (Skinner 1972: 407), and the context. In the social sciences there is one best interpretation of action, that which comes closest to that intended by the actor (Gibbons 1985: 785–86). In both cases the best interpretation is supplied by the initiator, the person who invented the text. Freudians, among others, would dispute this.

[27] Fish hopes to escape charges of relativism when he argues interpretation is not subjective because it is guided by the professional community. But his critics disagree: "If Fish has not made interpretation wholly subjective, the difference is not noticeable to the naked eye" (Dworkin 1983a: 295).

[28] One additional objection is that this theory fails to explain how challenges to interpretative communities ever arise or how legal interpretation changes over time (Norris 1988).

palatable, at least to conventional opinion, argues that "legal interpretations are constrained by rules that derive their authority from an interpretative community" (Fiss 1982: 762); this is sufficient to make truth claims.

Some efforts are being made by affirmative post-modernists to construct a post-modern law. Denouncing those that limit their critique to the presently existing state legality, Bonaventura Santos (1987) calls for a post-modern law that seeks to uncover "the latent or suppressed forms of legality in which more insidious and damaging forms of social and personal oppression frequently occur." He hopes his post-modern law will "become an edifying knowledge that, by enlarging and deepening our legal vistas, will contribute towards a radical democratisation of social and personal life. Only then will law be an unqualified human good" (Santos 1987: 299).[29] Handler (1986: 1030) also considers deconstructing the legal system to be emancipatory; he proposes a post-modern dialogic community, where dialogical relations, both transformative and constitutive, would give to law the job of righting wrongs, of helping the disadvantaged to be more successful vis-à-vis the state.

3. The Role of Reason and the Example of Post-Modern Planning

Broad confidence in reason and rationality are assumed by most versions of modern science, epistemology, and methodology (Meehan 1981), though this seems to be eroding not just in the social sciences but throughout society. Post-modernism is part of this larger erosive trend. In literature post-modern novels, such as Umberto Eco's *The Name of the Rose*, illustrate the futility of analytical reason and the naivety of causal explanation. Post-modern architecture revels in constructing buildings that at first glance cannot "reasonably" be expected to stand.[30] Qualifications to both reason and rationality have long been required in the social sciences by

---

Stanley Fish attempts an answer that is much too complicated to be summarized here (1989: chap. 7).

[29] Santos's project for a post-modern law actually confuses skeptical and affirmative post-modernism. He exhibits a passing fancy with Friedrich Nietzsche, Richard Rorty, and Harold Bloom's early work. But his proposals are also democratic and humanist. It would probably be greeted by the contemporary skeptical post-modernists as naive and logocentric.

[30] It might be assumed that architecture is immune to the extreme forms of post-modernism because buildings must respect the laws of science relating to gravity in order to be viable. But the avant garde of post-modern architecture today takes pride in "knowing nothing about materials" and in being willing to build "with chewing gum." One is said to have "built an officers' club, and the roof caved in during the dedication ceremonies." In other cases post-modern designs are abandoned because "they simply can't be built" (Seabrook 1991: 127, 129).

Popper's "falsifiability" (1959, 1962, 1979), by Kuhn's "paradigmatic" view (1970, 1971), and by Lakatos's competing "research programmes" (1970) and "rational reconstruction" (Brante 1986: 190–95). The post-modern challenge to reason is even more thoroughgoing, however, and thus more threatening to conventional social science.

There is considerable internal debate among post-modernists about how reason can best be "overcome," but most skeptics call for a "definitive fare-well" to modern reason (Borradori 1987–88).[31] They contend that, al-though an individual may reflect on a topic, employ "reasoned arguments," and go through the motion of rationally evaluating evidence, this yields preference rather than privileged insight (Baudrillard 1983c; Lyotard 1984; Vattimo 1988) because reason is "a matter of taste and feeling, know-how and connoisseurship" (Latour 1988). Within this understand-ing of reason modern science has no unique or special logic (Latour 1987; 1988: 179, 186 Latour and Woolgar 1979). Religions, cults, and witch-craft are elevated to the status of "rationalities" equal to science (Shweder 1986: 172). Logic and reason are "on the same footing" as myth and magic (Latour 1988: 146–50, 186, 212–13).

Several motives account for the general post-modern attack on reason. First, modern reason assumes universalism, unifying integration, the view that the same rules apply everywhere. Reasoned argument is assumed to be basically the same from country to country, culture to culture, and across historical periods. Post-modernism, on the contrary, argues that each situation is different and calls for special understanding. Post-mod-ernists assume that the "foundations change from one episteme to another" (Harland 1987: 106–7). There is no place for universal reason in a post-modern world where all paradigms are equal because each has its own logic. So if there is such a thing as post-modern reason, it is "scattered abroad and disseminated into heterogeneous forms" (Schrag 1988: 2); it is a "logic beyond any form of reason whatsoever" (Harland 1987: 140). Modern reason and rationality are said to be specific to situations, cultural artifices, internal to each system of thought and never examined critically (Henriques et al. 1984: 124). Reason is criticized for allowing "little room for cultural and personal idiosyncrasies" (Toulmin 1990: 200).

Second, reason is the product of the Enlightenment, modern science, and Western society, and as such for the post-modernists, it is guilty by association of all the errors attributed to them. Reason, like modern sci-ence, is understood to be dominating, oppressive, and totalitarian (Bern-stein 1986). Assuming a "best answer" or a "unique solution," it thus pre-

---

[31] Sometimes the skeptics' anti-reason statements are nuanced, but the consequences for the social sciences are the same. For example, does it really make any difference if, as Vattimo claims (1988: liii), he only intends to argue that there is no difference between reason and the irrational?

cludes diversity and tolerance (Toulmin 1990: 199–200). "Its reasonable ways are provisional and always brutally unfair to someone or other. In this sense irrationality is less mad than reason and order" (Corlett 1989: 215). The post-modernists focus on how reason and rationality are employed as legitimating devices to defend modern bureaucracy, law, economics, and politics (Wellmer 1985: 338–46). Reason "reduces the domains of indeterminacy, contingency, and democracy for reasons of efficiency, domination and power" (Ryan 1988: 565). Abandoning reason means, for post-modernists, liberation from modernity's preoccupation with authority, efficiency, hierarchy, power, technology, commerce (the business ethic), administration, social engineering (Ryan 1988: 563–65). It means release from modern science's concern for order, consistency, predictability, "institutionalized procedures dictated by the authority of an accepted paradigm" (Schrag 1988: 3). Thus reason is resisted because it leads to objectivity in science and power to the military and the government; they, in turn, are associated with violence, suffering, and alienation in the twentieth century, be it the Holocaust, world wars, Vietnam, Stalin's Gulag, or computer record keeping of information on individuals. As a product of the Enlightenment, reason is infused with the idea of progress and humanism. But reason, the post-modernists argue, has neither improved the human condition nor solved the problems of the homeless, women, Blacks, and other oppressed groups (Touraine 1988b). Even though good "reasons" have been given for every imaginable action, "the consequences have all too often been experienced as disastrous, immoral, or the fruit of inexcusable stupidity" (Edelman 1988: 109).

Third, reason and rationality are inconsistent with post-modern confidence in emotion, feeling, introspection and intuition, autonomy, creativity, imagination, fantasy, and contemplation. Post-modernists point out that to abandon their basic priorities and to countenance reason is to

> favor the head over the heart; the mechanical over the spiritual or the natural . . . , the inertly impersonal over the richly personal . . . , the banal collective over the uniquely individual, the dissociated anomic individual over the organic collective; the dead tradition over the living experiment; the positivist experiment over the living tradition; the static product over the dynamic process; the monotony of linear time over the timeless recurrence of myth; dull, sterile order over dynamic disorder; chaotic, entropic disorder over primordial order; the forces of death over the forces of life. (Graff 1979: 25)

Despite the intellectual incentives to abandon reason and rationality, affirmative post-modernists are more cautious, and many of them step back from the radical gesture of completely repudiating it. Some of them simply avoid the more rigid formulations of reason and rationality; others are inclined to accord almost absolute confidence to reason (Norris 1988: 188).

Many affirmative post-modernists call for flexibility, for contextual consideration of what is "reasoned" (Ryan 1988: 564), neither accepting rationality nor rejecting it (Ankersmit 1989: 140–42). They suggest that there are many different kinds of reason; some of them post-modernism should retain, and others it must reject. There is, of course, little agreement about the preferred order of reason (Touraine 1988b; Eco 1983a: 127–30; Agger 1990: 14, 23–24); the only agreement is that it should call modern science into question (Aronowitz 1981, 1988a: 131).[32] Instrumental or "scientific" reason, however, does appear especially objectionable (Bauman 1987: 191) inasmuch as it is rational, purposive, and subject centered and also because it emphasizes utility, efficiency, reliability, durability, superiority (Leiss 1983; Leiss et al. 1986).

Some affirmative post-modernists consider reason essential both to their own critique of modern social science and to the construction of positive post-modern projects that are both reasonable and logical (Griffin 1988a: 30), such as a post-modern science or the development of post-modern political and social movements. If they deny reason any legitimacy, then they are in a "predicament of having to use the resources of the heritage" that they question (Sarup 1989: 58). Some even conclude that the "tendency toward a displacement of reason . . . in postmodernism needs to be curtailed, for it invites a blatant irrationalism" (Schrag 1988: 3). Others contend that the real problem is that reason is absent in the modern world to begin with. They warn that the absence of reason is not cause for endorsing its demise (Agger 1990: 175). One feminist post-modernist proposes to avoid contradiction and ambivalence by deconstructing modern reason and then reconstructing a feminist rationality (Weedon 1987: 10).

An example from the fields of planning and organization theory illustrates how abandoning or even seriously doubting rationality and reason makes social science virtually impossible. Conventional versions of these fields presume, by definition, rationality; they are premised on logic and reason (Cooper and Burrell 1988). Complaints against reason and rationality are major points in deconstructing modern planning and organization theory. Both reason and rationality are, however, reintroduced when interest turns to constructing new post-modern versions of these fields.

Any presentation of post-modern planning and organization theory is generally preceded by a critique of modern, conventional versions and its assumptions as post-modernists attempt to break with the conception of planning as a "focus on large scale, technologically rational, austere and functionally efficient international style design" (Dear 1988). Modern

---

[32] Some affirmatives agree with the Frankfurt school's support for ethical substantive reason, its emancipatory character and its support for human rights, equality, and social justice. This view is closer to that of the post-Marxists than the post-modernists, however.

planning emphasizes efficiency, integration, coordination of policy, and revision in light of feedback (Meehan 1979). Post-modernists contend that this form of conventional planning leads to disorder, confusion, and the deterioration of life conditions. It is an absurdly narrow capitalist activity (Dear and Scott 1981) that presupposes an integrated system, a homogeneous whole that rejects diversity and difference.[33] A plan is the work of a central planning agency, of an hierarchical administrative body that claims expertise. It is said to have a rhetoric of instrumentalism, negotiation, and performance (Dear 1989). There is no room for the individual mind (Ryan 1982: 187). Reason and rationality are presumed to disguise power relations in the field of planning and organization studies. Post-modernism "reveals formal organization to be the ever-present expression of an autonomous power that masquerades as the supposedly rational constructions of modern institutions" (Cooper and Burrell 1988: 110).

But post-modern planning and post-modern organization theory are almost by definition a contradiction, and this may be why post-modernists in these fields are required either to compromise with modernity and reason instead of dismissing them entirely or to somehow limit themselves to critique. So Cooper and Burrell criticize the role of rational control and reasoned understanding in organization studies and sketch out new post-modern forms of formal organizations. Post-modern organizational studies are described as "process" and as "informal," as a "series of programmes, technologies, and as anti-functional strategies." But reason remains intact (Cooper and Burrell 1988: 105–10). Post-modern planning advocates the absence of a plan altogether or a situation where no plan is permitted to claim superiority. But most post-modern planners also retain reason and rationality while focusing their innovative energy on revision of other concepts. For example, they question space as objective, observable, tangible, controllable, and they offer a post-modernism view of space and time. They reject absolutist deconstructive relativism; they call not for the abolition of theory but for its re-formulation.

Ryan, a post-modernist with a post-Marxist orientation, offers a model of "anticentrist, antiabsolutist deconstructionist" planning that, while probably not acceptable to the skeptical post-modernists, departs equally

---

[33] The post-modern analysis that follows reverses the line of argument offered during the Cold War period when planning was understood to be socialist and capitalist-democracies were considered anti-planning (Lindblom 1959).

A "post-modern" critique of planning today is often phrased in Marxist terminology (classes and capitalism) (Harvey 1985, 1987; Dear and Scott 1981; Jameson 1984a; Zukin 1988), but post-modern planning gives up any aspirations of revolution, any instrumentalist theories of domination. Post-modern planners do, however, advance a "project." Many of them hope to reconstruct their discipline after having deconstructed it, to eventually provide planning with a new "master-narrative" appropriate for a post-modern age (Dear 1986: 376).

from modern, conventional views of the field (1982: 124–26). Its innovative qualities come not from abandoning reason so much as from other post-modern elements. He argues that this new form of planning for a post-modern world would have to be participatory and involve the social collectivity in all its heterogeneous form. "Multiple strategies, policies, and plans would have to be employed, all interrelated, with no one exclusively dominant. A principle of nonexclusion (which would integrate culture, politics, psychology) and nonisolation (which would not privilege economic optimality, abstractly conceived) follows from the deconstructive displacement of abstract formalism from the center of planning" (Ryan 1982: 188). "Post-modern planning would begin with participatory input, not with a centralizing, efficiency map . . . [that] focuses the social system toward the satisfaction of criteria." It would take "on the satisfaction of social needs." It "would emphasize 'interactive adaptation,' the role of uncertainty, the modifications imposed by diverse situations and different contexts, the need for inclusion, rather than exclusion, of variables, the wisdom of choosing policies over monolithic programs and the impossibility of mapping a whole reality." It would entail "multiple inputs based on needs, diversification of initiative, situational adaptation . . . , an emphasis on diverse, microstructural ground level plans to counter the theoreticist tendency of macro-structural, singular, global planning, and finally, immediate interfacing between sectors, rather than mediated relaying through the 'center' " (Ryan 1982: 191–93).

It is difficult to exaggerate the gravity for the social sciences of skeptical post-modernism's denial of reason and the affirmative post-modernists' ambivalence about it. Although one can understand post-modernism's tolerance, multiple realities, and pluralism, its repudiation of reason, and the vagueness of its standards of judgment (as discussed below) reduce its potential for the social sciences. In addition, rejecting reason requires that post-modernists make room within their ranks for those who, though they share some of its views, are questionable allies. For example, some of the New Age groups and those whose views of science are clearly mystical (a number of examples are found in Griffin 1990). Taken to the limit, the skeptical post-modernists' hostility to reason and rationality encourages anti-intellectualism. When the skeptics abandon reason and employ methods that reduce knowledge and meaning to "a rubble of signifiers," they also "produce a condition of nihilism,"[34] a state that may prepare "the ground for the re-emergence of a charismatic politics and even more simplistic propositions than those which were deconstructed" (Harvey 1989: 350). The affirmative post-modernist's ambivalence about reason "tends

[34] Nihilism is defined here as a denial of the possibility of any affirmation (Vattimo 1988) and the rejection of the very prospect of knowledge altogether (Hawkesworth 1989: 557).

also toward mysticism" and "begins to veer into nihilism" (Ryan 1988: 565). In some cases, it attracts individuals whose concern with religion, the transcendental, and the hermetic may invite intolerance (Levin and Kroker 1984: 16) and even prejudice (Ryan 1988: 565).

4. Standards of Judgment and Criteria of Evaluation

Critics allege that because post-modernists refuse either to apply established standards of inquiry or to be "governed by preestablished rules" (Lyotard 1984: 81) they are unable to evaluate intellectual production. Inspired by Heidegger (1962, 1972) post-modernists answer that there are no longer any rules or norms to guide inquiry, no overall validity, no universal, unequivocal basis for truth or taste (Bauman 1987: 197). If the basis of such judgments is well established for those who subscribe to modern social science, then this is not the case for all versions of post-modern social science, which may lack guidelines for choosing between discrepant theories or evaluating the overall quality of knowledge claims.[35]

a. Standards of Modern Social Science

Modern science specifies precise criteria for evaluating knowledge claims, even though these are not always met: it has guidelines for questioning theories and asserting counterclaims. Studies that respect specific rules of inquiry generate more confidence than inquiries that flagrantly ignore established procedures. At the same time it need not be assumed that "experiential evidence" assures definitive knowledge. The "liberalized empiricism" of modern social science merely contends that "the bearing of given evidence on scientific claims and thus on their truth is subject to appraisal and remains open to re-appraisal in the light of pertinent theories accepted as epistemically optimal at the time" (Hempel 1988: 26). Methodological errors—failure to follow the rules of method—are frequently the basis for discrediting knowledge claims in modern science, and they are often sufficient grounds for rejecting a specific set of research results. Consistency and general coherence lend support as does predictive capacity, though none of these alone is adequate. Tightly reasoned, rational, logical conclusions are given priority over contradictory, irrational, and illogical statements (Hoover 1980: 9–10).

---

[35] I do not mean to suggest that modern social science always seeks to settle on the one "best" theory. For example, in a policy-making situation it is sufficient that such judgment undertakes a simple comparison of outcomes to select the empirically and normatively preferable alternative (Meehan 1990: 78).

b. Post-Modernists on Standards, Criteria, and Evaluation

Post-modernists, and especially the skeptical post-modernists, argue that the very idea of strict evaluative standards goes against the whole philosophy of post-modernism (Kariel 1989: 128). They disparage modern social science's standards and its criteria for evaluating knowledge and all "accepted," conventional means to judge the results of intellectual inquiry in any form (study, research, and writing). They take aim at coherence because "false or otherwise wrong versions can hold together as well as right ones" (Goodman, 1984). They reject consistency as a criterion, calling for "a proliferation of inconsistent theories" rather than a weeding out of bad from good theories (Feyerabend 1975). Nothing can be proved; nothing can be falsified (Ferry and Renaut 1988: 175–90). They dismiss the possibility of evaluating theory on the basis of data, adding that if theory exists at all it must be liberated from data and observation (Gergen 1987: 2). Standards are not needed if one gives up the idea of truth-as-a-matter-of-matching-up-facts-to-theory and reconceptualizes it as a question of "discovering the range and scope of the interpretive standpoints that have won a place" (Toulmin 1983: 113).

Skeptical post-modernists argue that what they do is so distinctive that the standards, such as performativity, are inappropriate (Lyotard 1984).[36] Post-modern inquiry sets out to change "the meaning of the word knowledge. . . . It produces not the known, but the unknown [paralogy]" (Lyotard 1984: 60). Post-modern intellectual activity must be understood to be "risk taking," and no further claim can be made beyond that. If taste and judgment remain, then they are divested of any special privilege. If tentativeness and uncertainty result, then these simply have to be accepted. Post-modernists seek not to dispense knowledge, but rather to provide a basis for people to decide for themselves because truth outside the individual, independent of language, is impossible (Jacquard 1982: 195).

Accordingly, skeptical post-modernists neither argue for the superiority of their own analysis (Ashley and Walker 1990b: 368, 395, 398) nor propose permanent status for what they say or write. Some, in fact (Henry Kariel is an example), argue for the right to repudiate, at any time and without consequence, everything that they have written or said in the past. They never argue that "the post-modern mode constitutes an advance over the modern one." To do so would be to reestablish the idea of progress (Bauman 1987: 6).

Is there any real reason to try to establish criteria for evaluating this kind of post-modern knowledge? Kariel writes: "We [post-modernists] strive for no extrinsic objectives. Not seeking to be anywhere else, we act without

---

[36] See glossary for a definition of performativity and paralogy.

ulterior motives. Play suffices; it's intrinsically satisfying" (1989: xi). If this is so, then one may ask, Is there anything that qualifies as knowledge out there anyway? Or if all post-modernists offer as knowledge claims are simply "paralogy," as Lyotard (1984) expresses it, and if paralogy is, according to the dictionary, false or erroneous reasoning, then of what use are standards?[37]

The refusal or inability of post-modern social science to offer criteria for evaluating knowledge is in accord with other post-modern views, such as the contention that there is no "alternative ground" upon which knowledge might be established (Ashley 1989a: 278). It is consistent with post-modernism's epistemological view that reality is what we make of it, neither independent nor objective. Given this, no basis for definitively assessing the superiority of one theory over another can be established. Lacking any confidence in reason, rationality provides no help to post-modernists in determining the comparative excellence of varying perspectives. A denial of universal truth, or any approximation to it, follows logically.

Although skeptical post-modernists disclaim explicit criteria of judgment, the case can be made that they do indirectly, unintentionally, or by innuendo express implicit guidelines as they develop their own ideas and criticize those of others. Of course, these are not formally recognized and would probably be repudiated if they were publicly identified. But when skeptical post-modernists criticize modern science for being "contradictory" or "fraudulent," for avoiding counterevidence, for the logical fallacy of argument, for questionable definition of concepts, are they not evincing a respect, if not a preference, for the contrary? Skeptical post-modernists employ internalized guidelines, "criteria of evaluation," as they search for the "beauty" or "strength" in a text (Smith 1988: 106) or the "force" of a network (Latour 1988: 17). They advise us "to listen to, learn and put into practice all the unfolding possibilities hitherto denied." They seek to "impede, disrupt, and delay." They argue "it is incorrect to close one's ears to criticism" (Ashley and Walker 1990b: 395, 396, 414). They commend tension between "plot" and "narrative." They argue for the superiority of the writerly text over the readerly text, and they contend the written form is superior to oral voice (Derrida 1981). They acclaim a text that has elegance of expression and style, seductiveness of content, and simplicity of presentation (Feyerabend 1975: 157). They ask, What does a text tell us in terms of our personal experience and discrimination? In their own work they seek to "clarify the nature" of things, to "explore" multiple forms and functions,

---

[37] Lyotard contends post-modern work "cannot be judged according to a determining judgment, by applying familiar categories to the text or to the work" because it is precisely these rules and categories that the work "itself is looking for" (Lyotard 1984: 81). Few post-modernists have taken up this view, probably because they do not share his assumption that the "work itself" has such a project or that, if it did, it could succeed.

to devise descriptions and accounts "looking to the history of taste," in the context of "cultural dynamics and specific local conditions" without imagining "a monolithic intellectual project," all the while striving to avoid anything along the lines of the "comprehensive, unified, and objective" (Smith 1988: 28–29).

Affirmative post-modernists frequently employ terms such as oppression, exploitation, domination, liberation, freedom, insubordination, and resistance—all of which imply judgment or at least a normative frame of reference in which some definitive preferences are expressed. They hint that studying the local, the decentered, the marginal, and the excluded is superior to examining what is at the center. Some of them even go so far as to acknowledge that intellectual excellence, texts of quality, are marked by "coherence, comprehensiveness, penetration . . . , guiding and underlying intention in a work, thoroughness, appropriateness, contextuality, suggestiveness, and potential" (Madison 1988: 29–30). Others look to criteria set in community standards for determining value and assessing quality. Such "criteria" are, of course, vague and unsettled, but they do provide a glimmer of the terms for post-modern assessment. They are generally antitotalistic and nondefinitive; they seek to escape any hint of supposed superiority and avoid normative terms such as good and bad, consistent and inconsistent.

Explicit post-modern criteria are needed if post-modern inquiry is ever to become a viable alternative to modern social science. Can post-modernism survive for long in a methodological vacuum where all means for adjudication between opposing points of view are relinquished? Without clearly explicit criteria as a basis for evaluating their intellectual activity, for distinguishing between good and bad interpretations, post-modernism is of little value outside itself; it may be enjoyed and appreciated on a personal level but nothing more. It "abandons the communal sense of a shared inquiry in which individual perceptions are expected to be tested and shifted by others" (Ellis 1989: 1159). Without any standard or criteria of evaluation post-modern inquiry becomes a hopeless, perhaps even a worthless, enterprise.

5. Conclusion?

Modern social science makes for winners and losers. Its paradigms permit, at least in theory, only one of two contradictory theories to be considered "correct" in the long run (Kuhn 1970). It offers the interesting possibility of arbitrating, on the basis of evidence, between diametrically opposed views. If one respects its rules of evidence, one must accept the verdict, crushing as it may be at times, that one is simply mistaken. The analysis offered by modern social science is restricted in scope; the evidence it requires and its criteria for evaluating the results of inquiry are extremely narrow. Modern social science requires simplification. It surrenders richness of description and the feel for complexity in return for approximate answers to the questions, often limited in scope, that are eligible for consideration within its own terms. Modern social science's many foundationally relevant constraints confine the range of possible conclusions that can be drawn from research, often requiring so much qualification that broad and far-reaching interpretations are precluded. Those statements that are permitted sometimes appear trivial.

Post-modern social science for its part has the opposite problem. It rejects the Kuhnian model of science as a series of successive paradigms and announces the end of all paradigms. Only an absence of knowledge claims, an affirmation of multiple realities, and an acceptance of divergent interpretations remain. We can convince those who agree with us, but we have no basis for convincing those who dissent and no criteria to employ in arguing for the superiority of any particular view. Those who disagree with us can always argue that different interpretations must be accepted and that in a post-modern world one interpretation is as good as another. Post-modernists have little interest in convincing others that their view is best—the most just, appropriate, or true. In the end the problem with post-modern social science is that you can say anything you want, but so can everyone else. Some of what is said will be interesting and fascinating, but some will also be ridiculous and absurd. Post-modernism provides no means to distinguish between the two.

8

POST-MODERN POLITICAL ORIENTATIONS AND
SOCIAL SCIENCE

In certain forms deconstruction is "anti-working class, anticommunist, and even racist."
(Foley 1985: 118)

"Deconstruction has participated in the conservative
hegemony . . . close to the heart of the Reaganite legacy."
(Berman 1990: 8)

Deconstruction is "neither conservative nor revolutionary nor
progressive. . . . It makes distinctions of this kind irrelevant."
(Heller and Feher 1988: 139)

"Deconstruction is a philosophical pretext for a socialism that
would be radically democratic and egalitarian in nature. . . .
Deconstruction can be articulated with critical marxism."
(Ryan 1982: 41–43)

THE POLITICAL VIEWS of the skeptical and affirmative post-
modernists provide insight into their respective conceptions of
social science. We will see that the skeptic's political views are
such that they have little need for a highly complex post-modern social
science. But the affirmatives require a more developed, interventionist
social science to assist them in accomplishing their positive political
goals.

Whether post-modernism is inherently left-wing or right-wing is also
discussed below. Both cases have been argued. If either were true, serious
consequences for any post-modern social science would result. Of special
concern is the possibility that by adopting a post-modern approach one is
automatically committed to either a left-wing or a right-wing political
stance. I argue that this is not the case; while there may be many problems
with a post-modern social science, an automatic left-wing or right-wing
bias is not one of them.

1. Skeptical Post-Modernists on Politics: The Dark Side of Post-Modernism

A skeptical post-modern political orientation is grounded in a whole range of views presented in previous chapters. The skeptics embrace a political cynicism that is appropriate given their conception of modernity as a period of decay; the world as inevitably moving toward a final collapse, oblivion, and self-destruction that cannot be postponed (Jay 1988: 5–6; Redner 1987: 677). The skeptics ontological agnosticism urges them to relinquish any global political projects. Their epistemological relativism means their political views necessarily deny privilege. Decisive political conclusions almost always imply a foundational basis, and the skeptics shy away from such assertions. They call for tolerance of a range of meanings, a plurality of political beliefs without advocating any of them. These post-modernists struggle to survive in a normative void that therefore cannot go beyond political critique.

The skeptical post-modernists view the political as a "construction" in the sense that any political stance originates not in conclusive generalizations but in uncertainties, subjective interpretations, and contradictions. Political understandings are equally conditional and unsure because there is no basis for deciding one political strategy is "better" than another on the basis of fact, truth, or science; so a tentativeness results, and the political world is peopled by individuals, leaders, and followers, who themselves are "constructions" that originate in the eye of the observer (Edelman 1988: 123). There is no room here for justice or righteousness, or any desire to instill moral, self-sacrificing political beliefs, or any effort to incite exemplary forms of political action.

The most consistent skeptical post-modernists avoid judgment even when talking about modern conventional political orientations. They do not label them as "bad," "oppressive," "right-wing," or "left-wing." Any analysis that held modern political systems to be biased, distorted, or imperialist would be judgmental (Henriques et al. 1984: 1). Skeptical post-modernists strive to employ terms that do not imply anything pejorative when characterizing modern political systems as constituting, producing, regulating, classifying, or administering. They would not call for the overthrow of a political system, but they might propose to "unsettle" or deconstruct conventional political systems (Henriques et al. 1984: 11).

The skeptics' anti-representational and anti-democratic political views, outlined in Chapter 6, need not be repeated here. Many skeptics, it will be recalled, argue that nonparticipation in politics is a healthy, protest response to modern representation, to the corruption of representative democracy, to modern politics that is "inevitably remote, uninteresting and irrelevant" (Edelman 1988: 7–8).[1] These skeptics consider it better to withdraw approval from representative democracy (Ferry and Renaut 1985: 100, 164).

Given the skeptic's belief in the demise of a viable public sphere, the end of history, the absence of truth, and the death of the author (as a responsible agent), it is not surprising that they might refuse to advocate action, that they are anti-participatory or indifferent with respect to politics. Little results, they contend, from dramatic, heroic political commitment. Revolutions "have been betrayed, reforms have been counterproductive, and even resistance has been undone." Modern politicians are "worthless, corrupt, or absurd"; the political systems they direct are without redeeming qualities (Nelson 1987).[2] This pessimism applies not only to mainstream political participation but also to left and right political organizations and to the new social movements supported by the affirmative post-modernists and discussed below (Kellner 1989b: chap. 5; Sloterdijk 1987; Corlett 1989: 216–17). The skeptics interpret low levels of political participation (at least in the United States) as indicative of a refusal to be taken in (Edelman 1988: 7–8). To actively work for political or social change, to "bet on liberation, emancipation, the resurrection of the subject," is to act in accordance with the "political logic of the system." It is to play into the hands of the oppressor, to accept "subjecthood" (Levin and Kroker 1984: 15–16; Baudrillard 1983a: 107–9). It brings only marginal, temporary change that "acts as a balm" for those who engage in it (Edelman 1988: 130). If history has ended and if there is "no future" (Baudrillard 1989b: 34), then any struggle for social change is meaningless because individual human beings are powerless to influence government and society anyway.

To refuse to participate, to cultivate "ironic detachment" (Baudrillard 1983a: 108–9), becomes a positive, progressive political stance. The masses express genuine and authentically revolutionary sentiments, concrete resistance when their needs and desires are tapped, but it takes the form of a nonreception, of a refusal to participate (Baudrillard 1983a: 105–6). The masses reject the rational, reasoned logic of those who seek to mobilize them around modern political projects. They are simple, un-

[1] See Botwinick (1990) for an interesting exception. Seeking a synthesis of continental and American forms of post-modernism—perhaps of what are here called affirmative and skeptical post-modernism—this author suggests that because certainty is impossible, because there is no truth, because all interpretations are more or less interesting, all opinions must be taken seriously; this, therefore, results in a radical egalitarianism, and it is a "continually renewing impetus for the expansion of political participation."

[2] This, of course, violates the post-modern attempt to avoid judgment. This contradiction is discussed in Chapter 9.

complicated, intuitive, rightfully and justifiably cynical about politics. Strategic resistance in the form of indifference is a refuge against the kind of political engagement that could monopolize one's time and dominate one's life (Baudrillard 1983a: 39, 105–6).

In support of post-modern withdrawal, Edelman argues that high levels of political participation have lead to slaughter, repression, and genocide in the name of nationalism and patriotism. He concludes the world would be better off without any of it (Edelman 1988: 8). In the extreme we have Baudrillard who tells us that political participation makes little sense because everything of interest has already happened: the revolution has already taken place, the atomic bomb has already exploded so, therefore, why worry (1989b: 34–35)? It is too late to oppose the momentum of industrialized society. All one can do is abandon "extrinsic objectives. . . . Stay alert and cool in its midst . . . , be passionately impassive" (Kariel 1989: ix).

Critics argue there is something unhealthy about the political orientation of the skeptics—their turn inward and their concentration on the self. The skeptics are anti-determinist, pro-individualist, even narcissistic; they refuse all responsibility for what goes on in the society around them. Their retreat from the political may reflect their concern with self-development, self-expression, self-awareness, and self-affirmation, or it may simply be self-indulgent in the sense that each person decides for himself or herself what constitutes political truth.

The only forms of positive political action of interest to the skeptics are those that violate modern conceptions of the normal and those that display ironic contempt for the political. These forms of "detached" participation are not aimed at a positive project of establishing and maintaining. They, rather, incorporate the implicit goal of dissolving and attacking in forms that range from harmless playful pastimes to terrorism (Aronowitz 1988a: 49) and the darker preoccupation with death and suicide. Self-oriented narcissistic pursuits of life are all that make sense if there is "no alternative to it [modernity], no logical resolution. Only a logical exacerbation and a catastrophic resolution" (Baudrillard 1983a: 105–6).

One form of political activity attractive to some skeptics is euphoria and carnival (dressing up, comedy, the circus) (Kellner 1989b: chap. 4; Eagleton 1983a: 108–9). Inspired by Bakhtin's analysis of the medieval carnival where the everyday world is turned upside down by farce and play, the skeptics argue this is a healthy response to the post-modern situation (Bakhtin 1973; Todorov 1984: 78–90). The medieval carnival is "free; full of laughter, sacrileges, profanations of all things sacred, disparagement and unseemly behavior, familiar contact with everybody and everything" (Bakhtin quoted in Todorov 1984: 78–80). Sloterdijk offers an excellent example. He argues, and not all skeptical post-modernists would agree, for an affirmative form of cynicism that he calls "knyicism." This is satirical cynicism inspired by Diogenes. He tells us it has a "positive adversarial, counterstrategy" that seeks "existence in resistance, in laughter, in refusal, in the appeal to the whole of nature and a full life" (1987: 218). It focuses on the politics of the body, pleasure, risk, self-assertion, the individual's right to expect to be happy and to find joy and pleasure in life. Sloterdijk formulates a strategy effective for personal survival, but his solution is appropriate only for individuals. The forms of defense he envisions do not constitute a "project," an alternative to modernity; they are more in the line of anarchistic guerilla warfare waged against modernity. The body is "the primary locus of cognition . . . social protest and change" (Adelson 1984: 189). The example of Diogenes, Sloterdijk suggests, encourages us to urinate and masturbate in public. Although he criticizes the confirmed post-modern cynics, his quarrels with them are not really so serious as is evident in his definition of cynicism as enlightened false consciousness. He proposes an alternative to pessimism, a "light-hearted disrespect in pursuit of original task" (1984: 93).

Many skeptics assume that in a post-modern context political activity is necessarily random, unpredictable, and even pathological. These are Sorel's disillusioned optimists who turn to post-modern defeatism and terror out of pure frustration (Sorel 1987: 192–94). Acts of madness and insanity take on a new symbolic significance. Terrorism, violence, protest, insurrection are offered as anti-conventional post-modern forms of nonrepresentational political participation, as "deconstructive" alternatives to participation, as efforts to subvert representation and deny legitimacy (Baudrillard 1983a: 20–21, 54). Violence becomes a post-modern problematique, a "discourse and a semiotics . . . , a mode of interpretation . . . , an antitext," a post-modern language that "creates structure out of events, and events out of structure" (Apter 1987: 40–43).

A handful of the skeptical post-modernists are preoccupied with death and fascinated with destruction—preoccupations regarded as making a political statement (Scherpe 1986–87: 98; Baudrillard 1976; Kellner 1989b: 106–8; Wulf 1989). Post-modern fiction is said to "simulate death," to concentrate consciously on rehearsing death, to be the last site in the post-modern world where the living can learn anything about death (McHale 1987: 232). Poetry and art are not timeless expressions of genius, but rather reminders of mortality, disintegration, death (Vattimo 1988: 27). Living under the threat of nuclear catastrophe, a form of collective extermination, has led these skeptics to the very brink where everything evaporates and disappears. The difference between insanity and fantasy is bridged; "pandemonium and laughter [are] at the core of the igniting explosive mass" (Sloterdijk 1987: xxi).

For these skeptics the ultimate self-realization is the "apocalypse they can only carry out on themselves, a self-destruction" (Scherpe 1986–87: 123, summarizes a half dozen German post-modernists who adopt this perspective). Death, self-inflicted death, suicide, are affirmations of power that conquer rationality (Baudrillard 1976: 221), and these take on special significance in a post-modern world where powerlessness is the general rule. The absence of any hope for the future requires an anticipation of the end. The will to death becomes a positive attribute "when it is realized that only one strong enough to die can live, it becomes possible to embrace death as grace" (Taylor 1984: 73). Because no philosophical foundations remain for the skeptics, death becomes the only finality, a depository of all that is "great and beautiful" in the cumulative "life experience of past generations." Death is the "source of the few rules that can help us to move about our existence in a non-chaotic and undisorganized way while knowing that we are not headed anywhere" (Vattimo 1982: 25).

For the most extreme skeptics suicide becomes the only authentic political gesture left, the last and most revolutionary act, the culmination of post-modern resistance. It goes beyond recuperation and cooptation. It alone escapes the control of modernity and the object status that modernity imposes. The post-modern pushes us to transcend fear by "going beyond death," by controlling our own death, by "fantasizing life after death while still undead" (Wolfe 1988: 581).[3]

This dark side of post-modernism is disturbing when it encounters the challenge of the political and frighteningly explicit when it gains political expression. The skeptics represent a current of desperation and defeatism (Benhabib 1984: 125–26). By opting out of politics they leave power relations and formal authority untouched. This engenders a cynical, nihilist, and pessimistic political tone (Vattimo 1988). In their most cheery frame of mind they refuse political participation and celebrate the carnival. Their attraction to death and suicide evokes much the same message however: whatever political scenarios emerge, none is different enough from the status quo to matter to them. Given the history of the twentieth century, that is a powerful and frightening statement.

In considering the consequences of skeptical post-modern political orientations for social science the views of the extremist minority preoccupied by death and terrorism can be dealt with rather quickly. These post-modernists have no interest or need for a social science—be it modern or post-modern. The political views of the remaining skeptical post-modernists range from passivity to deliberate frivolity, and although they too may not require any social science at all, some of them are interested in a discursive,

---

[3] Suicide is closely linked to the post-modern appeal in Japan. Resistance within Japanese culture is minimal to begin with, and suicide "represents the capacity for the subject to resist without resisting, to undermine emptiness itself, to preempt death and destruction, or undo the end of history itself" (Wolfe 1988: 588).

literary social science. Such a social science would have little of importance to contribute to society. It would not need to play the role of conventional social science at any level. Nor would it be asked to provide theoretical insights in the form of new knowledge. It would not seek to enhance understanding because understanding assumes or promotes meta-narratives. Nor would it need to offer information as a basis for problem solving or policy making. What is a problem for conventional modern social science does not strike the skeptical post-modernists as worrisome. To formulate policy the skeptics would have to advance a point of view that something needs to be done and can be accomplished, and this they deny. All that is left for the skeptics is a social science that exhibits a passion for discourse, that serves as a means of self-exploration, self-reflection, and self-expression, but that is passive because it does not move beyond conversation.

2. Affirmative Post-Modernists on Politics: Activist, New Age, and Third World

Affirmative post-modernists exhibit a wide variety of political perspectives (Luke 1989b) that give rise to a fragmented, heterogeneous collection of political views that have little "common content" and often contradict one another (Ross 1988: xiv; Luke 1989c: chap. 8; Melucci 1990b: 14). They do however agree on several politically relevant dimensions: a rejection of modern science, a questioning of the modern idea of progress, a refusal to affiliate with any traditional, institutionalized political movements that have what they consider a "totalizing ideology" and an abandonment of logocentric foundational projects with comprehensive solutions—be they liberal, centrist, or conservative. They question official forms of knowledge, expertise, and "paper" qualifications. They are "post-proletarian, post-industrial, post-socialist, post-Marxist, and post-distributional" (Luke 1989c: 235).

The affirmative post-modernists encompass a more optimistic spirit than the skeptics, and they support a range of new political movements organized around everything from peace, ecology/environment, feminism, green politics, nationalism,[4] populism, and anarchism to "spiritual fitness disciplines," parapsychology, psychokinesis, and New Age movements. They encompass "communities of resistance," poor people's movements, and therapy groups. They bring together the oppressed, the mentally ill, citizens with disabilities, the homeless, and the generally disadvantaged (Falk 1990: 277–78; Huyssen 1984: 51). Some would add animal rights,

---

[4] Some post-modernists reject nationalist movements considering them to be modern along with socialist and liberal political movements (Walker 1988b: 28).

anti-abortion, gay and lesbian groups (Calhoun 1990). They are found not only in modern Western societies but in the Third World as well.

a. The Activist Affirmatives

Affirmatives, as indicated in Chapter 6, are not anti-democratic or opposed to political participation. They criticize representative democracy as rigid, as turning off the masses who withdraw and refuse to participate. But the affirmatives also call for a revival of genuine democracy, for the construction of authentic self-government; these provide opportunities for the new post-modern social movements and their post-modern projects of renewal that are directly or indirectly political. They were inspired by the world-wide outbreak of peace in the late 1980s (J. Rosenau 1990). They still believe that people can master their own destiny. They are cheered by the end of the Cold War and the increasing freedom in Eastern Europe, and they are dismayed by the 1991 war in the Persian Gulf.

Affirmative post-modernists may not vote because they see voting in a representative democracy as a pro forma "self-expression" that merely "legitimates" the state. But they, unlike the skeptics, understand nonvoting to be a democratic exercise. They do not vote because they live in a democracy that they believe is not really democratic. Even if they do not participate in elections they hold to their right to vote (Lipovetsky 1983: 187).

Although the skeptics are rendered politically passive by their understanding of the logic of modernity and their philosophical relativism, the affirmatives are fundamentally participatory. Many of them are political activists and political advocates. They adopt positive political positions based on explicitly stated values and goals. They move from deconstruction and reconstruction to construction, despite the intellectual logical contradiction involved in denying modern foundations and then positing one's own vision as in some ways "better." For example, although the skeptics and affirmatives both complain about pollution, poverty, civic disorder, and urban decline, the affirmatives are more likely to take action by proposing projects to prevent pollution and calling for public transportation, quality public housing for the poor, and better schools (Bauman 1987: 190). If modernity threatens the survival of the planet, this only urges them to attain higher levels of political participation and new forms of action. If their post-modernism is inspired by Marxism they are likely to emphasize oppression and insist on efficacious political strategies. If it is informed more by anarchism, then political action becomes an end in itself, important for its own sake.

The affirmative post-modernists emphasize grass-roots activity, voluntary associations, openness to other world views and divergent political orientations. They do not always argue for the superiority of their own group but rather work toward solidarity across groups in areas of politics, culture, and the arts; they seek out joint issue-specific commitments that encompasses various interests. But neither do they shy away from normative stands. Formulating value positions that are broad and inclusive is a delicate task; it requires considerable diplomacy and an exchange of views that does not attribute dogmatic authority to anyone.

Affirmative post-modern political and social movements (sometimes referred to in the literature as contemporary or critical social movements) have been defined as countermodels of all previously existing social movements (Calhoun 1990).[5] But they can also be viewed as an eclectic recombining of contradictory elements from a wide variety of social movements from the 1950s, 1960s, and 1970s. Whatever the case, post-modern social movements resemble neither the old left nor the new left. Post-modernists emphasize a tolerance and political pluralism that contrasts with both dogmatism and strict ideological standards of the past. These post-modernists have no faith in conventional political parties because they "are bound to become bureaucratic, corrupt, and undemocratic" (Tucker 1990: 76). Post-modern social movements are not interested in speaking for the working class (Heller and Feher 1989), which they consider reactionary or obsolete. The politics of redistribution is not part of their program. Nor do they struggle for the social benefits that were central to the old left, such as welfare or unemployment insurance. Such assistance, these post-modernists contend, just creates problems (Luke 1989c: 210). They look to new forms of politics that go beyond emancipation because the "enemies," if they exist at all (Vester 1990: 7; Walker 1988: 154), are no longer the bourgeoisie or the boss so much as the bureaucracy, centralized government, and "democratically" elected representatives (Melucci 1990a; Kellner 1989a: 220).

The affirmatives choose "life politics" over "emancipation." Emancipatory politics is rejected because so much of what the old social movements designated as emancipatory (seeking justice, freedom from inequality and oppression), the affirmatives argue, turned out to be oppressive. Besides, any plan for emancipation implies a "general prescription, a coherent plan, a program." The affirmative post-modernists look rather to "life politics," defined in admittedly vague terms as intimacy, globalization, self-actualization, and identity. They "seek to further the possibility of a fulfilling and satisfying life for all" (Giddens 1990: 150–55; Vester 1990).

Modern social movements, the old left for example, were characterized by a highly committed and homogeneous membership, a strategically effective hierarchical organizational structure, and clearly designated (hope-

---

[5] Some contend that old left and traditional right political movements are part of declining modern culture (Elkins 1989–90: 57).

fully) charismatic leadership; however, the new post-modern movements differ. Their membership is deliberately heterogeneous and cross-cuts societal categories such as class. They do not expect anything but part-time, temporary commitment from their membership. Lacking coherent organizational structures, they are decentered, local, disorganized, and fragmented. There is no stable post-modern leadership; leaders are often hard to identify at all. Modern social movements have long-term strategies and expect to be around for decades, while post-modern social movements have no such view. They are a "network of waxing and waning groups and strategies" (Vester 1990: 4).

The programs of modern social movements have been pragmatic and instrumental, but those of the post-modernists are seldom so reasoned and rational, almost never programmatic and directive (Vester 1990). If modern social movements look for material advantages for their members, then post-modern goals are more ambiguous. In general, however, they are anti-system and subversive in orientation. The hope of having an impact on culture and emotions sometimes substitutes for more material goals. If poverty moved the old left, then the post-modernists are touched by pain and anxiety (Offe 1987). They are less concerned with the success of a calculated strategy than they are with ongoing political practice (Agger 1990: 19; Walker 1988b: 117). They are peace-oriented and nonviolent in general (Falk 1990: 227). Critics, however, question their political effectiveness (Melucci 1990b: 15).

Post-modern political action is generally aimed at arousing aspirations, raising consciousness, exploring the politics of identity, and opening up opportunities for those who are marginal (Luke 1989c: 209, 235). In so doing it employs a new style, a new political agenda, and a very different content.[6] These post-modernists emphasize new conceptions of knowing and being, which make for a politics where more conscious attention is given to language and discourse. Post-modernists seek new ways of acting politically and new spaces for political action (Walker 1988a: 98–99). This means less concern with the state because they have no desire to "seize power" and more concern with the neighborhood, local, regional, and community levels. Small is beautiful, and autonomy is a prerequisite. Post-modern social movements are interpretive, connective (intertextual); they search to have an impact on seemingly remote structures of everyday life (Walker 1988b: 63, chap. 7). They call for the return of the subject, and in the field of politics the specific character of the new post-modern subject

[6] There is certainly little effective communication between the emerging post-modern movements and those who are part of the more modern political institutional structure (Melucci 1990a). Yet, post-modern movements do seem to have an impact on more structured political and formal organizations such as Worldwatch Institute, Amnesty International, and the Overseas Development Council (Falk 1989: 22).

takes shape: here the post-modern (subject) individual has no choice but to confront modern agency and authority.[7]

The affirmative post-modernists undertake joint political actions around specific issues rather than advocating a broad political platform. For example, in spring of 1988 when the University of California at Irvine permitted a franchise of Carl's Jr. Hamburgers to open on campus, a coalition of women, animal rights groups, Japanese Americans, lesbians, gays, and people with disabilities joined to organize a boycott and picket. The leaflets distributed indicated the diversity of motivations that brought these groups together: each had a different complaint, but they all agreed the Carl's Jr. had to go.

The political orientations of these activist affirmatives result in special demands being placed on social science. These post-modernists require a radically engaged social science. It has to go beyond modern social science, which is limited by formal rules and the guidance of rigorous methodological procedures. It must necessarily be an interventionist, spontaneous, and unpredictable social science. Because the affirmatives do not reject knowledge claims or reason in any absolute sense, many of them still value and employ a revitalized social science that substantially resembles its modern version.

b. New Age Affirmative Post-Modernists

Many New Age "sensibilities" are affirmative post-modernist, but their political orientations are very different from the other affirmatives.[8] New Age

[7] Not all post-modern social movements are directly committed to political action. For those that bridge affirmative and skeptical forms of post-modernism, linguistic, conceptual, and definitional matters often substitute for political action. In a sense this is inevitable for those who are truly allergic to coordinated, institutionalized, and organized political action. If they cannot formulate clear-cut goals, and if they believe it is pointless to speak specifically about "what is to be done" and "how" (Walker 1988b: 137, 154), then they have little choice but to emphasize linguistic nuances. For example, Walker (1988b: 117–28) explains how the post-modern peace movement has redefined "national security" by broadening it beyond military conceptions. This movement calls for an expanded definition of security and concern for it in new locations at local, regional, and personal sites. They focus security needs on people and away from the state, elites, and special interests. They associate security with greater and more authentic democracy, with more popular input in the formulation of defense policy in the area of national security. They ground national security on political community where violence is only the last resort. They accept the idea of "vulnerability" as part of the human condition, not as an indicator that more must be done to achieve "invulnerability." But this political action remains potential rather than realized. Reconceptualization and redefinition challenge, but they need not result in any concrete change, especially if they remain at the level of discourse.

[8] Post-modern opposition to reason—its relativism, individualism, and subjectivism—nurture New Age social movements that emphasize idealist fervor, religious experimentation,

post-modernists share a preference for the emotional, the irrational, the mystical, and the magical over the analytical, scientific, and reasoned (Capra 1982). They focus on all that modern science cannot explain, and so, for example, they offer guides to ghostly abodes and arrange visits to haunted houses. A belief in reincarnation is important, and they expend much energy to discover the details of past lives. The supernatural and the occult are popular, too. Noninstitutional religion, new spirituality, is a central focus; this is offered as an alternative to modern, organized mainstream Protestantism or the "one, universal, Catholic, or Jewish religion." Paganism and pantheism return as post-modern religions. Cosmic and mystical in character, both include a "celebration of the wisdom of ancient and primordial peoples' spirituality" (Fox 1990: 37). There is a fascination with the Black Goddess, the Sixth Sense, the secret, "lost" years of Jesus' life, astrology, astronomical pilgrimages, horoscopes, tarot, auras, dowsing, ESP, palm-reading numerology, vampires, werewolves, Big Foot, mummies that live.

Their efforts at post-modern pluralism and tolerance link up with special religious sentiments that differ from those of traditional religions and attempt to harmonize with the cosmos. Techniques such as "channeling" and "cleansing" are employed to develop the "powers," balancing and aligning one's psychic energy, that facilitate such linking up. Sometimes the search for religious experience focuses on out-of-body sensation, spiritual travel to another place or into the body of another person.

The New Age affirmative post-modernists search for deeper inspirational messages that come from inside the selves or outside the solar system. Meditation, the I Ching, sun signs, moon signs, mystical Eastern religions, several different kinds of Yoga, and ceremonial magic are all examples. The more conventional but still post-modern Church of Scientology and the Unification Church and their secular counterparts of Lifespring and EST (Erhard's Seminar Training) also share traces of a post-modern identity. Feminism has an impact in this area and draws attention to goddess religions, pre-Christian goddess worship, the search for feminine meaning in sun signs, and the role of good witches as healers.

Modern social science and natural science both have New Age post-modern counterparts. Affirmative post-modernists of a New Age bent are centered on personal relations, New Age psychology, and the therapy movements that provide the keys to self-discovery and personal "transformation." Although scientific knowledge is rejected, the preoccupation with the body remains; better health is sought through imaging and creative

---

millenarianism, and other similar phenomena (Bordewich 1988). For example, Derrida's writings are assigned reading in therapy groups (Anderson et al. 1988: 16), and both EST (Erhard's Seminar Training) and its successor, The Forum, draw heavily on Heidegger's philosophy (Gottlieb 1990: 23).

visualization, development of self-healing techniques, hands-on healing, discovery of human energy fields that are thought to cure. Post-modern aids for health can be found in stores that specialize in crystals and pyramids—the use of light that has transformative powers and can help one achieve "peak experience." Good magic, as opposed to Bad magic, is employed to improve health. The message is the same: do not trust the rational mind; modern medicine does more harm than good. A small but increasingly significant portion of the "modern population" of First World countries is turning to post-modern alternatives (homeopathetic medicine, witchcraft, and the laying on of hands), a protest against doctors more interested in profits than human lives. The "deep ecology" movement takes the environmental concerns of the affirmative post-modernists and adds a mystical religious dimension to the New Age incursions into the realm of natural science (Elkins 1989–90; Macy 1990). Inspired by Heidegger and ancient Chinese philosophy, "deep ecology" is anti-growth and holistic. It has confidence in the "wisdom of nature" and actively listens for that erudition to be expressed. This form of "ecological awareness is truly spiritual," said to be linked to the cosmos (Capra 1982: 412).

Rituals from the past are reinstated. For example, the search for the Holy Grail is renewed in Rhinebeck, New York, where organized weekends offer a return to the mystic realm of the Grail, to a world where storybook tales of physical transformation are given credence, where hermits, maidens, knights, and dragons are nearby as each individual seeks to "create" his or her own new spirituality and to be in touch with the past.[9]

New Age movements search ancient cults in hope of discovering something that might be relevant today. Books from the seventeenth, eighteenth, and nineteenth centuries on these matters are recent publishing successes. Initiation rites into secret societies of the nineteenth century are reprinted. Merlin's mystic life and rituals are studied. Texts about Celtic magic, the Runes, and their system of Nordic and Germanic religions are of substantial importance. Those from ancient India are equally popular, as are Astrals from the East. There is a search for information about ancient Black magic, poisons, potions, witchcraft, and demons. Educational programs teach how to lay a curse on an enemy, how to induce sleep or even death, and how to escape the spells others have inflicted on you. Prophets of the past such as Nostradamus are widely read.

These anti-rationalist post-modern New Age movements are explicitly affirmative and political. They stress "global unity, cooperation, tolerance and truth through self-understanding." Their political orientations are anti-intellectual because intellectuals transmit the values of modern science

[9] Ari L. Goldman, "Searching for the Holy Grail at an Adult Healing Camp," *New York Times*, August 21, 1989, B1, B4.

and reason. Many of them are millennialist; all are philosophical idealists, and this too influences their political attitudes. They reject traditional political parties. The Republicans are too attached to orthodox religions, the traditional family, and conventional morality. The Democratic party's commitment to social justice, secular humanism, government intervention makes it uninteresting to them. These New Age groups are not mobilized by issues that imply superior value systems (logocentric in character) such as racial justice, equal opportunity, and affirmative action. "New Age thinking generally regards such problems as a mere state of mind" (Bordewich 1988: 43).

New Agers argue that, although their social movements are presently dispersed and fragmented, new unified political formations will emerge once a "critical mass of awareness" is reached. And when they come together, they will form "a powerful force of social transformation" (Capra 1982: 45, 418). But even now, in geographic localities where there are a great many New Age post-modernists, they successfully support the political candidates who share their views.[10]

Members of New Age groups already exercise substantial power and influence in certain communities. New Age entrepreneurs and heads of private institutions support like-minded candidates for political office. Politicians with New Age connections propose programs that expand and enlarge their audiences and constituencies. In their capacity as elected public officials they are in a position to act on their views that spiritual development and testimony of personal transformation is as good an indicator of one's ability to "solve" social problems as a firm grasp of reality. In Boulder, Colorado, the board president of the Community Health Department, the nurse manager of medical units at the Community Hospital, administrators at local community colleges, elementary school principals, and teachers are all New Agers. Courses in the community colleges include channeling techniques, a crystal workshop, synchronicity, I Ching, transpersonal dimensions of astrology, and alchemy. Eastern meditation is taught in the elementary schools. Reputable businesses (50 percent of the Fortune 500 companies) hire "New Age Trainers" or buy products designed to improve employee performance and increase profits (Bordewich 1988: 42).

New Age affirmative post-modernists challenge the formal political system, but they are not all convinced that direct political action is effective. Some argue that nothing "out there" can be changed and that only personal transformation is worthwhile and fulfilling (Bordewich 1988); one

[10] Adherents to these movements come from the ranks of the American middle class. Their members are not viewed as eccentric or deviant in those communities where they are heavily concentrated such as Boulder, Colorado (Bordewich 1988).

must work to "change oneself." Others, also having given up on the present-day corrupt political infrastructure, work outside the "system" in "citizen diplomacy efforts." For example, in the early 1980s a New Age group with the hope of "placing a 'spiritual aura' of peace around the planet" brought Soviet scholars and members of the U.S. Department of Defense together to meditate. Educational programs, such as the "World Citizen curriculum," employ the "I Ching and out-of-body experiences as a way of visualizing a world without boundaries" (Bordewich 1988: 42).

New Age affirmative post-modernists are as intellectually inconsistent as the other affirmative post-modernists. Although modern meta-narratives are rejected, their own local-narratives, their personal "stories," are often all-encompassing. Although religious revival is part of New Age post-modernism—and generally they are ecumenical and pluralist—some are more fundamentalist (Heller and Feher 1988: 6). Although calling for tolerance, some New Age post-modern communities are exclusive and intolerant.

Some New Age post-modernists find a wide variety of social science forms important, but others reject social science by arguing their own religion or system of thought provides all the answers needed. The more electorally oriented New Age post-modernists do not hesitate to employ modern social science knowledge if it facilitates their election. If a post-modern social science could be constructed to include the mystical and magical, then they would probably welcome it. But the diversity of post-modern New Age sensibilities is so great that it is difficult to invent a social science acceptable or helpful to all of them.

c. Third World Affirmative Post-Modernists

On the surface post-modernism appears primarily of interest to the West and of little concern in the Third World (Calhoun 1990; Flax 1990: 190–93). But a closer look reveals that modern social and political movements in the Third World are giving way to new forms of political expression; in some cases what emerges is very much of an affirmative post-modern character. If modernity has failed the Third World, post-modernism appears in all its diversity and permissiveness to permit and encourage a selective attention to the past and an eclectic re-construction of the present.

The modern political crisis in the Third World may differ from that encountered elsewhere, but it seems likely to encourage post-modern social movements; the overall impact is potentially explosive. Detente and the rapprochement of the USSR and the United States may mean that the Third World is forgotten; neither superpower needs to compete for its support. The fiscal demands of the Western states seem to be enlarging as a result of, among other things, debt and military expenditures during the cold war. All this, too, results in cutbacks in foreign aid to the Third World. As the plight of these Third World countries deepens, one can reasonably ask if the appeal of post-modernism will not increase.

The appearance of post-modernism in the Third World is yet to be studied systematically. Certainly it appeals, as in the West, to the affluent, the desperate, and the disillusioned. But more must be said. Post-modernism is never heard about in Shanghai, but mixed with spiritualism it rumbles across the landscape in unexpected forms in Calcutta. The failure of Third World socialist liberation movements, modernist in style and conviction, seems to have provided an opening to anti-systemic and anti-democratic post-modern movements. Post-modern social movements in the Third World today are increasingly cynical about efforts to seize control of the state because, they argue, Marxist and socialist national liberation movements (the old left) produced little of consequence where they succeeded in gaining power (Arrighi et al. 1989).[11]

Post-modern themes—including anti-Enlightenment views, anti-modern attitudes, a return to fundamentalist indigenous spirituality, anti-science sentiments, and opposition to modern technology—are generating a growing interest throughout the Third World. Salman Rushdie provides an illustration of Third World post-modern discourse along these lines in his novel, *The Satanic Verses*. A fictional fundamentalist religious leader broadcasting by radio from London to his followers in the Middle East contends that modern history, progress, and Western conceptions of time must be denounced. "History the intoxicant, the creation and possession of the Devil, of the great Shaitan, the greatest of lies—progress, science, rights. . . . History is deviation from the Path, Knowledge is a delusion, because the sum of knowledge was complete on the day Allah finished his revelation to Mahound. We will unmake the veil of history. . . . And when it is unravelled, we will see Paradise standing there, in all its glory and light!" And on time: "Death to the tyranny . . . of calenders, of America, of time! We seek the eternity, the timelessness of God. . . . Burn the books and trust the Book" (Rushdie 1989: 210–11).

Post-modernists in the Third World argue that Western ideas, assumed synonymous with "the modern," have had a corrupting effect on the purity of their original indigenous cultures. These post-modernists speak of a return to the past: recapturing all that was valued and sacred in their own, now lost, primitive traditions, renouncing all that the colonial powers required, retrieving all that decades of Western imperialism negated and made a shambles of. Post-modern social movements in the Third World

---

[11] Many Communist parties in the Third World are revising their roles. In Mozambique the Communist party declared itself to be not the Vanguard party of the working class, but the Vanguard of All of the People. The Sandinistas in Nicaragua have set aside Marx and Lenin and now emphasize anti-Americanism and nationalism.

are expressions of a still remembered, if idealized, traditional society that has been passed on through generations and is now being re-affirmed. Post-modernism encourages this reminiscence for the past as a way to overcome the modern (Vattimo 1988: chap. 10). What results is not a duplication of the past, not a simple reaffirmation of traditionalism (Baykan 1990: 137), but, rather, something qualitatively new and different. Sometimes it takes the form of an incoherent combination of the modern and the irrational. For example, fundamentalist Muslim students major in modern medicine and computer science. Any discrepancy between these modern meta-narratives and their own religious belief systems is ignored.

These Third World forms of post-modernism are intellectually contradictory in another respect. Although rejecting Western truth claims, Third World post-modernists do not hesitate to assert their own truth and argue its superiority over any other. They denounce any special voice for the colonizer. But rather than deconstruct and dismiss it, they seek to replace it with an equally hegemonic, though indigenous, author. For instance, Gayatri Spivak, an Indian feminist post-modernist, criticizes the way modern authors represent the Third World. Drawing more from Derrida than Foucault, she argues that Hindu law has been misunderstood by the British colonial powers. She contends that these misinterpretations cannot be corrected with the help of modern social science. They must be deconstructed, overturned, and re-revealed by an understanding of the "mechanics of constitution of the Other." She offers sati (or suttee), the religious norm that encourages the Hindu widow to ascend the funeral pyre of her dead husband and immolate herself upon it, as an illustration. British colonial officials, she tells us, misunderstood and were misguided in saving these women; to do so was to impose British values upon them, and it denied the women any voice of their own. A woman who carried out this act saw it as her own praiseworthy choice, an example of exemplary conduct, a sign of moral superiority (Spivak 1988: 271–313). Spivak gives full voice to these women while maintaining that she does not intend to defend sati; her explicit intention is to be neutral vis-à-vis sati. The post-modern reluctance to judge does not permit Spivak to make such explicit assessment anyway. But the political implications of her analysis would not prohibit a re-legalization of sati, and this is indeed a frightening prospect.

Modern values question many traditional social institutions in the Third World that post-modern relativism and tolerance encourage. Serious moral questions emerge. The role of women in general is an example. Post-modernism in the Third World provides a justification for requiring women to adopt forms of dress that were abandoned by their grandmothers. It allows for reestablishing the subservience of women in traditional marriage roles. It is being used to restore male prerogatives at a time when the first measures for female equality are just beginning to have some effect. "There's a reaction against women. If there's unemployment, it's because women are taking jobs. If there's delinquency, it's because women are leaving the home to work. If there's no room on the buses, it's because women are filling them on their way to work."[12] Post-modernism in the Third World is surely not solely responsible for these trends, but it is being employed to encourage fundamentalism and reaction.

Post-modernism in the Third World emphasizes the style of political participation over effectiveness. If "life politics" is stressed over "emancipatory" political action in a Western, post-scarcity society, the repercussions are far less severe than in the Third World where the priority to life politics over emancipatory politics could prolong pain and suffering (Larsen 1990: xlvi).

The politics of Third World post-modernism has consequences for the social sciences. There is little of value in modern social science for those countries where these forms of post-modernism are widespread and hegemonic. Modern social science may, of course, continue to exist in peaceful contradiction, alongside fundamentally incompatible and even hostile political and social movements in the Third World, just as religious fundamentalists from these countries become computer experts despite discrepant sets of beliefs and assumptions underlying each. But in the long run modern social science is unlikely to have much impact in Third World countries dominated by post-modernists. Unless social science is stripped of all expectation that it can do more than "tell stories," it may not even be tolerated. It would never be permitted to challenge the dominant religious system. Post-modern versions of social science compatible with Third World post-modernism may be invented. None exists today.

3. Is Post-Modernism Left-Wing or Right-Wing?

It is easy to make the case that post-modernism is a political phenomenon, but it is harder to make a convincing case that it is inherently left-wing (Cantor 1989) or right-wing (Foley 1985). Both cases have been competently argued (Huyssen 1984: 49; Jameson 1984b: 55). The divergence of views on this question may indicate that post-modernism (or deconstruction) is either a-political, anti-political, politically ambiguous (Agger 1989b: 103–15; Dews 1986; Malkan 1987: 129–35), or politically ambivalent (Fraser 1984: 142–43; Gitlin 1989: 56).

In 1987 and 1988 the whole question of the dark side of the post-modern political orientation was brought to public attention by the Heidegger

[12] Hoda Badran, secretary general of the National Council for Childhood and Motherhood in Egypt, was quoted in the *New York Times*, September 23, 1989, 4.

affair in Germany and France and the de Man affair in the United States. Heidegger inspired post-modern methods, and de Man is credited with bringing Derrida's formulation of deconstruction in the field of literature and literary criticism to the United States and indirectly influenced its application to the social sciences. What do we now know about these men? Both actively supported the Nazis. Both were found to have deliberately disguised or denied the extent of their Nazi involvement (Farias 1989; Wiener 1988; Lehman 1988). De Man never publicly admitted his Nazi connection (Donoghue 1989: 36); neither he nor Heidegger ever spoke out to repudiate Nazism or Hitler (Atlas 1988:69).[13] This raises the question, Is post-modernism itself somehow inherently biased, inherently right-wing, because of Heidegger's and de Man's influence on it?

In the discussion about the political orientation of post-modernism that follows it seems clear that not everyone talking about the politics of post-modernism is discussing the same post-modernism. The distinction between skeptical and affirmative post-modernism is of some help, but these differences do not provide clear-cut insights in all cases. Agger, for example, argues that establishment forms of post-modernism are right-wing, detached from social praxis and quieting political activity. Radical forms of post-modernism are left-wing and subversive, and in this form it fulfills the "ambitions of the Enlightenment—reason, freedom, justice" (Agger 1990: 10–19, 33, 44–45).

The terms "left" and "right" are themselves plagued with definitional problems. The distinctions between them that seemed so evident in the 1930s have clouded over in the interim; today they are muddied, confused. The meanings of left and right have evolved and even been reversed in some cases.[14] In addition, sometimes authors, issues, and concepts can be read from either a left or a right point of view.[15] Neither are specific issue

---

[13] Invited reactions to the de Man affair have been collected in Hamacher et al. 1989, and from it we see that De Man has not gone without defenders. J. Hillis Miller explicitly denies the allegations with respect to de Man (1988: 676). Derrida similarly says that in the context, de Man's behavior was understandable if "not laudable" (Derrida 1988). See Walter Kendrick (1988:7) for an inventory and a much longer list of defenders. Francois Fedier (1988) responds to Heidegger's critics. These defenses have taken a number of different forms, but, to be sure, no one argues so as to justify Nazism itself.

[14] Historically the left emphasized the interests of the collective over those of the individual; the right favored individual liberty, individual rights, and individual initiative even if they were costly to the collective. The left encouraged activist, interventionist government; the right argued for the minimalist state. The right had confidence in competition, in the freedom of the market mechanism to assure a healthy economy and the maximum quality of life for all. The left preferred government intervention, planning, legislation of policies to redistribute society's resources more equally. Any consensus about these matters disappeared years ago. Revolutionary Marxists, for example, would argue against this left position and favor the withering away of the state.

[15] Emphasizing objectivity used to be considered left-wing, but today it is said to be con-

positions any longer the exclusive territory of the left or the right. Those opposing the military draft, the participation of women in the armed forces, and pornography are drawn from the entire left-right political spectrum. Much the same can be said for the pro-choice position on abortion. Left and right political orientation no longer predicts whether one favors or opposes increased political participation for the disadvantaged (Rosenau and Paehkle 1990).

Despite the Heidegger and de Man Nazi connections, I find it very difficult to argue that post-modernism is inherently biased; its ontology and its deep epistemology, especially that associated with skeptical post-modernism and deconstruction, can be (and have been) interpreted in both left-wing and right-wing fashions.[16] Post-modernism permits different readings with contradictory political implications. Therefore, those who choose to embrace a post-modern perspective need not worry about also adopting a left-wing or a right-wing perspective along with their post-modernism. But lacking a specific political identity does not signify political neutrality. Some on the left regard post-modern analysis as left-wing, although many of their left political comrades are fully convinced that it is basically right-wing. Those on the right who have spoken to the question are similarly divided (see Rosenau, forthcoming).

a. Some Marxists Criticize Post-Modern Methods

Some Marxists, especially the deductivist (orthodox) Marxists, materialist Marxists, and Marxist-Leninists reject post-modernism.[17] Those emphasiz-

---

servative (Graff 1983: 150–53; Gibbons 1985). Likewise, those whose philosophy inspires skeptical post-modernism, Nietzsche and Heidegger, were once assumed to be right-wing philosophers. In the early 1980s there was considerable respect for them on the left (Graff 1983: 151). A convincing case can be made that they both can be read as either left or right (Norris 1988: 190). Consider another example: pluralist interpretation has been held to be conservative, but others argue it permits an "anything goes" methodology that is not conservative but rather empty of politics and quite appropriate for post-modernism (Gibbons 1985: 777).

[16] I do not mean to say that in the cases of Heidegger and de Man there is no connection between ideas and action, philosophy and practice; often enough there are close links between thought and political choices. Dissociating abstract ideas from concrete action is very difficult. Once a value orientation is specified, a context designated, the favorable or unfavorable conditions of application outlined, then the left and right consequences of more abstract principles become clear. In addition, much depends on the level of abstraction of presentation. Certainly the embodiment of a doctrine in the life of its creators—Heidegger and de Man in this case—is an important consideration in discovering its consequences; but this evidence is hardly ever the only piece. Although both these individuals were influential in forming post-modernism and deconstruction, they did not single-handedly control its development.

[17] Few Marxists discussed here recognize a distinction between skeptical and affirmative forms of post-modernism, and, as we will see, these do not enter their discussion.

ing the continuity between their own views and the writings of Marx, Engels, and Lenin (Vaillancourt 1986a) might agree with post-modern criticism of "bourgeois modernity" (that is, its principles, practices, and categories are repressive and maintained in a hegemonic status through coercion), but they find fault with post-modern deconstruction and charge that this method tries to be critical without paying attention to the content of the discussion. They say it takes no notice of the concrete reality of human oppression. These Marxists consider post-modernism itself decadent, politically regressive (Davis 1985: 109), even reactionary (Eagleton 1981; Foley 1985: 114, 118; Malkan 1987: 154). Post-modernism is said to fit with the culture and ideology of the new conservatism and the global wave of religious fundamentalism. Its pessimism and its anti-bureaucracy—its opposition to hierarchy, state power, and administrative regimes—go along with specific conservative social policies such as de-regulation, privatization, and the reduction of social welfare. It is little more than a "decadent trope of massified modernism, a sympathetic correlation of Reaganism" (Davis 1985: 114), a cultural defense of capitalism (Harvey 1987).[18] Marxists give priority to economic variables; post-modern analysis emphasizes language, discourse, and culture. Marxists deny language is autonomous by arguing that it is intertwined with ideology, class, context, and history. They contend that the narrow post-modern focus on language reduces everything to discourse, and this makes post-modernism frivolous and anti-political. They claim post-modernism's strict attention to writing leads it "to set up language as an alternative to the social problems which plague society" (Eagleton 1983).

The anti-post-modern Marxists hold the author/subject responsible for his/her political actions, and they complain that deconstruction is not designed to explore this dimension. They do not hesitate to attribute blame for exploitation and oppression, to attribute causality and political agency to specific roles. They point out that when post-modernists do away with the author, they severely limit the possibilities of attributing obligation, thus shielding those with responsibility for working class exploitation (Wood 1986). They object that when post-modernists set aside authorial motivation when analyzing a text, they direct attention away from power relations involving the author who may employ the text as a context of

[18] Some Marxists do acknowledge that, in its most critical form, deconstruction reveals the plight of the disadvantaged (Agger 1990: 203, 213; Harvey 1987: 279–80). On occasion it denies legitimacy to the discourse of dominance. It demystifies and criticizes ideology, and it breaks the male/female dichotomy (Eagleton 1981, 1983). But none of this, they say, reflects its major thrust. Even if post-modernism is radical in the sense that it encourages self-expression and self-affirmation, this does not make it left-wing because it has lost all sense of social justice (Bauman 1986–87: 64–68).

dissimulation and manipulation. Without an author, without agency, a Marxist revolution is impossible (Eagleton 1981: 109).

Many of these orthodox Marxists argue with post-modern epistemology; their argument centers on the dialectic. Most of them are epistemological objectivists; reality is independent of the observer; they consider post-modernists to be philosophical idealists (Foley 1985: 125–30; Larsen 1990). These Marxists employ a concrete dialectical method (Vaillancourt 1986b) that post-modernism does not recognize. Derrida's deconstruction abolishes oppositions in the form of bipolar, dichotomous elements but without proposing a third category. Derrida says to do so would be to set up an equally exclusive, objectionable compromise position. Instead he calls for abolishing all such logocentric categories. But Marx's dialectic requires this third term in the form of a synthesis that follows the conflict of the thesis and anti-thesis, which in turn is replaced by another set of bipolar oppositions. Marxist dialectics and Derridian deconstruction are incompatible (Foley 1985: 121, 127).

Orthodox Marxists criticize post-modernism's relativism (Sarup 1989), its refusal to make value assertions (Comay 1986), its support for "anti-foundationalism." They see post-modernism as providing "a reading," not "answers," and they require answers. These Marxists argue that interpretation is political and takes place in a political context that effects and limits it (Eagleton 1983). They reject the post-modern views that all interpretations are equal and that there are an infinity of equally interesting interpretations (Said 1979, 1982). Asserting the superiority of their own normative positions, their own anti-capitalist value statements (Latimer 1984), and the necessity to establish meaning and knowledge, these Marxists criticize post-modernists for abandoning the "search for universal standards of truth, justice and taste" (Bauman 1986–87: 85; Wolin 1984–85: 28). Their argument continues along the following lines. Relativism makes for a lack of any political engagement,[19] and post-modernism by default supports the status quo (Kurzweil 1980; Said 1982). This absence of resistance or its transformation into private personal forms (see Hartsock 1987: 190) accounts for the skeptical post-modernist's refusal to "participate in collective projects designed to overthrow or transform the status quo"; it permits inequality and the abuse of power. "Ironic detachment" allows an acceptance of social injustice (Callinicos 1985: 99). In the worst case, the absence of normative values and an excessive tolerance is said to leave post-modernism vulnerable to nihilism and Nazism. These orthodox Marxists agree that the post-modern rejection of all meta-narratives, all theories

---

[19] Some post-modernists who defend deconstruction argue it is, itself, a form of praxis, a theoretical form of political practice.

without regard to merit, opens the way for totalitarianism, especially if all more responsible alternatives are rejected.

b. Some Post-Marxists and Neo-Marxists Favor Post-Modern Analysis

A broad range of those on the left support substantive post-modern positions.[20] The move in this direction has been accelerated by the broad global crisis of authoritarian, dogmatic Marxism. These Marxists must contend with both the languishing of liberal reforms of the 1930s and the flagging of the totalizing truths such as humanism or existentialism in the 1960s. The waning of the Communist party in socialist countries in the 1980s and 1990s is also a cause for crisis, leading some on the left to embrace post-modernism.

Two Marxists tendencies are attracted to post-modernism: the post-Marxists and the neo-Marxists.[21] The post-Marxists abandon many principles central to Marxism; they adjust their Marxist perspective so that it conforms to a post-modern frame of reference. Some of them read post-modernism as a radical, critical continuation of Marxism, as socially and politically progressive. Post-Marxists also adopt post-modernism to express their discontent with both modernity and orthodox Marxism. The writings of Ernesto Laclau, Chantel Mouffe, Stanley Aronowitz, and Scott Lash are post-Marxist. The post-Marxist leftists, like the post-modernists, are anti-state (Laclau and Mouffe 1985), anti-hierarchy (Lash and Urry 1987), and anti-centralization (Ryan 1982). They question any privileged voice for state officials. Some feel that deconstruction acts to correct Marxism, assuring the "economic and political institutions required in egalitarian and non-hierarchical socialist construction" (Ryan 1982: 44).

The neo-Marxists maintain their essential identity and primary affiliation with a Hegelian form of Marxism (Aronowitz 1981), but they look to

[20] They share post-modern reservations about humanism, the subject, objectivity (Laclau and Mouffe 1985), authority, bureaucracy, science (Aronowitz 1981). These leftists estimate support for such concepts to be a politically right-wing orientation, and they reason that post-modern opposition to all these concepts is left-wing (Graff 1983: 151–52). Some are suspicious of reason and rationality as symbols of closure, as indicators of unified thought (Laclau and Mouffe 1985). They see post-modern suspicion of reason and rationality as consistent with their own socialist politics because "capitalism requires rationalism, and such rationalism is incompatible with the social form of socialism" (Ryan 1982: 158). They argue that socialist forms, much like post-modernism, seek to go beyond "rationalist limits" (Ryan 1982: 158). The Western Marxists agree with post-modern opposition to orthodox communism, central planning, and the vanguard political party that monopolizes authority. The anarchist left is especially attracted to this post-modern orientation, extending it to mean that new forms of workplace organization are needed.

[21] It is not always easy to distinguish between neo-Marxists and post-Marxists, though both orientations are left of center. They are best conceived of as overlapping categories that permit individuals to move between them over time.

post-modernism for inspiration to reinvigorate, revive, and expand Marxism (Stephanson and Jameson 1988; Woodiwiss 1990). They suggest post-modernism is constructive because it alerts the left to the weaknesses of its own assumptions (Bauman 1986–87: 87–88). Examples of neo-Marxist post-modernists include Fredric Jameson and E. W. Soja.[22]

These pro-deconstruction leftists make the case that deconstruction is critical, left-wing, and revolutionary. The neo-Marxist post-modernists read Derrida as having declared publicly that he was a communist (Ryan 1981: 161; 1982).[23] Deconstruction is understood to have a left political content, to open the path to revolution, to destabilize the status quo (Gayatri Spivak, quoted in English in Fraser 1984: 129–31), to challenge hegemonic discourse, and to question hierarchy and bureaucracy. It offers a nonrepressive conception of "order"; and it is radical in the sense that it goes to the roots (Murphy 1987a). It is assumed to provide an opening for marginal groups, women, non-Western groups, blacks, the dominated, the mentally ill, the homeless, and all those oppressed by capitalism.

Some of these Marxists consider Marx himself to have anticipated Derrida (Ryan 1981, 1982), to have been the first deconstructionist (Spivak 1980).[24] At minimum, there is strong support for the view that Marxism and deconstruction can learn from each other (Ryan 1981, 1982) or that deconstruction can serve Marxism (Spivak quoted in Fraser 1984 and in Foley 1985: 122–23). For example, Ryan suggests that by drawing attention to the antagonistic forces and contradictions in capitalism, deconstruction can revise the dialectic so that it is less linear and fatalistic about progress toward socialism, thus making the Marxist dialectic more provisional (1982: 43).

The post-Marxists put post-modernism first and justify this with a whole range of arguments. Marx himself, they conclude, was open, intellectually flexible, rejecting truth and finality; much the same is true of post-modernism (Ryan 1982). Some post-Marxists argue, however, that the relation-

[22] All the neo-Marxists or post-Marxists who employ post-modern analysis or make concessions to it, are criticized as "revisionists," "anti-revolutionary," and pro-anarchist by the anti-post-modern Marxists (Foley 1985: 115–33).

[23] Ryan says that Derrida took the opposite point of view in the past. But he says that Derrida has changed, that if deconstruction is not viewed as inherently left-wing in the United States it is because the Yale school of literary criticism and other departments of literature misappropriated Derrida (much as Stalin misappropriated Marx) and presented deconstruction as a-political and exclusively aesthetic (1982). Norris agrees with Ryan (1982: 91); contending that Derrida has much evolved of late (Norris 1988); while Derrida used to be a-political and relativist (guilty as charged), he has become more politically conscious of what he writes since the revelations about Paul de Man's Nazi connections.

[24] Agger convincingly argues that "Marxist post-modernists forget that Marx would have reserved the term 'postmodernity' only for the end of prehistory—socialism" (1990: 19).

ship goes in the other direction; they propose to deconstruct Marxism and, by implication, perhaps, abandon it altogether (Laclau 1988).

On some points the neo-Marxists and the post-Marxists have important differences. Post-modernism rejects meta-narratives (logocentric theories with specific universal truth-claims). Marxism seems to be an obvious example, and in his early work Derrida singled it out as especially objectionable. Post-Marxists tend to also consider meta-narratives as totalizing, even totalitarian.[25] But the neo-Marxists respond that without a meta-narrative there is no possibility of "transforming a whole social system" (Jameson 1988: 347).[26]

The neo-Marxists and post-Marxists have different views on many of Marx's concepts, and they disagree about the appropriateness of Marxist concepts for a post-modern analysis. The post-Marxists give up most Marxist terminology and categories of analysis. They require adjustments in Marx's "original axioms" in the light of contemporary political situations, which they understand to be very different from those of Marx's time. They contend that if Marx were alive today, he would be the first to agree with this move (Ryan 1982: 21). The neo-Marxists retain Marxist terminology but are willing to abandon certain, less essential Marxist con-

[25] They also argue that Lenin (or Engels) developed Marxism into a global theory, a closed meta-narrative, and that this was never Marx's intention. They denounce Leninism and/or Marxism-Leninism with its singular direction to history (Laclau and Mouffe 1985) because it is "exclusive, elitist, hierarchical, disciplinarian" (Ryan 1982: xiv). Lash and Urry (1987: 279) conclude that the Marxist theory of capitalism is no longer valid because it has become "disorganized." Some of them simply grant that Marxism is an antiquated and old fashioned meta-narrative, "rooted in old, surpassed assumptions," and they propose to move beyond it (Aronowitz 1981: 126).

[26] The neo-Marxists give priority to Marxism on this point. They say post-modernists are mistaken in their critique of meta-narratives. They contend Marxism offers a unified theory, which although not perfect, is superior to others, and they propose to reformulate it in ways appropriate to a post-modern world. They develop new theories of capitalism that, although not orthodox, still imply the category of capitalism and its eventual collapse; thus, they reaffirm Marxist theory rather than repudiating it. Jameson develops an innovative Marxist meta-narrative that incorporates much post-modern thought, including Baudrillard's critique of consumer society (1985, 1981), which he does not like but admits is accurate. For Jameson the post-modern world is "the cultural logic of late capitalism," a distorted, decentered, global network that constitutes a third stage of capitalism, a "mode of production," and the present successor to modern capitalism (1984a; 1989: 40). He sees in the post-modern world a potentially popular and democratic opening that may permit the entry of new forms of political practice moving on to the construction of a Marxist society (Stephanson and Jameson 1988). Jameson's proposal, however, is severely criticized. Some contend that if he keeps the totality and a meta-narrative, then it will lead him to Stalinism and Leninism. Others on the left attack him for making too many concessions to post-modernism and accuse him of "apolitical millenarianism" (P. Anderson 1985, 1988; B. Anderson 1987–88). Davis (1985) says Jameson is overly sympathetic to post-modernism when he defines it as a sign of capitalist energy rather than as merely a symptom of global crisis.

cepts. Jameson, for example, proposes Marxist views of time and space are no longer relevant and therefore adopts post-modern conceptualizations of these dimensions. Soja (1989: 75) retains Marxist categories but supplements them with post-modern concepts.

Adjusting the concept of class to post-modern analysis presents special problems for those on the left who favor post-modernism. The post-Marxists are generally opposed to class analysis, and they permit no special role for the working class (Laclau and Mouffe 1985; Aronowitz 1988a: 57–61). Thus, they have no argument with its absence from post-modern analysis. For example, Lash and Urry (1987) argue that a Marxist definition of the working class and its role is less valid today and that post-modernism is helpful in revising this out-dated Marxist conceptual apparatus. The neo-Marxists, however, are more reluctant to abandon class analysis. They make certain adjustments, but in the end they argue for retaining it. For example, Soja (1989) seeks to uncover class exploitation, "gender and racial domination, cultural and personal disempowerment, and environmental degradation" within a post-modern analysis. Jameson (1988) also argues he can be a post-modernist and still keep the concept of class-identity that he feels is essential to understanding. In an attempt at compromise Bauman argues (1987: 195) that the class struggle continues but that the rich and poor work together in a post-modern world.[27] Finally, it is reasonable to argue that while post-modernism may deny the legitimacy of the working class, this is not a problem because it offers a substitute: those on the margins form a "surrogate proletariat."

Post-modern analysis questions authority, and this means questioning Marxist author(ity). Although the left has always challenged the authority of others (be it Jesus Christ, the Founding Fathers, or the hegemonic discourse of the modern state), it has been less willing to question its own authorities. Neo-Marxists have more problems with post-modernism in this respect than is the case with the post-Marxists. Post-Marxists see post-modernism as subverting authority, decentering the subject (individual). They do, however, substitute agency in the form of "permutations of language, in discursive formations" (Laclau and Mouffe 1985). They retain the author but permit him/her little importance. The neo-Marxists are more sympathetic to the author and sensitive to the importance of agency that is so essential to their understanding of political struggle and to revolutionary activity (Jameson 1984a: 84; 1989: 41).

Post-modernism offers no privilege to any particular variable or approach; thus, it questions Marx's emphasis on the economy as a primary

[27] Bauman (1986–87: 93) argues that the model of "major revolution," so closely associated with Leninism, shows that such revolutions are shortcuts forcing change; reforms are more acceptable because people are better prepared to accept the shifts required.

category of analysis.[28] Few neo-Marxists or post-Marxists have any objection because most of them ceased to be preoccupied by economic factors long ago. Aronowitz argues that Marxism is economist and "logocentric" (1981: 127; 1988a: 57–61) and urges more attention to culture. He maintains that this view does not compromise his socialist goals (1988a). Jameson (1984a) sees culture as having become autonomous in the post-modern world, although he feels this was not the case historically under modern capitalism. Laclau and Mouffe (1985) note that since the 1930s efforts to move away from economism within Marxism were stifled, a factor contributing to its overall decline. Had this not been the case, they say, Marxists would have come to post-modern conclusions much sooner.

c. Many on the Right Oppose Post-Modernism

Many on the right severely criticize post-modernism.[29] They argue it is decadent, amoral, hedonistic, opportunistic, (Kramer 1982b: 40), disruptive (Bell 1976: 54), destabilizing (Graff 1983), anarchist, left-wing (Pacom 1989: 61; Bell 1976), a refuge for ex-Marxists (Gitlin 1989), eroding respect for authority and "striking at the motivational and psychic-reward system," the competitive spirit, so very necessary for capitalism (Huyssen 1984). They understand it to undermine customary, established family structure and traditional religious values. In the social sciences post-modernism is said to overthrow traditional methods and research orientations without replacing them with anything else (Kramer 1984).

These conservatives disagree with post-modernism on essential points. They believe in the possibility of truth, in reason, and in the importance of history as the discipline that transmits human traditions from generation to generation. Certain of their own values, they oppose post-modernism's value relativism because it erases the difference between right and wrong, good and bad, true and false. Some on the right agree with those on the left who complain that post-modernism is a-political and overlooks the political content of a text and the importance of political orientation as a valid motivation for interpretation (Davie 1983).

For certain conservatives the appearance of post-modernism indicates that something has gone seriously awry. It is said to represent a "collapse

---

[28] Jameson, a neo-Marxist, protests this (1988: 347) by suggesting that because post-modernism desperately needs a theory of history it should look to Marxism for inspiration and completion of its project (1989: 34).

[29] Those on the right who criticize post-modernism are split regarding modernity. Some argue modernity is characterized "by high purposes and moral grandeur" (Kramer 1982b: 42). Others argue the modern is as unacceptable as the post-modern. All that is modern is exhausted, and traditional religion is needed to restore positive societal relations (Bell 1976: 28–30).

of critical standards, the undesirable heritage of the 1960s radicalism" (Kramer 1982a: 2; 1982b; Sayres et al. 1984: 10–11).

d. Some on the Right Favor Post-Modernism

Right-wing support for post-modernism exists, although it is not well developed. The problem is that, while various sectors of the right may find occasional points of substantial agreement with post-modernism, this does not lead to serious political alliances between the post-modernists and the right because impressive areas of disagreement remain. In the 1970s, for example, the "new philosophers" movement in France opposed reason just as do the post-modernists. Right-of-center political scientists in the United States in the 1960s offered pluralism as an alternative to "socialist" planning; their definition of pluralism was not very different from that of post-modernism—ever-changing groups of citizens that form, disaggregate, and reform alliances across various political issues.

Certain conservatives share political perspectives with post-modernism, though perhaps not always for the same reasons. Both conservatives and post-modernists are anti-state, anti-bureaucracy; both call for "minimal government," the elimination of big government, dismantling the welfare state, doing away with the power of the central government (Berman 1986–87: 62–67). Both approve of deregulation, increasing individual freedom of choice and personal liberty (Aronowitz 1988a: 49; Rosenau and Paehlke 1990). Some in both camps argue strongly for the "end of history" (Fukuyama 1989).

There are even a few cases of post-modernists who are publicly known to be politically right-wing. For example, Stanley Fish supported Barry Goldwater. In the 1970s through post-modernism he attacked the established order, which he saw as politically left in character (Berman 1986–87: 62; Johnson et al. 1985: 89). In an approving manner Fish argues that post-modernism discourages change. Post-modernism's value relativism does not offend his right-of-center political perspective because he argues that truth remains for specific intellectual communities, and it is unimportant that truths are not universal.

4. Conclusion

A great variety of political perspectives exists within post-modernism. Some are politically active, others more passive. Some consider post-modernism politically left-wing; others feel it is right-wing. Because of this diversity the consequences for social science are not straightforward.

Political views of most post-modernists would require a seriously transformed social science. Some skeptics would find any social science, even a revised post-modern form of social science, of little importance. Others might find it of interest if it were restructured as merely discursive, intellectual activity. The activist affirmative post-modernists, because they envision post-modern political projects that do not reject all modern assumptions, could put social science knowledge to use in attaining their goals. For the New Age affirmative post-modernists and the Third World affirmatives, results are more mixed.

Post-modernism is not inherently left-wing or right-wing. Those who employ it, therefore, are not unconsciously subscribing to a political ideology along with it. But this reassurance should not be too comforting. It does not signal political neutrality. It may only indicate that post-modernism is so abstract and obscurantist that it can be manipulated to fit any political orientation.

9

ELEMENTS FOR AN ASSESSMENT

I N THIS CHAPTER I present a summary sketch of post-modern social science based on what has been learned in previous chapters. I
assess some of the difficult choices social scientists must make vis-à-vis
post-modern forms of inquiry. In addition, I review selected criticisms of
post-modernism not covered elsewhere and consider various scenarios for
the future of post-modernism in the social sciences.

In a plural(ist) world any conclusion is inevitably inadequate, and that
offered here is no exception.[1] The reader may choose to defer, postpone,
or defy conclusions altogether in the spirit of Derrida's *différance*. After all,
conclusions aim to establish hierarchy, to be authoritative. Or the reader
may simply rewrite this one, reinventing it through the process of reading.
But this will not be an easy task because this is a "readerly" finale.[2] It does
not encourage post-modern liberties of interpretation. This author, in a
modernist demeanor, asserts her sovereign presence and refuses to be ignored.

Post-modernism is an ambiguous bequest of the humanities to the social
sciences. It pleases some, frightens others, and leaves few untouched. But
is it appropriate for the social sciences? Some social scientists are contented
beneficiaries and accept it without hesitation. Others are more ambivalent
heirs. Still others are defiant and want no part of any such inheritance.

Post-modernism emerged in the humanities, and, perhaps too often, its
application in the social sciences is grounded on the assumption that there
is little difference between the two. Post-modernists make this case to justify employing a post-modern approach in the social sciences. Those
who champion post-modern law, for example, argue that legal texts and
literary texts are identical. Post-modern anthropology merges ethnography
and poetry (Tyler 1984; 1986: 138; Clifford and Marcus 1986: 4).[3]

[1] Jane Flax (1990) says that post-modernism permits no conclusions.

[2] As indicated in the glossary, a "readerly" text assumes a passive reader seeking to understand an author's intentions. It is the opposite of a "writerly" text that is purposely vague,
open to many interpretations, and deliberately encouraging the reader to rewrite the contents
of the text.

[3] This argument extends to natural science as well: post-modernists argue there is no distinction between science and literature, no special reality to which either can appeal. Both are
said to be fiction. Both are texts (Latour 1988: 189; Latour and Woolgar 1979: 252–61).
Both are mere rhetoric (Vattimo 1988). See Rosenau for an analysis of post-modern science
(1992).

But the opposite case can be made, and it gives pause. The application of post-modernism to the humanities, literature, and the arts may be without undue consequences, but its appropriateness for the social sciences is a question of another order. In the humanities subjectivity and speculation may be playful and interesting, but the social sciences need to be more rigorous and analytical, grounding conclusions on reason and evidence of one sort or another. A case can be made that there are dramatic differences in the "truth conditions" of the social sciences and fictional texts (Norris 1988: 16–21). In the social sciences, research results are encrusted in power relations (Hoy 1985b: 167). At least part of the time, they are relevant for policy making, and this is of enormous import. It matters less in the humanities if the author refuses to accept responsibility for his or her text-event. No one cares very much if authority disappears, if agency cannot be established. But it seems imperative in the social sciences that decision makers assume responsibility. An inadequate decision or the refusal to decide may have serious repercussions on human life conditions and the environment. Such is not the case in the humanities; this allows one to be more cavalier about matters without incurring such serious consequences.

In literature the advance of post-modernism has meant the loss of definitional meaning. Literature is de-stabilized. Parameters are removed. No determinate readings remain (Hassan 1987: 201). And often a harmless, fascinating form of magic results. Modern time, space, and history can be dispensed within post-modern literature, and the results are entertaining. But this is not always the case in the social sciences. The social sciences often enough confront problems that do not permit a retreat into agnosticism, nihilism, linguistic relativism, or a stance holding human communication impossible.

Any assessment of post-modernism in the social sciences needs to be qualified, according to the dimension of knowledge and the form of post-modernism being considered. Post-modernism may have a contribution to make on *substantive* themes, and, indeed, it often provides fascinating insights across a wide range of topics because it focuses on what is nonobvious, left out, and generally forgotten in a text and examines what is unsaid, overlooked, understated, and never overtly recognized. For example, in the field of international relations, a special issue of a major journal considered from a post-modern point of view "surveillance, simulation and computer-assisted war gaming, the acceleration of weapons delivery, alliance politics, arms transfers, the local politics of ecological and anti-nuclear movements, the politics of international debt, and the production and transformation of political institutions, to name only a few" (Ashley and Walker 1990a: 265). The results are innovative and challenging.

The prognosis is more qualified with respect to its *methodological* reconstruction. From a modernist perspective, it is seriously flawed and epistemologically dubious. In its most *extreme*, uncompromised formulations post-modernism yields results that appear frivolous. Consider, for example, its posture toward modern science. Despite its errors and inconsistencies, the costs and benefits of modern science must be weighed. More people are alive today than ever before, and a good many of them live better and longer than in the past. Even if all this was accomplished in the presence of philosophical inadequacy and a possibly misguided belief in linear progress, it still remains a remarkable accomplishment. To question the philosophic and intellectual tradition that gives rise and sustains this achievement, as the affirmative post-modernists do, is one thing; but to dismiss it altogether, as so many skeptical post-modernists do, is quite another. The latter offer an unbalanced view, without nuance and qualification, thereby undermining the credibility of the whole of post-modernism. Viewed in this way, post-modernism risks being dismissed as just another anti-modern intellectual current (Lechner 1990; Kellner 1989b: 208–9), part of the fin-de-siècle fringe movement (Jay 1988).

1. The Substance of Post-Modern Social Science: A Summary

Post-modern social science is in its infancy, and thus, like many incipient paradigms, its overall shape and character is vague, its substantive contribution still shadowy and fragmentary, mixed and uneven. The affirmatives seek to formulate a new post-modern social science with goals and methods substantially different from those of modern social science.[4] But the skeptics, pessimistic about the possibility of a new revitalized post-modern social science, envision a very limited role for it—that of criticizing and deconstructing. Because of this any attempt to outline a post-modern social science will, on balance, depend more on the affirmatives than the skeptics. Yet, one thing seems clear, post-modernism in all its forms shakes us loose of our preconceptions, our "normal" way of doing social science. It asks some of the most potent questions we are capable of phrasing.

The affirmatives look to a post-modern social science that would be broad-gauged and descriptive rather than predictive and policy-oriented. Their social science would underscore novelty and reflexivity as it looks to the richness of difference and concentrates on the unusual, the singular, and the original (Hirschman 1987). For these post-modernists the pursuit of knowledge results in a sense of wonder and amazement (Murphy 1988). It is an encounter with the unexpected, a "voyage into the unforeseen" (Graff 1979).

[4] Modern social science emphasizes the cumulation of knowledge. Efforts are made to build on what has already been accomplished. The affirmatives' post-modern model expects no such privileged body of already available knowledge.

Skeptical post-modernists view the universe as impossible to understand, and this discourages them from efforts at building a post-modern social science. They conceive of the world as fragmented, disrupted, disordered, interrupted, and in search of instabilities. Contemplating the universe they are struck by "undecidables, the limits of precise control, conflicts characterized by incomplete information, 'fracta,' catastrophes, and pragmatic paradoxes" (Lyotard 1984: 60; Latour 1988: 164; Latour and Woolgar 1979: chaps. 1, 6).[5]

In any new post-modern social science the active post-modern reader would be a powerful figure, required to toil and labor for any answers in the text, as none would be provided in advance. Post-modern social science, encouraging interpretation, is marked by an absence of the author as agent or authority. We could expect post-modern social science texts to be more open and less definitive and to ignore the origins of phenomena. The role of the researcher as author would be eliminated as far as the skeptics are concerned. No indisputable results would derive from post-modern research, only disputable description. Readers would be expected to sort out the meaning in the text for themselves, to accept that whatever conclusions they reach would be of little value to anyone else, and to refrain from imposing their impressions on others. The goal would be to explore (rather than explain) and to produce texts that avoid definitive judgment and closure. Though the skeptical post-modern author has little clout and no authority, s/he does take pride in form, style, and presentation. S/he consciously strives to cultivate an indefinite, unsettled text. The affirma-

[5] Chaos theory is often said to support the skeptical post-modernists' view of science, but "disorder, chaos, the discontinuous, the erratic and the irregular" can also be incorporated into modern science. A "science of process rather than state, of becoming rather than being," is turning attention to elements of motion, oscillation, and wild swirls. It hopes to uncover new laws that encompass these patterns, that "make strong claims about the universal behavior of complexity." The scientists studying these phenomena "speculate about determinism and free will, about evolution, about the nature of conscious intelligence." But they also agree that chaos is part of reality, that systems exhibiting chaos "settle down"; "islands of structure," or "shapes embedded in the fabric of motion," can be observed within these forms of complexity and are waiting to be revealed. In the end they seem to agree that "order arises spontaneously in those systems." Even when "no point or pattern of points ever recurred," a new kind of order appeared; pattern [is] born amid formlessness." When these scientists talk of chaos they mean a special complex kind of prediction or probability assessment is called for, not that "prediction" is impossible because these remain "deterministic systems" and "harmonies" are there to be "discovered." "Turbulence and disorder coincide; what seem like infinite and wild cascades are 'rich with structure.' " "The modern study of chaos began with the creeping realization in the 1960s that quite simple mathematical equations could model systems every bit as violent as a waterfall." "There were no tools for analyzing irregularity as a building block of life. Now those tools exist." Chaos means not the end of modern science but rather "the genealogy of . . . a new science" that improves on the old and makes it even more powerful (Gleick 1987: 3–8, 30, 56, 118, 153, 211, 240, 299, 300). Also see Holden (1986) and Prigogine and Stengers (1984) for further work along these lines.

tives, however, reduce the power of the author without doing away with authorship, thus preserving some small role for the author as interpreter. They do not see all texts as absolutely arbitrary.

Human beings as individuals are absent from the skeptics' post-modern-ism, and there would be no place for the humanist subject, for "heroic" figures in their social science. The post-modern individual is a shadowy substitute. Advocacy is prohibited, and only a few skeptics dare to contem-plate institutional and societal reconstruction along lines compatible with the views of their post-modern individual. Those who do, for example, call for a community that does not impose collective choices or democratic decisions on its members (Corlett 1989). The affirmatives' "return of the subject" has taken their version of post-modern social science in the direc-tion of compromise with the modern subject, revision rather than outright rejection. Their post-modern social science is process-oriented. It leaves room for a socially sensitive, active human being, groping for a new post-modern politics, religion, and life in general: New Age, New Wave, new post-modern social movements.

If skeptics were to rewrite social science, it would be a present-oriented enterprise. There would be little role for conventional history. The affir-matives would retain history as a form of storytelling, as a local narrative without privilege, and they would deprive it of much prestige and influ-ence. There could be as many different and conflicting histories as there are consumers of the historical text. Efforts to "learn" from history would necessarily be discarded by the skeptics. The affirmatives would argue that such "lessons" may exist but are never very clear. At best they would pro-duce temporary, local lessons, and different people could be expected to derive distinct and disparate lessons from the historical record.

Post-modernists reject modern views of linear time and predictable space (geography). Some skeptics substitute post-modern versions (for ex-ample, hyper-space), or they concentrate on denying the legitimacy of modern versions. It is hard to imagine modern social science under these circumstances: without modern time and space, absence and presence be-come arbitrary, causality an impossibility, reality an invention. The affir-matives question linear time to a lesser extent. One of their main goals is to expose the oppressive dimensions of modern temporal assumptions. They substitute an emphasis on local space and a respect for the space-of-the-other for modern views of space.

As far as the skeptics are concerned, social science would have to do without representation, without objects or subjects who represent and are represented; research as now known would be rendered improbable. It could never "map" the social world in the sense of re-presenting it. Neither would it acknowledge the possibility of representing what is to be studied so as to permit comparative analysis. Post-modern anti-representationalism in methodology results in surrendering knowledge claims, so that for the most extreme post-modernists ethnography, anthropology, and sociology, for example, would be merely literary endeavors, more comfortable in the humanities and arts than the social sciences.

The skeptics' logic—their rejection of modern epistemology, of conventional social science methodology, and of all formal rules of inquiry—results in their limiting the role of any post-modern social science to that of critique (via deconstruction). They would be inclined to renounce efforts to construct new knowledge in the social sciences.[6] The skeptics' logic includes a view of the social universe as absolutely intertextual, a commitment to irreducible uncertainty, and epistemological impossibilism, or "anything goes." Any version of social science they propose must necessarily be very constricted.

The skeptics reject modern foundational assumptions of reason and all formal criteria for judging knowledge claims. But their own alternative perspective, the vague indefinite criteria they actually employ when evaluating texts, restrains any positive contribution of a new post-modern social science. Although self-conscious about their own social science, the skeptics are inclined to say that they do not intend to provide "clear reasoned defense." They tell us their texts offer "no consistent argument" and that "not all points made are 'necessary.' " They boast that by design "some essential matters are forgotten" (Corlett 1989: chap. 1). The skeptics' epistemology and methodology lead them to disclaim an interest "in imposing a general interpretation as a guide" (Ashley 1987; 1988: 95). They aim to "destabilize and render open to question all claims to an absolute foundation" (Ashley 1989a: 278). Their post-modern project is to "ceaselessly query and interrogate," rather than to "affirm a new identity, authenticity, or disciplinary purity" (Der Derian 1989a: 8). They contend that most questions modern social scientists seek to answer are simply undecidable. Their post-modern social science aspires to offer only "rigorously sustained integrity of theoretical intellect" (Ashley 1989a: 279).

The affirmatives criticize modern epistemology and methodology as they seek to revise rather than to dismiss them. The affirmatives are more ambivalent than the skeptics about reason and the need for some criteria for evaluating knowledge. Consequently, their critique of modern social science is less absolute than that of the skeptics, and they are therefore better positioned to contribute to the formation of an alternative post-modern social science, one that consciously avoids being predictive, positivist, scientific, or causal and instead emphasizes faith, emotion, and personal fulfillment. This post-modern social science would not offer any accumulation of knowledge or synthesis and generalization so much as

---

[6] This is not to accept the skeptics' contention that they have no logic, no meta-narrative.

complexity, interrelationships, a focus on difference in the absolute sense, the unique, and the local (Calhoun forthcoming b: 44). Although they may revise modern views along any number of dimensions, the affirmative post-modernists seem to reject absolute relativism, and they necessarily retain reason and rationality to some degree.

The affirmatives' post-modern social science is likely to be influenced by their substantive focus on the margins, the excluded, those who have no control over their lives, and those who have never known what it is to be either an author in modernist terms (in control) or a post-modernist reader (active, creative, and inventive). Their goal is to speak for those who have never been the subject (active, human), but who are rather so often assumed to be objects (observed, studied). They would include new voices and new forms of local narrative but not in an attempt to impose discipline or responsibility.

The political orientations of the post-modernists are internally heterogeneous and diverse, so that in the end political ideology does not directly dictate opinion upon post-modern social science. Examining left-wing and right-wing assessments of post-modern approaches revealed that those on the left are divided for and against post-modernism. Most of those on the right oppose it, but cases of support and elements of common accord do exist. In short, post-modernism is inherently neither left-wing nor right-wing; just as it denies any special privilege to any interpretation, so does it defy strict political classification.

New post-modern political movements are on the agenda of at least some affirmatives, as are broader and more authentic forms of participation and democracy. Although little agreement has emerged about what these forms will look like, there is a consensus that they will be interventionist and process-oriented. If it is to be problem solving, post-modern social science would have to be involved, relevant, and activist, not afraid to tackle problems, take positions, or intercede on behalf of certain interests and intrude on the state of nature. Other less participatory affirmatives and the New Age affirmatives need a post-modern social science that emphasizes emotion, personal fulfillment, even faith, spirituality, and the irrational, but that is neither preoccupied by methodological rules or epistemological consistency nor overly concerned with rigor, reason, discipline, and responsibility. This may very well require branching out into as yet unpredictable areas not before considered legitimate or appropriate for any post-modern social science. If the political needs of affirmatives say anything, the message is twofold: post-modernists have diverse expectations for any social science they may invent; and it will be difficult for any single version to fully satisfy all of them.

Although the inadequacies of modern social science are evident and few would quarrel with the need for some correction, it is difficult to tell if post-modern social science will be able to offer viable alternatives. Certainly it is unlikely that any form of post-modern social science will gain undisputed acceptance in the immediate future. At best skeptical post-modernism is minimal in terms of content—offering limited description and critique, sometimes transmitting a dismal negativism. In some cases it would concentrate on difference and on deconstructing all it encounters without any effort to replace what was dismantled. At other points it refers to a destructive form of nihilism. Some skeptics might be more comfortable without any post-modern social science at all. Affirmative post-modernism offers any number of imaginative alternatives, including a synthesis of post-modern science and theology, an opening up of social science to the metaphysical and the mystical. But no consensus emerges, and the consequences of all these various options are at best controversial.

2. The Trade-Off of Internal Consistency versus Relevance

Post-modernism in the social sciences raises some challenging questions and may require some difficult choices. Among the most important is the choice between skeptical and affirmative forms of post-modernism. In this section I weigh the advantages and disadvantages of each of them. Fringe versions of either type of post-modernism, such as the New Age affirmatives and the skeptics preoccupied with death and violence, are of less interest to social science than the more standard variations. Hence we focus on the more moderate forms of each.

Within its own terms, skeptical post-modernism can seem irresistible, coherent, and even reason(able). Its internal logic can be forceful, especially if one suspends modern assumptions.[7] For example, doing away with the subject logically coincides with the death of the author. Symbolically removing the author is liberating for all concerned, even if the author is relieved of any "responsibility" for the text. Elevating the role of the reader represents no contradiction within the terms of post-modernism because readers are plural, and different readings express post-modern multiple realities. Many interpretations are possible, and all are equally valid. Such textual openness gives flight to the imagination. In the extreme one can even accept the counterintuitive views: the reader is created by the text (for indeed, by definition there can be no reader in the absence of a text), and

---

[7] Skeptical post-modernism is characterized by internal consistency, but this does not mean contradiction is altogether absent. Consideration of these inconsistencies is reserved for the next section because even holding post-modernists to standards of consistency is considered by some post-modernists to be "unfair" inasmuch as this implies a modern point of view.

at the same time the text is written by the reader, just as the world around us is created by discourse.

Once the initial premises are agreed upon, skeptical post-modernism creates a circle of logic, a world of its own, out of which it is almost impossible to break. It is hardly fair to pose the modernist query, How do we know if one interpretation is better than another? because within a post-modernist framework no single element in a set of dichotomous oppositions can be judged superior. Good/bad criteria are simply unavailable, and all post-modern interpretations are presumed equally interesting. In addition, these approaches deny the goal of establishing any truth claims, and the question assumes this goal. Critics charge that post-modernism is destructive, that it deconstructs (tears down), but fails to produce alternative theories. This seems unjust if, according to its own assumptions, knowledge is impossible.

The affirmatives are philosophically conscious and less concerned with categorical epistemological rigor or total coherence. They relinquish intellectual consistency in exchange for political relevance and a positive commitment to new projects such as post-modern science, post-modern politics, and post-modern religious movements. The contradictions the affirmatives face are clear. If they call for radical democracy, then they must have a foundational framework, something hardly reasonable within a skeptical post-modern point of view (Aronowitz 1988a: 52). If they advocate New Age religion, they necessarily imply its superiority to traditional organized forms of religion, and this violates the post-modern allergy to judgment. If they compromise with post-modern doubts about reason and rationality, then they risk contradiction. But if they reject reason, they dismiss one important ground for criticizing modern social science (see Chapter 7, section 3). If they embrace relativism—say, to deny privilege to the voice of the oppressor—then they cannot claim that their own voice (or that of the oppressed) merits special attention. They are inconsistent because it is not possible to argue that one's own views are objective and then apply the post-modern philosophy of radical indeterminacy to others (Chapter 7, section 3c). Despite their criticism of modern meta-narratives and their intention to avoid logocentric political projects, the affirmatives hint at a renewed political context and a new, nonmaterial political praxis that involves them in a sort of double standard.

If their initial premises are accepted, the skeptical post-modern perspective possesses a compelling internal logic; but in exchange we are drawn into a circle of absolute uncertainty. Affirmative post-modernists, however, offer a substantive contribution of revision and renewal, but at the same time this requires significant compromises, some of which make for intellectual inconsistency and may even open social science up to the irrational and the metaphysical.

3. Some Critical Afterthoughts: The Unreflexive Dimension of Post-Modernism

Post-modernists sometimes fail to examine their own assumptions or follow their own advice. They also fail to apply their well-honed critical capacities to their own intellectual production. Such an incapacity to address their own presuppositions or fully consider the consequences of their own assumptions must be addressed. Self-deconstruction is seldom on the post-modern agenda, but if it were, such activity would reveal at least the following seven contradictions in addition to those already discussed in previous chapters (especially Chapter 7, section 2b). First, post-modernism devalues any pretensions to theory building. But an anti-theory position is itself a theoretical stand. If theory is futile and if every attempt to associate truth with theory must be denied, then such premises must also apply to every "form of theoretical endeavor, including such attempts to discredit other kinds of theory while smuggling one's own back in, so to speak, by the side entrance" (Norris 1988: 147). Second, although stressing the importance of the irrational and expressing grave doubts about the Enlightenment's intellectual tools of reason, logic, and rationality, post-modernists employ these latter instruments in their own analysis. Deconstruction, for example, is a highly logical, reasoned, and analytical process. Third, post-modernists neither judge nor evaluate interpretations as good or bad. But does their suggestion that social science focus on the excluded, the neglected, the marginal, and the silenced, not indicate an internal value structure implicitly favoring certain groups or certain perspectives over others? And does this not conflict with their supposed refusal to prioritize? If post-modernism focuses on the forgotten and the isolated and if it calls for a de-centering of social science theory, does this not make for neglect of the center? Does it not discourage focusing attention on the conspicuous, the integrated, and the evident, thus risking the creation of a whole new set of lacuna? If the post-modernists assume, by definition, that their own view is superior to that of the Enlightenment, are they not judging their own interpretation as privileged over any other? Fourth, post-modernists emphasize intertextuality, but many of its versions, especially those inspired by Derrida, treat the text in isolation.[8] Fifth, many post-modern-

---

[8] Not all post-modernists are committed to considering the text in absolute isolation. Foucault called for balance and criticized Derrida for attributing too much autonomy to language and missing the historical and political implications of the text. He emphasized the relation-

ists reject modern criteria for assessing theory. But if post-modernists draw conclusions of any sort, such as the undecidability of questions modern social science seeks to answer, they cannot argue that there are no valid criteria for judging. They themselves must have criteria, implicit perhaps, on which they make such pronouncements. And if such criteria exist, then post-modernists are making a statement to the effect that there is some certainty in the world. Sixth, although warning of modernity's inconsistencies, they reject being held to consistency norms themselves. They openly deny that they need make any special effort to avoid self-contradiction (Culler 1979: 173); this hardly seems fair. Seventh, post-modernists contend that anything they say or write is itself only a local narrative, relevant only for its own constituency. But very few post-modernists entirely relinquish the truth claims of what they write, and this also makes for self-contradiction.

Post-modernism is criticized for simultaneously both espousing linguistic determinism and proposing linguistic indeterminacy. Linguistic determinism is the view that language explains everything.[9] In such instances language becomes a world unto itself, constituting the essence of post-modern reality. The logical consequences are important: if language determines everything, then post-modernists err because they construct a hierarchy, attributing a privileged position to language and relegating the social to an inferior station. But post-modernists emphasize the indeterminacy of language when they argue that words are empty of content, when they define language as nonreferential and nondenotational, without material constraint (Harland 1987: 5; Vattimo 1988). Critics charge that this post-modernist perspective multiplies and manipulates language so that it is devoid of all meaning (Anderson 1984: 43). The consequences of linguistic indeterminacy are equally serious. If language is relative or arbitrary, then our knowledge claims are without foundation. Once again post-modernists disagree about what this means. Affirmatives interpret it to mean that words cannot represent certifiable truths, hardly a dubious proposition. But the skeptical post-modernists suggest that words have no meaning, and none can legitimately be uttered. And this would leave the social sciences without much to say.

Post-modern views of language undermine meaning and question the ability of human beings to communicate effectively with each other. Social science is grounded in language even though, of course, the communication of facts and ideas is never perfect. But there is a difference between

---

ship of the text to power and the many forces that influence its production and final form (Foucault 1972).

[9] This is not the same form of linguistic determinism that has been called "linguistic fundamentalism," that assumes "an infallible author, a perfect language and a timeless context" (Scholes 1989: 52).

those affirmative post-modernists who stress the difficulty inherent in communication and the more extreme skeptical post-modernists who argue that words never mean what we think, that all attempts to communicate are fruitless because communication is imperfect. Once again the tendency is for the skeptics to look only at communication failures and to take for granted or ignore instances of success. It seems intuitively reasonable, however, to conclude that in normal usage language is not so equivocal and contested. People succeed in understanding each other quite effectively most of the time (Bouveresse 1984: 133). If this were not the case, then how did we get from yesterday to today? And what hope is there that we might even negotiate our way into tomorrow and beyond?

If post-modernists were consistent and true to the linguistic relativism they expound, and if they really believed successful communication was impossible, then they would cease to deconstruct what others wrote or said. To avoid being hypocritical, they would have to remain silent (Weber 1990: 143). If post-modernists were sincere when they stated that no statements are privileged, not even their own, then they would have to give up their right to speak without authority. Only this would assure internal consistency.

It has also been suggested that if post-modernists see intercommunication as impossible, it may be because they do not extend themselves to use words precisely.[10] Are the vital and intriguing forms of post-modern style and presentation not also sometimes obscurantist, even obfuscationist (Ferry and Renaut 1990: 12–13)? Who benefits from "a text where the connections are so elusive as to become private, a text which moves sideways and backwards in an exhausting—and impossible—effort to say everything in one single, discursive operation" (Moi 1988: 21)? If one has something of substance to say, then clarity and lucidity of style and presentation need not be scorned. And yet some post-modernists state explicitly that "clarity and precision" are of secondary importance to them (e.g., Shapiro 1988: xii), that "ambiguity, uncertainty, and the ceaseless questioning of identity" are their key "resources" (Ashley and Walker 1990a: 263). Both strategic and philosophical reasons justify this position. Strategically, an ambiguous presentation permits, even encourages, an "infinity of interpretations." From a post-modern point of view this is an asset. It is philosophically acceptable because a less than lucidly written post-modern text reflects the impossibility of representation.

Much of what has been said about post-modernism up to this point implies its highly unorthodox nature, but this too must be questioned. Post-

---

[10] Some critics observe a deliberate attempt on the part of post-modern writers to avoid being understood (Ferry and Renaut 1990: 12–13), to preserve ambiguity and unfamiliarity (Ellis 1989: 134).

modernism initially appears to require radical reform and innovation in the social sciences, but on occasion and quite surprisingly, sometimes it merely strengthens conventional social science views.[11] Post-modernism can be employed to defend positions already adopted by those committed to modern approaches, consistent with a point of view that is well within the traditional parameters of the social sciences. As I suggested in Chapters 2 and 3, post-modernism, in its more moderate presentations, parallels structuralism and systems analysis. There is nothing very novel in suggesting we give up any claim for a perfect author who is never misunderstood or reinterpreted, or cease to strive to produce a perfectly translucent text comprehensible to all readers, or forsake the hope for a text written so that its meaning never changes.

In addition post-modernists are not the first to suggest the importance of the reader. Many social scientists have long been aware of the importance of reader's reactions to a text, and they have been sensitive to the possibility of different readings. Marketing research and studies of audience reaction to election campaigns are examples. Conventional social scientists directly investigate the variety of reader responses to a "text."[12]

Similarly, in Chapter 4 the similarities between skeptical post-modernism and the End-of-History philosophy and between the affirmative post-modernists and the New History movement were outlined. In Chapters 6 and 7 we discovered that the post-modernists are not the first in the social sciences to suggest erasing the barrier between the representing (subject) and the represented (object) of inquiry (Heller 1990: 77–78) or to propose that post-modern social scientists "go among the people" and simply let them "speak for themselves" (Pratt 1986: 32). This method may be a post-modern strategy designed to end the "illusion of objectivity," but Paulo Freire (1970) employed it more than twenty years ago in both his literacy campaigns and his efforts to raise political consciousness.

Yet, to say that post-modernism offers nothing new is, in another sense, to underestimate it. Certainly in the case of the affirmatives, post-modern forms have been anticipated by others. But the skeptical post-modernists' rejection of modern foundations of knowledge in its most absolute presentation is no mere repetition, at least not in the social sciences. It has far

[11] Calhoun, a sociologist, argues modernity is so diverse that what is called post-modern is really just a subtype of the modern that does not merit a special new label because it is not a different category. "Post-modernism is an internal product of modernity, not its true opponent" (forthcoming a, forthcoming b).

[12] But unlike post-modernism, mainstream social scientists employ the results of such studies to modify a message or text so as to achieve more perfect communication, to present a more convincing impression (vote for candidate A instead of B) with a specific goal (getting their candidate elected). Such goal-specific intentions are usually absent from post-modern analysis.

greater consequences. Even if particular components of the post-modern critique of conventional social science are, when taken alone, not especially offensive, once all the elements of a post-modern critique (especially those offered by the skeptics) are assembled together and presented in their more extreme form, they cannot but strike one as both threatening and absurd. It would be a mistake to underestimate the radical potential of the post-modern challenge for the future of the social sciences even though this challenge is not always entirely original.

4. Post-Modern Social Science: Looking Toward the Next Millennium

The future of post-modernism in the social sciences is open to a number of potential scenarios. The exact outcome, or combination of outcomes, of the struggle between the modern and post-modern in the social sciences is probably impossible to predict with any certainty, but trends, already apparent, are not independent of the larger worldwide social, political, and economic evolution.

a. No Compromise—Disciplinary Division or Minority Status

The very real possibility exists that the post-modern challenge to social science will eventually divide each of its disciplines into two separate fields: one inspired by the natural sciences, and the other derived from the humanities (post-modernism); one dedicated to discovering the causes of social phenomena, and the other preoccupied with criticism and the exploration of language and meaning.[13]

This outcome is not altogether undesirable. It would permit both contemporary social science and post-modern social science to concentrate on the positive production/construction of their separate projects rather than expend energy on the debate between them. In the last instance, this debate may be futile because of the absence of shared assumptions requisite for fruitful exchange. In the end, according to this scenario, it is preferable that post-modernists and modernists simply agree to disagree and go their own ways.

Disciplinary division is not without costs; such divorces are unlikely to be particularly amiable. Declining all compromise with conventional social

---

[13] Post-modern concerns would not be absent from a modern social science inspired by the natural sciences. Post-modernism would be something to be studied and predicted or a "descriptive category" (Turner 1989), but it would not be a special perspective, a unique and different methodology, or a novel epistemology.

science may lead post-modernists into enduring conflict with their more conventional disciplinary counterparts. Retaining intellectual purity might result not in disciplinary division so much as permanent minority status and academic isolation for post-modernists. They may end up talking only to one another, professionally marginalized. This may be the price of intellectual integrity.[14]

b. Integration and Compromise

Another scenario aims for the integration of post-modernism into mainstream social science. The affirmative post-modernists are most likely to compromise with modern social science. To some extent they have already done so. Again, implementing this strategy of concession and settlement also incurs substantial penalty, with the post-modernists likely to pay the higher fee. Making post-modernism "interesting" or "relevant" for conventional social science may require relinquishing the integrity of a post-modern point of view, the coherence that serves to strengthen its initial assumptions, positions, and insights that so effectively ward off challenges by denying them any legitimacy. Each concession made opens up the entire structure to internal contradiction and potentially introduces incoherence and renders it more vulnerable to external critique. For example, if post-modern social scientists accept the view that some interpretations are better, more powerful, than others, then the question, How do you tell which is the best interpretation? returns as a nagging and now distressing matter of concern. And there is no acceptable answer within the terms of both modern and post-modern frameworks. As a result of the extreme openness, tolerance, and pluralism of affirmative post-modernism, so much is conceded that it risks not only losing its identity, but it may also lose the ability to defend itself against the charlatans (cults, New Age philosophy, mythology, and witchcraft) who would literally make social science little more than a carnival.

The strategy of reconciliation involves abandoning those post-modern assumptions that appear most absurd to conventional social science and harmonizing the remainder. A parallel openness from the other side might modify the requirements for social science, qualify claims of scientific objectivity, and bring about a broader recognition of the legitimacy of subjective and relativist innovative methodologies. The resulting combination would join inquiry based on rigor and reason on one hand with that linked to emotion and intuition on the other (Bonnefoy 1984). Certainly these

---

[14] This could result in another scenario, one not discussed here, the return to hegemonic status of the modern approach to the social sciences and the complete elimination of the post-modern. This outcome was judged improbable and so not given special consideration.

projects are not without value. Fruitful interchange and mutual enrichment might result.

The affirmatives would probably agree to "reconstruct" social science disciplines, but the skeptics are likely to argue that this amounts to abandoning an authentic post-modern viewpoint. The skeptics charge that any project to "reconstruct" is a project to set up an alternative hegemonic model that post-modernists cannot undertake if they are consistent with their own critique of modernism. The more tempered voice of the affirmatives is likely to take the lead if any compromise with modern social sciences comes to pass.

Compromise with certain elements of the original post-modern formulations in the humanities is being explored. Social scientists pursuing this strategy of eclecticism have produced some exciting post-modernist texts as they strive to make these approaches relevant to their particular concerns. Some of these efforts have been reviewed in this book.

c. Future Trends

Those most likely to be disappointed by the future contribution of post-modernism to the social sciences are those whose initial expectations were too grandiose. Post-modernism has not compensated for the weaknesses of structuralism, realism, systems analysis, or any other major conventional paradigms in the social sciences. Neither Marxists, feminists, or socialists who turn to post-modernism to invigorate their social analysis are likely to be completely satisfied with the results of such a fusion. Although there are points of affinity, all these groups are likely to find some forms of post-modernism to be enemies as much as allies.

Events in the larger world may also have an effect on the future of post-modern social science. These could go either way. Forces at work may facilitate the development and expansion of post-modernism, but others may curtail its evolution in the social sciences. On the one hand, the cultural and societal forces that brought post-modernism to the forefront have been at work for a long time, and they are still vigorous. Many feel that they are unlikely to fade away very quickly (Gitlin 1989). For example, the war in the Persian Gulf and the human and ecological disaster it represents offer a dismal perspective on the future. The uncontrolled rapid change and extraordinary technological advances that pose ethical and moral dilemmas for which we are ill-prepared are also among these forces. Nor are the professional crises that continue to promote the intrusion of post-modernism likely to disappear in the near future. Whatever the choice—integration and intellectual compromise or isolation and intellectual purity—the post-modern repudiation of contemporary social science is unlikely to be without residual effects (Schwartz 1990: 33).

On the other hand, the half-life of paradigms appears shorter and shorter as human affairs become increasingly complex. Certainly indicators suggest the influence of the skeptical post-modernists in the social sciences is waning. The absurdity of the skeptics' analysis draws ridicule rather than praise. The decline of military dictatorship across Latin America, the rise of the democratic possibility in Eastern Europe, the hopes of Glasnost and Perestroika even if not realized, and the reduced probability of nuclear holocaust all make the skeptics' pessimism seem out of place, left over from the 1970s or the new cold war mentality of the early 1980s. The feelings of apocalyptic destruction advanced by the most extreme skeptics, such as Baudrillard (1983a, 1983b) and Kamper and Wulf (1989), are also on the decline. To be sure, problems of the environment could still confirm the worst scenario of the skeptics, but the broad concern and public awareness of even these problems make for optimism.

The results of struggles within the post-modern community itself cannot but affect its future. For example, the political implications of post-modern views of representation are such that post-modern social scientists will have a difficult time relating to and explaining the increasing worldwide demands for greater political representation in the form of democratic, multiparty systems and citizen voting rights. If the skeptics prevail, their extreme anti-representationalism will lead to a situation where post-modernism appears less relevant to society. If it continues to run counter to major intellectual currents, to ignore global political trends, as in the case of representation, it may suffer a decline.

None of this means that post-modernism will disappear, that the questioning of science and reason will come to an abrupt end. But it suggests that the moderate affirmative post-modernists will have a greater impact if we ever get beyond a mentality that argues for "giving war a chance." In a climate of international peace, attention can be given to the affirmatives' call for self-fulfillment, tolerance, and humanizing technology. If an era of peace and calm were to develop, flourish, and endure, then the prestige of the affirmatives might be enhanced, and their influence on modern social science would be greater than that of the skeptics. But even in the case of the skeptics, who are exclusively critical and refuse to "construct," there is a potential positive contribution. The skeptical post-modernist attack may force modern social science to sharpen its defenses and tighten its priorities. This would be no small accomplishment even if it is largely unintended (Meehan 1991).

If the social sciences of tomorrow, already manifest today, are not postmodern, then what traces of this encounter with a post-modern perspective will they bear? At the very least they will esteem and employ science more critically and less naively than in the past. They may even lower their expectations of the value and products of science. They may come to more widely recognize the economic, social, and political context of science, its uses and abuses. A broader acceptance and appreciation of the qualitative may emerge and gain a greater audience.

Some would say all this was in the works long before anyone in the social sciences ever heard the word "post-modern." One may, of course, credit all this to a backlash of decades of dominance by the scientific paradigm. Or one may describe it as merely the normal swing of the paradigmatic pendulum rather than as motion initiated by post-modernism. But whatever the case it would be an error to dismiss entirely the impact of post-modernism on the social sciences. For even if post-modernism only intensifies tendencies already in effect, it may push the arc of the pendulum further than usual; that might, just possibly, expand horizons in the social sciences.

BIBLIOGRAPHY

Abrams, M. H. 1981. *A Glossary of Literary Terms*. 4th ed. New York: Holt, Rinehart and Winston.

Adelson, Leslie. 1984. "Introductory Note to Sloterdijk." *New German Critique*, no. 33 (Fall): 189–90.

Agger, Ben. 1989a. *Socio(ont)logy*. Urbana: University of Illinois Press.

———. 1989b. *Fast Capitalism: A Critical Theory of Significance*. Champaign: University of Illinois Press.

———. 1990. *The Decline of Discourse: Reading, Writing, and Resistence in Postmodern Capitalism*. New York: Falmer Press.

Alker, Hayward, and David Sylvan. 1986. "Political Discourse Analysis." Paper delivered at the American Political Science Association, annual meeting, Washington, D.C., August.

Allen, Robert C. 1987. "Reader-Oriented Criticism and Television." In *Channels of Discourse*, ed. Robert C. Allen. Chapel Hill: University of North Carolina Press.

Allison, David, ed. 1977. *The New Nietzsche*. New York: Dell Publishing.

Alter, Robert. 1989. *The Pleasures of Reading*. New York: Simon and Schuster.

Althusser, Louis. 1971. *Lenin and Philosophy*. London: New Left Books.

Anderson, Bron. 1987–88. "The Gospel According to Jameson." *Telos*, no. 74 (Winter): 116–25.

Anderson, Ken, Paul Piccone, Fred Siegel, and Michael Taves. 1988. "Roundtable on Communitarianism." *Telos*, no. 76 (Summer): 2–33.

Anderson, Perry. 1984. *In the Tracks of Historical Materialism*. London: Verso.

———. 1988. "Modernity and Revolution." In *Marxism and the Interpretation of Culture*, ed. Cary Nelson and Lawrence Grossberg. Chicago: University of Illinois Press.

Angenot, Marc. 1984. "Le discours social; problématique et ensemble." *Cahiers de recherche sociologique* 2 (1): 1–21.

Ankersmit, F. R. 1989. "Historiography and Postmodernism." *History and Theory* 28 (2): 137–53.

———. 1990. "Reply to Professor Zagorin." *History and Theory* 29 (3): 275–96.

Anonymous. 1982. "Architecture as a Corporate Asset." *Business Week*, October 4, 124–26.

Apter, David. 1987. *Rethinking Development: Modernization Dependency and Postmodern Politics*. Newbury Park, Calif.: Sage.

Arac, Jonathan. 1986. "Introduction." In *Postmodernism and Politics*, ed. Jonathan Arac. Theory and History of Literature series, vol. 28. Minneapolis: University of Minnesota Press.

———. 1987. *Critical Genealogies: Historical Situations for Postmodern Literary Studies*. New York: Columbia University Press.

Aronowitz, Stanley. 1981. *The Crisis in Historical Materialism*. New York: Praeger.

Aronowitz, Stanley. 1988a. "Postmodernism and Politics." In *Universal Abandon?: The Politics of Postmodernism*, ed. A. Ross. Minneapolis: University of Minnesota Press.

———. 1988b. "The Production of Scientific Knowledge: Science, Ideology and Marxism." In *Marxism and the Interpretation of Culture*, ed. Cary Nelson and Lawrence Grossberg. Chicago: University of Illinois Press.

Arrighi, Giovanni, Terence Hopkins, and Immanuel Wallerstein. 1989. *Antisystemic Movements*. New York: Verso.

Arrington, C. Edward, and Jere R. Francis. 1989. "Letting the Chat Out of the Bag: Deconstruction, Privilege and Accounting Research." *Accounting, Organizations and Society* 14 (1/2): 1–28.

Asher, Kenneth. 1984–85. "Deconstruction's Use and Abuse of Nietzsche." *Telos*, no. 62 (Winter): 169–77.

———. 1989–90. "The Moral Blindness of Paul de Man." *Telos*, no. 84 (Winter): 197–205.

Ashley, David. 1990. "Habermas and the Completion of 'The Project of Modernity.' " In *Theories of Modernity and Postmodernity*, ed. Bryan S. Turner. Newbury Park, Calif.: Sage.

Ashley, Richard. 1984. "The Poverty of Neo-Realism." *International Organization* 38 (2): 225–86.

———. 1987. "The Geopolitics of Geopolitical Space: Toward a Critical Social Theory of International Politics." *Alternatives* 12 (4): 403–34.

———. 1988. "Geopolitics, Supplementary Criticism: A Reply to Professors Roy and Walker." *Alternatives* 13 (1): 88–102.

———. 1989a. "Living on Border Lines: Man, Poststructuralism, and War." In *International/Intertextual Relations: Postmodern Readings of World Politics*, ed. James Der Derian and Michael J. Shapiro. Lexington, Mass.: Lexington Books.

———. 1989b. "Imposing International Purpose: Notes on a Problematic of Governance." In *Global Changes and Theoretical Challenges: Approaches to World Politics for the 1990s*, ed. Ernst-Otto Czempiel and James N. Rosenau. Lexington, Mass.: Lexington Books.

———. Forthcoming. "The Powers of Anarchy: Theory, Sovereignty, and the Domestication of Global Life." In *Anarchy, Power, Community: Understanding International Collaboration*, ed. Hayward Alker and Richard Ashley.

Ashley, Richard, and R.B.J. Walker. 1990a. "Speaking the Language of Exile: Dissident Thought In International Studies." *International Studies Quarterly* 34 (3): 259–68.

———. 1990b. "Reading Dissidence/Writing the Discipline: Crisis and the Question of Sovereignty in International Studies." *International Studies Quarterly* 34 (3): 259–68.

Atlas, James. 1988. "The Case of Paul de Man." *New York Times Magazine*, August 28, 36–69.

———. 1989. "What is Fukuyama Saying?" *New York Times Magazine*, October 22, 38.

Bakhtin, Mikhail. 1973. *Problems of Dostoyevsky's Poetics*. Ann Arbor, Mich.: Ardis.

Ball, Terence, ed. 1987. *Idioms of Inquiry*. Albany: State University of New York Press.

———. 1988. *Transforming Political Discourse*. London: Blackwell.

Barilleaux, Ryan. 1988. *The Post-Modern Presidency: The Office after Ronald Reagan*. New York: Praeger.

Barth, John. 1980. "The Literature of Replenishment: Postmodern Fiction." *Atlantic Monthly*, January, 65–71.

Barthes, Roland. 1970. *S/Z*. Paris: Seuil.

———. 1975. *The Pleasure of the Text*. New York: Hill and Wang.

———. 1977. "The Death of the Author" and "Writers, Intellectuals, Teachers." In *Images, Music, Text*, ed. R. Barthes. New York: Hill and Wang.

———. 1979. "From Work to Text." In *Textual Strategies: Perspectives in Post-structuralist Criticism*, ed. Josue Harari. Ithaca, N.Y.: Cornell University Press.

Baudrillard, J. 1976. *L'échange symbolique et la mort*. Paris: Gallimard.

———. 1981. *For a Critique of the Political Economy of the Sign*. St. Louis, Mo.: Telos Press.

———. 1983a. *In the Shadow of the Silent Majorities*. New York: Semiotext(e).

———. 1983b. *Les stratégies fatales*. Paris: Bernard Grasset.

———. 1983c. *Simulations*. New York: Semiotext(e).

———. 1985. "Modernité." In *Encyclopaedia Universalis*, corpus 12: 424–26.

———. 1986. "Forgetting Baudrillard." *Social Text*, no. 15 (Fall): 140–44.

———. 1987. "Modernity." *Canadian Journal of Political and Social Theory* 11 (3): 63–72.

———. 1988. "Hunting Nazis and Losing Reality." *New Statesmen*, February 19, 16–17.

———. 1989a. *America*. London: Verso.

———. 1989b. "The Anorexic Ruins." In *Looking Back on the End of the World*, ed. D. Kamper and C. Wulf. New York: Semiotext(e).

Bauman, Zygmunt. 1986–87. "The Left as the Counter-Culture of Modernity." *Telos*, no. 70 (Winter): 81–93.

———. 1987. *Legislators and Interpreters: Modernity, Post-modernity and Intellectuals*. Ithaca, N.Y.: Cornell University Press.

———. 1988. "Is There a Postmodern Sociology?" *Theory, Culture and Society* 5 (2–3): 217–39.

———. 1989. *Modernity and the Holocaust*. Ithaca, N.Y.: Cornell University Press.

———. 1990. "Philosophical Affinities of Postmodern Sociology." *The Sociological Review* 38 (3): 411–44.

Baykan, Ayşegül. 1990. "Women between Fundamentalism and Modernity." In *Theories of Modernity and Postmodernity*, ed. Bryan S. Turner. Newbury Park, Calif.: Sage.

Beaudry, Lucille. 1990. "Quelques idées du post-modernisme, aspect d'une réversion du rapport de l'art au politique." In *Les avenues de la science politique*, ed. L. Beaudry, Chantal Maille, L. Oliver. Montreal: Association canadienne-française pour l'avancement des sciences.

Bell, Daniel. 1973. *The Coming of Post-Industrial Society*. New York: Basic Books.

———. 1976. *The Cultural Contradictions of Capitalism*. New York: Basic Books.

Benhabib, Seyla. 1984. "Epistemologies of Post-modernism: A Rejoinder to Jean-Francois Lyotard." *New German Critique*, no. 33 (Fall): 103–26.

Bensman, Joseph. 1988. "The Crises of Confidence in Modern Politics." *International Journal of Politics, Culture, and Society* 2 (1): 15–35.

Berger, Peter, and Thomas Luckmann. 1966. *The Social Construction of Reality.* New York: Doubleday.

Bergson, Henri. 1896. *Données immédiates de la conscience.* Paris: F. Alcan.

Berman, Russell. 1986–87. "The Routinization of Charismatic Modernism and the Problem of Post-modernity." *Cultural Critique*, no. 5 (Winter): 49–68.

———. 1990. "Troping to Pretoria: The Rise and Fall of Deconstruction." *Telos*, no. 85 (Fall): 4–16.

Bernstein, Richard J. 1985. *Beyond Objectivism and Relativism: Science, Hermeneutics, and Praxis.* Philadelphia: University of Pennsylvania Press.

———. 1986. "The Rage Against Reason." *Philosophy and Literature* 10 (2): 186–210.

Bertaux, Daniel. 1980. "L'approche biographique. Sa validité méthodologique, ses potentialitiés." *Cahiers internationaux de sociologie* 69: 197–225.

———. 1985. "L'imagination méthodologique." *Recherche sociologique* 16 (2): 269–79.

Bierstedt, Robert. 1959. "Normal and Real Definitions in Sociological Theory." In *Symposium in Sociological Theory*, ed. L. Gross. New York: Harper & Row.

Birch, Charles. 1988a. "The Postmodern Challenge to Biology." In *The Reenchantment of Science: Postmodern Proposals*, ed. D. R. Griffin. Albany: State University of New York Press.

———. 1988b. "Eight Fallacies of the Modern World and Five Axioms for a Postmodern Worldview." *Perspectives in Biology and Medicine* 32 (1): 12–30.

Blonsky, Marshall. 1985. *On Signs.* Baltimore, Md.: Johns Hopkins University Press.

Bohm, David. 1988. "Postmodern Science and a Postmodern World." In *The Reenchantment of Science: Postmodern Proposals*, ed. D. R. Griffin. Albany: State University of New York Press.

Bonnefoy, Yves. 1984. "Image and Presence." *New Literary History* 15 (3): 433–51.

Bookchin, Murray. 1989–90. "Introduction to Elkins." *Telos*, no. 82 (Winter): 47–51.

Booth, David. 1985. "Nietzsche on 'the Subject as Multiplicity.' " *Man and World: International Philosophical Review* 18 (2): 121–46.

Bordewich, Fergus M. 1988. "Colorado's Thriving Cults." *New York Times Magazine*, May 1, 37–43.

Borradori, Giovanna. 1987–88. " 'Weak Thought' and Postmodernism: The Italian Departure from Deconstruction." *Social Text*, no. 18: 39–49.

Botwinick, Aryeh. 1990. *Skepticism and Political Participation.* Philadelphia: Temple University Press.

Bouchard, Donald, ed. 1977. "What is an Author?" *Language, Counter-Memory, Practice.* Ithaca, N.Y.: Cornell University Press.

Bourdieu, Pierre. 1984. *Distinction: A Social Critique of the Judgment of Taste*. Cambridge: Harvard University Press.

Bouveresse, Jacques. 1984. *Rationalité et cynisme*. Paris: Minuit.

Bove, Paul. 1990. "Discourse." In *Critical Terms for Literary Study*, ed. Frank Lentricchia and Thomas McLaughlin. Chicago: University of Chicago Press.

Boyne, Roy. 1990. *Foucault and Derrida: the Other Side of Reason*. Winchester, Mass.: Unwin and Hyman.

Brante, Thomas. 1986. "Changing Perspectives in the Sociology of Science." In *Sociology: From Crisis to Science?* ed. Ulf Himmelstrand. London: Sage.

Braudel, Fernand. 1972. *The Mediterranean*. Vol 1. New York: Harper & Row.

Bruckner, D.J.R. 1988. "How to Kill Readers." [An interview with Milorad Pavic.] *New York Times Book Review Section*, November 20, 15.

Burgin, Victor. 1986. *The End of Art Theory: Criticism and Postmodernity*. Atlantic Highlands, N.J.: Humanities Press International.

Burman, Erica. 1990. "Differing with Deconstruction: A Feminist Critique." In *Deconstructing Social Psychology*, ed. Ian Parker and John Shotter. London: Routledge.

Burrell, Gibson. 1988. "Modernism, Post Modernism, and Organizational Analysis 2: The Contribution of Michel Foucault." *Organizational Studies* 9 (2): 221–35.

Cahoone, Lawrence E. 1988. *The Dilemma of Modernity*. Albany: State University of New York Press.

Caldwell, Lynton K. 1975. "Managing the Transition to Post-Modern Society." *Public Administration Review* 35 (6): 567–72.

Calhoun, Craig. 1990. "Postmodernism, Critical Theory and Social Action." Paper presented at the World Congress of Sociology, Madrid, July 9–14.

———. Forthcoming a. "The Infrastructure of Modernity: Indirect Social Relationships, Information Technology, and Social Integration." In *Social Change and Modernization*, ed. Neil Smelser and Hans Haberkamp. Berkeley: University of California Press.

———. Forthcoming b. "Culture, History, and the Problem of Specificity in Social Theory." In *Postmodernism and General Social Theory*, ed. S. Seidman and D. Wagner. New York: Basil Blackwell.

———. Forthcoming c. "Introduction: Habermas and the Public Sphere." In *Habermas and the Public Sphere*, ed. Craig Calhoun. Boston: MIT Press.

Calinescu, Matei. 1987. *Five Faces of Modernity*. Durham, N.C.: Duke University Press.

Calinescu, Matei, and Douwe Fokkema, eds. 1987. *Exploring Postmodernism*. Amsterdam: John Benjamin Publishing Company.

Callinicos, Alex. 1985. "Postmodernism, Post-Structuralism, Post-Marxism?" *Theory, Culture and Society* 2 (3): 85–101.

———. 1989. *Against Post-Modernism*. London: Blackwell.

Cantor, Norman. 1989. *Twentieth-Century Culture: Modernism to Deconstruction*. New York: Peter Lang.

Capra, Fritjof. 1982. *The Turning Point: Science, Society, and the Rising Culture*. New York: Simon and Schuster.

Carravetta, Peter. 1988. "On Gianni Vattimo's Postmodern Hermeneutics." *Theory, Culture and Society* 5 (2–3): 395–99.

Carroll, David. 1978. "The Subject of Archaeology of the Sovereignty of the Episteme." *Modern Language Notes* 93: 695–722.

Carter, Pippa, and Norman Jackson. 1987. "Management, Myth, and Metatheory—From Scarcity to Postscarcity." *International Studies of Management and Organization* 17 (3): 64–89.

Castoriadis, C. 1986. "Les mouvements des années soixante." *Pouvoir* 39: 107–16.

Chabot, C. Barry. 1988. "The Problem of the Postmodern." *New Literary History* Autumn 20 (1): 1–20.

Clark, Stuart. 1985. "The Annales in History." In *The Return of Grand Theory in the Human Sciences*, ed. Quentin Skinner. Cambridge: Cambridge University Press.

Clifford, James. 1988. *The Predicament of Culture*. Cambridge: Harvard University Press.

Clifford, James, and George E. Marcus, eds. 1986. *Writing Culture: The Poetics and Politics of Ethnography*. Berkeley: University of California Press.

Cobb, John B., Jr. 1988. "Ecology, Science, and Religion: Toward a Postmodern Worldview." In *The Reenchantment of Science: Postmodern Proposals*, ed. D. R. Griffin. Albany: State University of New York Press.

Comay, Rebecca. 1986. "Interpreting the Conversation: Notes on Rorty." *Telos*, no. 69 (Fall): 119–30.

Connolly, William E. 1988. *Political Theory and Modernity*. Oxford: Basil Blackwell.

Connor, S. 1989. *Postmodernist Culture: An Introduction to Theories of the Contemporary*. Cambridge, Mass.: Basil Blackwell.

Cooke, Philip. 1988. "Modernity, Postmodernity and the City." *Theory, Culture and Society* 5 (2–3): 475–92.

———. 1989. "Postmodern Condition and the City." *Comparative Urban and Community Research* 2: 62–80.

Cooper, Robert, and Gibson Burrell. 1988. "Modernism, Postmodernism and Organizational Analysis: An Introduction, Part I." *Organization Studies* 9 (1): 91–112.

Coover, Robert. 1988. "He Thinks the Way We Dream." *New York Times Book Review Section*, November 20, 15.

Corlett, William. 1989. *Community without Unity: A Politics of Derridian Extravagance*. Durham, N.C.: Duke University Press.

Coward, Rosalind, and John Ellis. 1977. *Language and Materialism*. London: Routledge and Kegan Paul.

Cox, Harvey. 1984. *Religion in the Secular City: Toward a Postmodern Theology*. New York: Simon and Schuster.

Crane, D. 1972. *Invisible Colleges*. Chicago: University of Chicago Press.

Cronbach, L. J. 1986. "Social Inquiry by and for Earthlings." In *Metatheory in Social Science*, ed. D. W. Fiske and R. A. Shweder. Chicago: University of Chicago Press.

Crooks, Cheryl. 1984. "Changes for Amusement's Sake at Six Flag." *Corporate Design* 3 (2): 74–77.

Culler, Jonathan. 1979. "Jacques Derrida." In *Structuralism and Since: From Lévi-Strauss to Derrida*, ed. John Sturrock. Oxford: Oxford University Press.

———. 1982. *On Deconstruction: Theory and Criticism after Structuralism*. Ithaca, N.Y.: Cornell University Press.

———. 1983. *Barthes*. Glasgow: William Collin Sons.

———. 1988. "Its Time to Set the Record Straight about Paul de Man and His Wartime Articles for a Pro-Fascist Newspaper." *The Chronicle of Higher Education*, July 13, B1.

Dahrendorf, Ralf. 1979. "Towards the Hegemony of Post-Modern Values," *New Society* 50, no. 893 November 15, 360–62.

Dallmayr, Fred. 1981. *Twilight of Subjectivity*. Amherst: University of Massachusetts Press.

———. 1987. "Political Inquiry: Beyond Empiricism and Hermeneutics." In *Idioms of Inquiry*, ed. Terence Ball. Albany: State University of New York Press.

———. 1989. *Margins of Political Discourse*. Albany: State University of New York Press.

Davenport, Edward. 1983. "Literature as Thought Experiment (On Aiding and Abetting the Muse)." *Philosophy of the Social Science* 13: 279–306.

———. 1985. "Scientific Method as Literary Criticism." *Et Cetera* (Winter): 331–50.

Davie, Donald A. 1983. "Poet: Patriot: Interpreter." In *The Politics of Interpretation*, ed. W.J.T. Mitchell. Chicago: University of Chicago Press.

Davis, Mike. 1985. "Urban Renaissance and the Spirit of Postmodernism." *New Left Review*, no. 151 (May–June): 106–13.

Deak, Istvan. 1989. "The Incomprehensible Holocaust." *New York Review of Books*, September 28, 63–72.

Dear, Michael. 1986. "Postmodernism and Planning." *Environment and Planning D: Society and Space* 4: 367–84.

———. 1988. "The Postmodern Challenge: Reconstructing Human Geography." *Transactions of the Institute of British Geographers* 13 (Dec.): 1–13.

———. 1989. "Survey 16: Privatization and the Rhetoric of Planning Practice." *Environment and Planning D: Society and Space* 7: 449–62.

Dear, M.J., and A. J. Scott, eds. 1981. *Urbanization and Urban Planning in Capitalist Societies*. New York: Methuen.

De Certeau, Michel. 1984. *The Practices of Everyday Life*. Los Angeles: University of California Press.

Deleuze, Gilles. 1983. *Nietzsche and Philosophy*. New York: Columbia University Press.

Deleuze, Gilles, and Felix Guattari. 1983. *Anti-Oedipus: Capitalism and Schizophrenia*. Minneapolis: University of Minnesota Press.

de Man, Paul. 1979. *Allegories of Reading*. New Haven: Yale University Press.

———. 1983. *Blindness and Insight*. Minneapolis: University of Minnesota Press.

———. 1986. *The Resistance to Theory*. Minneapolis: University of Minnesota Press.

———. 1989. *Wartime Journalism: 1939–43*. Lincoln: University of Nebraska Press.

Denzin, Norman K. 1986. "Postmodern Social Theory." *Sociological Theory* 4 (Fall): 194–204.

Denzin, Norman K. 1990. "Reading 'Wall Street': Postmodern Contradictions in the American Social Structure." In *Theories of Modernity and Postmodernity*, ed. Bryan S. Turner. Newbury Park, Calif.: Sage.

Der Derian, James. 1988a. "Introducing Philosophical Traditions in International Relations." *Millennium Journal of International Studies* 17 (2): 189–93.

———. 1988b. "The Importance of Shredding in Earnest: Reading the National Security Culture and Terrorism." In *Cultural Politics in Contemporary America*, ed. Sut Jhally and Ian Angus. New York: Routledge, Chapman and Hall.

———. 1989a. "The Boundaries of Knowledge and Power in International Relations." In *International/ Intertextual Relations: Postmodern Readings of World Politics*, ed. James Der Derian and Michael J. Shapiro. Lexington, Mass.: Lexington Books.

———. 1989b. "Spy vs. Spy: The Intertextual Power of International Intrigue." In *International/ Intertextual Relations: Postmodern Readings of World Politics*, ed. James Der Derian and Michael J. Shapiro. Lexington, Mass.: Lexington Books.

———. 1990. "The (S)pace of International Relations: Simulation, Surveillance, and Speed." *International Studies Quarterly* 34 (3): 295–310.

Der Derian, James, and Michael J. Shapiro, eds. 1989. *International/ Intertextual Relations: Postmodern Readings of World Politics*. Lexington, Mass.: Lexington Books.

Derrida, Jacques. 1972. *Marges*. Paris: Editions de Minut.

———. 1974a. *Glas*. Paris: Galilée.

———. 1974b. "White Mythology: Metaphor in the Text of Philosophy." *New Literary History* 6 (1): 5–74.

———. 1976. *Of Grammatology*, trans. G. Spivak. Baltimore, Md.: Johns Hopkins University Press.

———. 1978. *Writing and Difference*. London: Routledge and Kegan Paul.

———. 1979. *Spurs: Nietzsche's Styles*. Chicago: University of Chicago Press.

———. 1981. *Positions*. Chicago: University of Chicago Press.

———. 1982. "Sending: On Representation." *Social Research* 49 (Summer): 294–326.

———. 1985. *The Ear of the Other*. New York: Schocken.

———. 1987. *De L'esprit, Heidegger et la question*. Paris: Galilée.

———. 1988. "Like the Sound of the Sea Deep within a Shell: Paul de Man's War." *Critical Inquiry* 14 (Spring): 590–652.

Descombes, Vincent. 1980. *Modern French Philosophy*, trans. L. Scott-Fox and J. M. Harding. London: Cambridge University Press.

Dews, Peter. 1986. "Adorno, Post-Structuralism and the Critique of Identity." *New Left Review*, no. 157 (May/June): 28–44.

———. 1987. *Logic of Disintegration—Post-Structuralist Thought and the Claims of Critical Theory*. New York: Verso.

———. 1989. "The Return of the Subject in Late Foucault." *Radical Philosophy*, no. 51 (Spring): 37–41.

Di Stefano, Christine. 1990. "Dilemmas of Difference: Feminism, Modernity, and

Postmodernism." In *Feminism/Postmodernism*, ed. Linda J. Nicholson. New York: Routledge.

Donoghue, Denis. 1980. "Deconstructing Deconstruction." *New York Review of Books*, June 12, 37–43.

———. 1989. "The Strange Case of Paul de Man." *New York Review of Books*, June 29, 32–37.

Dowling, William. 1984. *Jameson, Althusser, Marx*. Ithaca, N.Y.: Cornell University Press.

Dreyfus, Hubert, and Paul Rabinow. 1983. *Michel Foucault, Beyond Structuralism and Hermeneutics*. 2d ed. Chicago: University of Chicago Press.

Dumm, Thomas. 1988. "II: The Politics of Post-modern Aesthetics: Habermas Contra Foucault." *Political Theory* 16 (2): 209–25.

Dworkin, Ronald. 1983a. "My Reply to Stanley Fish (and Walter Benn Michaels): Please Don't Talk about Objectivity Any More." In *The Politics of Interpretation*, ed. W.J.T. Mitchell. Chicago: University of Chicago Press.

———. 1983b. "Law as Interpretation." In *The Politics of Interpretation*, ed. W.J.T. Mitchell. Chicago: University of Chicago Press.

Eagleton, Terry. 1981. *Walter Benjamin or Towards a Revolutionary Criticism*. London: New Left Books.

———. 1983. *Literary Theory*. Minneapolis: University of Minnesota Press.

———. 1985. "Capitalism, Modernism and Postmodernism." *New Left Review*, no. 152 (July/August): 60–73.

Eco, Umberto. 1980. *The Name of the Rose*. New York: Warner Books.

———. 1983a. *Travels in Hyper Reality*. San Diego, Calif.: Harcourt, Brace and Jovanovich.

———. 1983b. *Postscript to the Name of the Rose*. Orlando, Fla.: Harcourt, Brace and Jovanovich.

Edelman, Murray. 1977. *Political Language: Words that Succeed and Policies that Fail*. New York: Academic Press.

———. 1988. *Constructing the Political Spectacle*. Chicago: University of Chicago Press.

Eldridge, Richard. 1985. "Deconstruction and Its Alternatives." *Man and World* 18: 147–70.

Elgin, Catherine Z. 1984. "Representation, Comprehension and Competence." *Social Research* 51 (4): 905–26.

Elkins, Stephan. 1989–90. "The Politics of Mystical Ecology." *Telos*, no. 82 (Winter): 52–70.

Ellis, John. 1989. *Against Deconstruction*. Princeton, N.J.: Princeton University Press.

Falk, Richard. 1988. "Religion and Politics: Verging on the Postmodern." *Alternatives* 13 (3): 379–94.

———. 1989. "A Postmodern Presidency for a Postmodern World." Paper presented at the "Toward a Postmodern Presidency" conference, sponsored by the Center for a Postmodern World, Santa Barbara, June 30–July 4.

———. 1990. "Culture, Modernism, Postmodernism: A Challenge to International Relations." In *Culture and International Relations*, ed. Jongsuk Chay. Westport, Conn.: Praeger.

Farias, Victor. 1989. *Heidegger and Nazism*. Philadelphia: Temple University Press.

Fay, Brian. 1975. *Social Theory and Political Practice*. Boston: Allen and Unwin.

Featherstone, Mike. 1988. "In Pursuit of the Postmodern: An Introduction." *Theory, Culture and Society* 5 (2–3): 195–217.

———. 1989. "Towards a Sociology of Postmodern Culture." In *Social Structure and Culture*, ed. Hans Haferkamp. New York: Walter de Gruyter.

Fedier, Francois. 1988. *Heidegger, anatomie d'un scandale*. Paris: Robert Laffont.

Feigl, Herbert. 1953a. "The Scientific Outlook: Naturalism and Humanism." In *Readings in the Philosophy of Science*, ed. Herbert Feigl and May Brodbeck. New York: Appleton-Century-Crofts.

———. 1953b. "Unity of Science and Unitary Science." In *Readings in the Philosophy of Science*, ed. Herbert Feigl and May Brodbeck. New York: Appleton-Century-Crofts.

Fekete, John, ed. 1984. *The Structural Allegory: Reconstructive Encounters with the New French Thought*. Minneapolis: University of Minnesota Press.

Ferre, Frederick. 1988. "Religious World Modeling and Postmodern Science." In *The Reenchantment of Science: Postmodern Proposals*, ed. D. R. Griffin. Albany: State University of New York Press.

Ferry, Luc, and Alain Renaut. 1985. *La pensée 68, Essai sur l'anti-humanisme contemporain*. Paris: Gallimard.

———. 1987. *68–86 Itinéraires de l'individu*. Paris: Gallimard.

———. 1988. *Heidegger et les modernes*. Paris: Grasset.

———. 1990. *French Philosophy of the Sixties* [English version of Ferry and Renaut 1985]. Amherst: University of Massachusetts Press.

Feyerabend, P. 1975. *Against Method: Outline of an Anarchistic Theory of Knowledge*. London: New Left Books.

Fish, Stanley. 1976. "Interpreting the Variorum." *Critical Inquiry* 3: 465–85.

———. 1980. *Is There a Text in This Class: The Authority of Interpretive Communities*. Cambridge: Harvard University Press.

———. 1984. "Fish v. Fiss." *Stanford Law Review* 36: 1325–47.

———. 1987. "Dennis Martinez and the Uses of Theory." *Yale Law Review* 96: 1773–1800.

———. 1989. *Doing What Comes Naturally*. Durham, N.C.: Duke University Press.

Fiske, D. W., and R. A. Shweder. 1986. "Pluralisms and Subjectivities." In *Metatheory in Social Science*, ed. Donald W. Fiske and Richard A. Shweder. Chicago: University of Chicago Press.

Fiss, Owen. 1982. "Objectivity and Interpretation." *Stanford Law Review* 34 (4): 739–73.

Flax, Jane. 1990. *Thinking Fragments: Psychoanalysis, Feminism, and Postmodernism in the Contemporary West*. Berkeley: University of California Press.

Fokkema, Doune. 1984. *Literary History, Modernism and Postmodernism*. Amsterdam: John Benjamin Publishing Company.

Foley, Barbara. 1985. "The Politics of Deconstruction." In *Rhetoric and Form: Deconstruction at Yale*, ed. R. C. Davis and R. Schleifer. Norman: University of Oklahoma Press.

Fortin, Alfred J. 1989. "Notes on Terrorist Text: A Critical Use of Roland Barthes' Textual Analysis in the Interpretation of Political Meaning." In *International/ Intertextual Relations: Postmodern Readings of World Politics*, ed. James Der Derian and Michael J. Shapiro. Lexington, Mass.: Lexington Books.

Foster, Hal. 1983. "Postmodernism: A Preface." In *The Anti-Aesthetic: Essays on Postmodern Culture*, ed. Hal Foster. Port Townsend, Wash.: Bay Press.

———. 1984. "(Post)Modern Polemics." *New German Critique*, no. 33 (Fall): 67–79.

Foucault, Michel. 1967. *Nietzsche*. Paris: Minuit.

———. 1970. *The Order of Things: An Archaeology of the Human Sciences*. New York: Vintage.

———. 1971. *L'Ordre du discours*. Paris: Gallimard.

———. 1972. *Histoire de la folie*. Paris: Gallimard.

———. 1973. *The Birth of the Clinic*. London: Tavistock.

———. 1975. *Surveiller et punir: naissance de la prison* [English translation, *Discipline and Punish*]. Paris: Gallimard.

———. 1976. *Histoire de la sexualité, vol. 1 La Volonté de savoir* [English translation, *The History of Sexuality*]. Paris: Gallimard.

———. 1977. "Nietzsche, Genealogy, History." In *Language, Counter-Memory, Practice*, ed. Donald Bouchard. Ithaca, N.Y.: Cornell University Press.

———. 1979. "What Is an Author?" In *Textual Strategies: Perspectives in Post-structuralist Criticism*, ed. Josue Harari. Ithaca, N.Y.: Cornell University Press.

———. 1980. *Power/Knowledge*. Ed. C. Gordon; trans. C. Gordon, L. Marshall, J. Mepham, and K. Soper. New York: Pantheon Books.

———. 1982. "A Discussion of the Work of Michel Foucault." *Skyline*, March, 18.

———. 1983a. "How We Behave." *Vanity Fair*, November, 62.

———. 1983b. "The Subject and Power." In *Michel Foucault, Beyond Structuralism and Hermeneutics*, ed. Hubert Dreyfus and Paul Rabinow. Chicago: University of Chicago Press.

———. 1984. *The Foucault Reader*. New York: Pantheon.

———. 1987. "What Is Enlightenment?" In *Interpretive Social Science, A Second Look*, ed. Paul Rabinow and William M. Sullivan. Berkeley: University of California Press.

Fowler, Roger. 1987. *A Dictionary of Modern Critical Terms*. New York: Routledge and Kegan Paul.

Fox, Matthew. 1990. "A Mystical Cosmology: Toward a Postmodern Spirituality." In *Sacred Interconnections; Postmodern Spirituality, Political Economy, and Art*, ed. David Griffin. Albany: State University of New York Press.

Frank, Manfred. 1983. *Was ist Neostrukturalismus?* Frankfurt: Suhrkamp Verlag.

———. 1988. *L'Ultime raison du sujet*. Paris: Michel Guerin.

Fraser, Nancy. 1984. "The French Derrideans: Politicizing Deconstruction or Deconstructing the Political." *New German Critique*, no. 33: 127–55.

———. 1985. "What's Critical about Critical Theory?" *New German Critique*, no. 35: 99–131.

———. 1989. *Unruly Practices: Power, Discourse and Gender in Contemporary Social Theory*. Minneapolis: University of Minnesota Press.

Fraser, Nancy. Forthcoming. "Rethinking the Public Sphere: A Contribution to the Critique of Actually Existing Democracy." In *Habermas and the Public Sphere*, ed. Craig Calhoun. Boston: MIT Press.

Fraser, Nancy, and Linda Nicholson. 1988. "Social Criticism without Philosophy: An Encounter between Feminism and Postmodernism." *Theory, Culture and Society* 5 (2–3): 374–94.

Freire, Paulo. 1970. "Cultural Action and Conscientization." *Harvard Educational Review* 40 (3): 452–77.

Freund, Elizabeth. 1987. *The Return of the Reader*. New York: Methuen.

Friedman, Jonathan. 1988. "Cultural Logics of the Global System: A Sketch." *Theory, Culture and Society* 5: 447–60.

Fukuyama, Francis. 1989. "The End of History?" *The National Interest*, no. 16 (Summer): 3–19.

———. 1989–90. "A Reply to My Critics." *The National Interest*, no. 18 (Winter): 21–28.

Furet, Francois, and Mona Ozouf, eds. 1988. *A Critical Dictionary of the French Revolution*. Cambridge: Belknap and Harvard University Press.

Garfinkel, H. 1967. *Studies in Ethnomethodology*. Englewood Cliffs, N.J.: Prentice Hall.

Gebauer, Gunter. 1989. "The Place of Beginning and End: Caves and Their Systems of Symbols." In *Looking Back on the End of the World*, ed. Dietmar Kamper and Christoph Wulf. New York: Semiotext(e).

Geertz, Clifford. 1973a. "Thick Description: Toward an Interpretive Theory of Cultures." In *The Interpretation of Cultures*, ed. C. Geertz. New York: Basic Books.

———. 1973b. *The Interpretation of Culture*. New York: Basic Books.

———. 1983. *Local Knowledge: Further Essays in Interpretive Anthropology*. New York: Basic Books.

Geras, Norman. 1987. "Post-Marxism?" *New Left Review*, no. 167 (May/June): 40–82.

Gergen, K. J. 1986. "Correspondence versus Autonomy in the Language of Understanding Human Action." In *Metatheory in Social Science*, ed. Donald W. Fiske and Richard A. Shweder. Chicago: University of Chicago Press.

Gergen, K. J. 1987. "Introduction: Toward Metapsychology." In *The Analysis of Psychological Theory: Meta-psychological Perspectives*, ed. H. J. Stam et al. Washington, D.C.: Hemisphere Publishing Corporation.

Gibbins, John R. 1989. "Contemporary Political Cultures: An introduction." In *Contemporary Political Culture*, ed. John R. Gibbins. Newbury Park, Calif.: Sage.

Gibbons, Michael T. 1985. "Interpretation, Conservatism & Political Practice." *Polity* 17 (4): 777–94.

———. 1987. "Interpretations, Genealogy and Human Agency." In *Idioms of Inquiry*, ed. Terence Ball. Albany: State University of New York Press.

Giddens, Anthony. 1984. *The Constitution of Society: Outline of the Theory of Structuration*. Berkeley: University of California Press.

———. 1987. "Structuralism, Post-structuralism and the Production of Culture."

In *Social Theory Today*, ed. A. Giddens and Jonathan Turner. Oxford: Polity Press.

———. 1990. *Consequences of Modernity*. Stanford, Calif.: Stanford University Press.

Giovannini, Joseph. 1988. "Breaking All the Rules." *New York Times*, June 12, 43.

Gitlin, Todd. 1989. "Postmodernism: Roots and Politics." *Dissent* (Winter): 100–108. [Abridged and summarized in *Ute Reader*, July/Aug 1989.]

Glassner, Barry 1989. "Fitness and the Postmodern Self." *Journal of Health and Social Behavior* 30 (June): 180–91.

Gleick, James. 1987. *Chaos*. New York: Viking.

Goffman, Erving. 1959. *The Presentation of Self in Everyday Life*. New York: Doubleday.

Goleman, Daniel. 1989. "The Dalai Lama Has Ideas for Neuroscience." *New York Times*, October 8, 6.

Goodman, Nelson. 1984. *Of Mind and Other Matters*. Cambridge: Harvard University Press.

Gottlieb, Anthony. 1990. "Heidegger For Fun and Profit." *New York Times Book Review*, January 7, 1, 22–23.

Gould, Stephen Jay. 1983. *Hen's Teeth and Horse's Toes*. New York: Norton.

Gouldner, Alvin. 1973. *For Sociology*. London: Allen Lane.

Graff, Gerald. 1979. *Literature Against Itself*. Chicago: University of Chicago Press.

———. 1983. "The Pseudo-Politics of Interpretation." In *The Politics of Interpretation*, ed. W.J.T. Mitchell. Chicago: University of Chicago Press.

———. 1989. "Looking Past the de Man Case." In *Responses: On Paul de Man's Wartime Journalism*, ed. W. Harnacher, N. Hertz, and T. Kennan. Lincoln: University of Nebraska Press.

———. 1990. "Determinacy/Indeterminacy." In *Critical Terms for Literary Study*, ed. Frank Lentricchia and Thomas McLaughlin. Chicago: University of Chicago Press.

Granier, Jean. 1977. "Nietzsche's Conception of Chaos." In *The New Nietzsche*, ed. David Allison. New York: Dell Publishing.

Gregory, Bruce. 1988. *Inventing Reality: Physics as Language*. New York: John Wiley and Sons.

Gregory, Derek. 1989. "Areal Differentiation and Post-Modern Human Geography." In *Horizons in Human Geography*, ed. Derek Gregory and Rex Walford. London: Macmillan.

Gregory, Derek, and Rex Walford, eds. 1989. *Horizons in Human Geography*. London: Macmillan.

Griffin, David R., ed. 1988a. *The Reenchantment of Science: Postmodern Proposals*. Albany: State University of New York Press.

———. 1988b. "Of Minds and Molecules: Postmodern Medicine in a Psychosomatic Universe." In *The Reenchantment of Science: Postmodern Proposals*, ed. D. R. Griffin. Albany: State University of New York Press.

———, ed. 1988c. *Spirituality and Society: Postmodern Visions*. Albany: State University Press of New York.

Griffin, David R. 1989. *God and Religion in the Postmodern World: Essays in Post-modern Theology*. Albany: State University of New York Press.

———, ed. 1990. *Sacred Interconnections: Postmodern Spirituality, Political Economy, and Art*. Albany: State University of New York Press.

Grunbaum, A. 1953. "Causality and the Science of Human Behavior." In *Readings in the Philosophy of Science*, ed. H. Feigl and M. Brodbeck. New York: Appleton-Century-Crofts.

Gunnell, John. 1988. "After Political Theory." Paper presented to the American Political Science Association, annual meeting, Washington, D.C., September 1–4.

Habermas, Jürgen. 1974. "The Public Sphere, An Encyclopedia Article (1964)." *New German Critique*, no. 3 (Fall): 49–55.

———. 1978. *L'espace public: archéologie de la publicité comme dimension constitutive de la société bourgeoise*. Paris: Payot.

———. 1981. "Modernity Versus Post Modernity." *New German Critique*, no. 22 (Winter): 3–14.

———. 1983. "Modernity—An Incomplete Project." In *The Anti-Aesthetic: Essays on Postmodern Culture*, ed. Hal Foster. Townsend, Wash.: Bay Press.

———. 1985. *The Theory of Communicative Action. Vol. 1: Reason and the Rationalization of Society*. Boston: Beacon Press.

———. 1986. *Autonomy and Solidarity*. London: Verso.

———. 1987a. *The Philosophical Discourse of Modernity*. Boston: MIT Press.

———. 1987b. *The Theory of Communicative Action. Vol. 2: Lifeword and System*. Boston: Beacon Press.

———. 1989a. "Work and Weltanschauung: The Heidegger Controversy from a German Perspective." *Critical Inquiry* 15 (2): 431–56.

———. 1989b. *The Structural Transformation of the Public Sphere*, trans. Thomas Burger. Cambridge: MIT Press.

Halliday, M. A. K. 1979. *Language as Social Semiotic: The Social Interpretation of Language and Meaning*. London: Arnold.

Hamacher, Werner, Neil Hertz, and Thomas Keenan, ed. (1989). *Responses: On Paul de Man's Wartime Journalism*. Lincoln: University of Nebraska Press.

Hancher, Michael. 1982. "Dead Letters: Wills and Poems." *Texas Law Review* 60 (3): 507–26.

Handler, Joel. 1986. "Dependent People, the State and the Modern/Postmodern Search for the Dialogic Community." *UCLA Law Review* 35 (6): 999–1113.

Hanson, Allan. 1989. "The Making of the Maori: Culture Invention and Its Logic." *American Anthropologist* 91: 890–902.

Harari, Josue. 1979. "Critical Factions/Critical Fictions." In *Textual Strategies: Perspectives in Post-structuralist Criticism*, ed. Josue Harari. Ithaca, N.Y.: Cornell University Press.

Harding, Sandra. 1990. "Feminism, Science, and the Anti-Enlightenment Critique." In *Feminism/Postmodernism*, ed. Linda J. Nicholson. New York: Routledge.

Hare-Mustin, Rachel, and Jeanne Marecek. 1988. "The Meaning of Difference:

Gender Theory, Postmodernism, and Psychology." *American Psychologist* 43 (6): 455–64.

Harlan, David. 1989. "Intellectual History and the Return of Literature." *American Historical Review* 94 (3): 581–609.

Harland, Richard. 1987. *Superstructuralism: The Philosophy of Structuralism and Post-Structuralism*. London: Methuen.

Harman, Willis W. 1988. "The Postmodern Heresy: Consciousness as Causal." In *The Reenchantment of Science: Postmodern Proposals*, ed. D. R. Griffin. Albany: State University of New York Press.

Hartman, Geoffrey. 1988. "Paul de Man, Fascism and Deconstruction: Blindness and Insight." *New Republic*, March 7, 26–27.

Hartsock, Nancy. 1987. "Rethinking Modernism: Minority vs. Majority Theories." *Cultural Critique*, no. 7 (Fall): 187–206.

Hartsock, Nancy. 1988. "Epistemology and Politics: Developing Alternatives to Western Political Thought." Paper delivered to the International Political Science Association, Washington, D.C., August.

Harvey, David. 1985. *Consciousness and the Urban Experience*. Baltimore, Md.: Johns Hopkins University Press.

———. 1987. "Flexible Accumulation through Urbanization: Reflections on 'Post-Modernism' in the American City." *Antipode* 19 (3): 260–86.

———. 1989. *The Condition of Postmodernity: An Enquiry into the Origins of Cultural Change*. Cambridge, Mass.: Basil Blackwell.

Hassan, Ihab. 1985. "The Culture of Post-modernism." *Theory, Culture and Society* 2 (3): 119–31.

———. 1987. *The Postmodern Turn*. Columbus: Ohio State University Press.

Hatch, Elvin. 1987. "Comment." *Current Anthropology* 28 (3): 271–72.

Hawkesworth, Mary. 1989. "Knowers, Knowing, Known: Feminist Theory and Claims of Truth." *Signs* 14 (3): 533–49.

Hawking, Stephen. 1988. *A Brief History of Time From the Big Bang to Black Holes*. New York: Bantam Books.

Heidegger, Martin. 1962. *Being and Time*, trans. John Macquarrie and Edward Robinson. New York: Harper & Row.

———. 1972. *On Time and Being*, trans. Joan Stambaugh. New York: Harper & Row.

———. 1973. *The End of Philosophy*, trans. Joan Stambaugh. New York: Harper & Row.

———. 1977. *The Question Concerning Technology: And Other Essays*, trans. William Lovitt. New York: Harper & Row.

Heller, Agnes. 1984. *Everyday Life*. London: Routledge and Kegan Paul.

———. 1986. "The Sociology of Everyday Life." In *The Sociology of Structure and Action*, ed. Ulf Himmelstrand. Newbury Park, Calif.: Sage.

———. 1987. "Mouvements culturels et changements des modèles de vie quotidienne depuis la deuxième guerre." In *La radicalité du quotidien*, ed. Andre Corten and Marie-Blanche Tahon. Montréal: VLB éditeur.

———. 1990. *Can Modernity Survive?* Berkeley: University of California Press.

Heller, Agnes, and Ferenc Feher. 1989. *The Post-Modern Political Condition*. New York: Columbia University Press.

Hempel, Carl. 1988. "On the Cognitive Status and the Rationale of Scientific Methodology." *Poetics* 9 (1): 5–26.

Henriques, Julian, Wendy Holoway, Cathy Urwin, Couze Venn, and Valerie Walkerdine. 1984. *Changing the Subject: Psychology, Social Regulation, and Subjectivity*. New York: Methuen.

Himmelfarb, Gertrude. 1987. *The New History and the Old*. Cambridge: Harvard University Press.

———. 1989a. "Some Reflections of the New History." *American Historical Review* 94 (3): 661–70.

———. 1989b. "Responses to Fukuyama." *The National Interest*, no. 16 (Summer): 24–26.

Hirsch, E. D. 1967. *The Aims of Interpretation*. Chicago: University of Chicago Press.

———. 1973. *Validity in Interpretation*. New Haven, Conn.: Yale University Press.

Hirschman, Axel O. 1987. "The Search for Paradigms as a Hindrance to Understanding." In *Interpretive Social Sciences, A Second Look*, ed. Paul Rabinow and William M. Sullivan. Berkeley: University of California Press.

Hobson, Marian. 1982. "Deconstructing, Empiricism and the Postal Services." *French Studies* 36 (July): 290–314.

Hohendahl, Peter U. 1986. "Habermas' Philosophical Discourse of Modernity." *Telos*, no. 69 (Fall): 49–65.

Holden, Arun V., ed. 1986. *Chaos*. Princeton, N.J.: Princeton University Press.

Hollinger, David. 1989. "The Return of the Prodigal: the Persistence of Historical Knowing." *American Historical Review* 94 (3): 610–21.

Honneth, Axel. 1985. "An Aversion Against the Universal." *Theory, Culture and Society* 2 (3): 147–57.

Hoover, Kenneth. 1980. *The Elements of Social Scientific Thinking*. New York: St. Martin's Press.

Horkheimer, Max, and Theodor Adorno. 1972. *Dialectic of Enlightenment*. New York: Herder and Herder.

Howard, George S. 1991. "Culture Tales: A Narrative Approach to Thinking, Cross-Cultural Psychology, and Psychotherapy." *American Psychologist* 46 (3): 187–97.

Hoy, David Couzens. 1985a. "Jacques Derrida." In *The Return of Grand Theory in the Human Sciences*, ed. Quentin Skinner. Boston: Cambridge University Press.

———. 1985b. "Interpreting the Law: Hermeneutical and Poststructuralist Perspectives." *Southern California Law Review* 58 (1): 135–76.

———. 1989. "Splitting the Difference: Habermas's Critique of Derrida." *Praxis International* 8 (4): 447–64.

Hughs, Robert. 1989. "*America*: The Patron Saint of Neo-Pop." *The New York Review of Books*, June 1, 29–32.

Hunt, Linda., ed. 1989. *The New Cultural History*. Berkeley: University of California Press.

Hurwitz, Roger. 1989. "Strategic and Social Fictions in the Prisoner's Dilemma."

In *International/Intertextual Relations: Postmodern Readings of World Politics*, ed. James Der Derian and Michael J. Shapiro. Lexington, Mass.: Lexington Books.

Husserl, Edmund. 1960. *Cartesian Meditations*. The Hague: Nijhoff.

Hutcheon, Linda. 1986–87. "The Politics of Postmodernism: Parody and History." *Cultural Critique*, no. 5 (Winter): 179–208.

———. 1989. *The Politics of Postmodernism*. London: Routledge.

Hutchinson, Allan, ed. 1988. *Critical Legal Studies*. Totowa, N.J.: Rowman & Littlefield.

Huyssen, Andreas. 1984. "Mapping the Postmodern." *New German Critique*, no. 33 (Fall): 22–52.

———. 1986. *After the Great Divide: Modernism, Mass Culture, Postmodernism*. Bloomington: Indiana University Press.

Ingarden, Roman. 1973. *The Literary Work of Art*, trans. George Graabowicz. Evanston, Ill.: Northwestern University Press.

Iser, Wolfgang. 1978. *The Act of Reading: A Theory of Aesthetic Response*. Baltimore, Md.: Johns Hopkins University Press.

Jacquard, Albert. 1978. *Éloge de la différence; la génétique et les hommes*. Paris: Editions du Seuil.

———. 1982. *Au péril de la science? Interrogations d'un généticien*. Paris: Editions du Seuil.

Jameson, Fredric. 1972. *The Prison-House of Language*. Princeton, N.J.: Princeton University Press.

———. 1981. *The Political Unconscious: Narrative as a Socially Symbolic Act*. London: Methuen.

———. 1983. "Postmodernism and Consumer Society." In *The Anti-Aesthetic: Essays on Postmodern Culture*, ed. Hal Foster. Port Townsend, Wash.: Bay Press.

———. 1984a. "Postmodernism, or the Cultural Logic of Late Capitalism." *New Left Review*, no. 146 (July/August): 53–92.

———. 1984b. "The Politics of Theory: Ideological Positions in the Postmodern Debate." *New German Critique*, no. 33 (Fall): 53–65.

———. 1985. "Postmodernism and Consumer Society." In *Postmodern Culture*, ed. Hal Foster. London: Pluto Press.

———. 1988. "Cognitive Mapping." In *Marxism and the Interpretation of Culture*, ed. Cary Nelson and Lawrence Grossberg. Chicago: University of Illinois Press.

———. 1989. "Marxism and Postmodernism." *New Left Review*, no. 176 (July/August): 31–45.

Jay, Martin. 1985. "Habermas and Modernism." In *Habermas and Modernity*, ed. Richard Bernstein. Cambridge: MIT Press.

———. 1988. "Fin-de-Siècle Socialism." *Praxis International* 8 (1): 1–13.

Jefferson, Ann. 1982. "Structuralism and Post-structuralism." In *Modern Literary Theory: A Comparative Introduction*, ed. Ann Jefferson and David Robey. Totowa N.J.: Barnes and Noble.

Jefferson, Ann, and David Robey, ed. 1982. *Modern Literary Theory; A Comparative Introduction*. Totowa, N.J.: Barnes and Noble.

Jencks, Charles. 1980. *Late-Modern Architecture and Other Essays*. London: Academy Editions.

Jencks, Charles. 1986. *What is Post-Modernism?* New York: St. Martin's Press.

Johnson, Barbara. 1980. *The Critical Difference*. Baltimore, Md.: Johns Hopkins University Press.

Johnson, Barbara, Louis Mackey, and J. Hillis Miller. 1985. "Marxism and Deconstruction: Symposium." In *Rhetoric and Form: Deconstruction at Yale*, ed. R. C. Davis and R. Schleifer. Norman: University of Oklahoma Press.

Judovitz, Dalia. 1988. "Representation and Its Limits in Descartes." In *Postmodernism and Continental Philosophy*, ed. Hugh J. Silverman and Donn Walton. Albany: State University of New York Press.

Kamper, Dietmar. 1989. "Between Simulation and Negentrophy." In *Looking Back on the End of the World*, ed. D. Kamper and C. Wulf. New York: Semiotext(e).

Kamper, D., and C. Wulf, ed. 1989. *Looking Back on the End of the World*. New York: Semiotext(e).

Kamuf, Peggy. 1989. "Impositions: A Violent Dawn at *Le Soir*." In *Responses: On Paul de Man's Wartime Journalism*, ed. W. Harnacher, N. Hertz, and T. Kennan. Lincoln: University of Nebraska Press.

Kariel, H. 1988a. "Bringing Postmodernism into Being." Paper delivered at the American Political Science Association, annual meeting: Washington, D.C., September 1–4.

———. 1988b. "Praxis, the Repressed Potential of Political Science." *Polity* 21 (2): 401–8.

———. 1989. *The Desperate Politics of Postmodernism*. Amherst: University of Massachusetts Press.

Karnoouh, Claude. 1986. "The Lost Paradise of Regionalism: The Crisis of Postmodernity in France." *Telos*, no. 67 (Spring): 11–26.

Ke, Gang. 1990. "A Comparative Study of the Representational Paradigms: Between Liberalism and Socialism." *Philosphy of the Social Sciences* 20 (1): 5–34.

Kellner, Douglas. 1989a. *Critical Theory, Marxism and Modernity*. Baltimore, Md.: Johns Hopkins University Press.

———. 1989b. *Jean Baudrillard: From Marxism to Postmodernism and Beyond*. Stanford, Calif.: Stanford University Press.

Kellner, Hans. 1987. "Narrativity in History: Post-Structuralism and Since." *History and Theory* 26 (4): 1–29.

Kendrick, Walter. 1988. "De Man that Got Away." *Village Voice Literary Supplement*, April 12, 6–8.

Klein, Bradley S. 1989. "The Textual Strategies of the Military: Or, Have You Read Any Good Defense Manuals Lately?" In *International/ Intertextual Relations: Postmodern Readings of World Politics*, ed. James Der Derian and Michael J. Shapiro. Lexington, Mass.: Lexington Books.

———. 1990. "How the West Was One: Representational Politics of NATO." *International Studies Quarterly* 34 (3): 311–25.

Knapp, Steven, and Walter Benn Michaels. 1982. "Against Theory." *Critical Inquiry* 8 (4): 723–42.

———. 1987. "Against Theory 2: Hermeneutics and Deconstruction." *Critical Inquiry* 14 (Autumn): 49–68.

Kolakowski, Leszek. 1990. *Modernity on Endless Trial*. Chicago: University of Chicago Press.

Kramer, Hilton. 1982a. "A Note on *The New Criterion*." *The New Criterion* 1 (September): 1–5.

———. 1982b. "Postmodern: Art and Culture in the 1980's." *The New Criterion* 1 (September): 36–42.

———. 1984. "The MLA Centennial Follies." *The New Criterion* 2 (February): 1–8.

Kratochwil, Friedrich, and John Gerard Ruggie. 1986. "International Organization: A State of the Art on an Art of the State." *International Organization* 40 (4): 753–76.

Krieger, Murray, ed. 1987. *The Aims of Representation: Subject/Text/History*. New York: Columbia University Press.

Krippner, Stanley. 1988. "Parapsychology and Postmodern Science." In *The Reenchantment of Science: Postmodern Proposals*, ed. D. R. Griffin. Albany: State University of New York Press.

Kristeva, Julia. 1974. *La révolution du language poétique*. Paris: Seuil. [Portions published in English in *Revolution in Poetics Language*. 1984. Trans. Margaret Waller. New York: Columbia University Press; and The Kristeva Reader (see below)].

———. 1980. *Desire in Language*. Oxford: Basil Blackwell.

———. 1981. "Women Can Never Be Defined." In *New French Feminisms*, ed. Elaine Marks and Isabelle de Courtivron. New York: Shocken Books.

———. 1986. *The Kristeva Reader/Julia Kristeva*, ed. Toril Moi. New York: Columbia University Press.

Kroker, Arthur. 1985. "Baudrillard's Marx." *Theory, Culture, and Society* 2 (3): 69–83.

Kroker, Arthur, and David Cook. 1986. *The Postmodern Scene: Excremental Culture and Hyper-Aesthetics*. New York: St. Martin's Press.

Kugler, Paul. 1988. "From Modernism to Post-modernism: Some Implications for a Depth Psychology of Dreams." *Psychiatric Journal of the University of Ottawa* 13 (2): 60–65.

Kuhn, Thomas. 1970. *The Structure of Scientific Revolutions*. Chicago: University of Chicago Press.

———. 1971. "Notes on Lakatos." In *Proceedings of the 1970 Biennial Meeting, Philosophy of Science Association*, ed. R. C. Buck and R. S. Cohen. Higham, Mass.: D. Reidal Publishing.

Kundera, Milan. 1984. *The Unbearable Lightness of Being*. New York: Harper & Row.

Kurzweil, Edith. 1980. *The Age of Structuralism: Lévi-Strauss to Foucault*. New York: Columbia University Press.

Laçan, Jacques. 1977. *Écrits*. New York: Alan Sheridan.

Laclau, Ernesto. 1988. "Building a New Left: An Interview." *Strategies: A Journal of Theory, Culture, and Politics* 10 (Fall): 29.

Laclau, Ernesto, and Chantal Mouffe. 1985. *Hegemony and Socialist Strategy: Toward a Radical Democratic Politics*. London: Verso.

Lacoue-Labarthe, P. 1987. *La fiction du politique: Heidegger, l'art et la politique.* Paris: Christian Bourgeois.

Laffey, John. 1987. "The Politics at Modernism's Funeral." *Canadian Journal of Political and Social Theory* 11 (3): 89–98.

Lakatos, I. 1970. "Falsification and the Methodology of Scientific Research." In *Criticism and the Growth of Knowledge*, ed. A. Musgrove and I. Lakatos. Cambridge: Cambridge University Press.

———. 1978. "Mathematics, Science and Epistemology." In *Philosophical Papers.* Vol. 2. Cambridge: Cambridge University Press.

Lambropoulos, Vassilis. 1986. "Polis, Semiotics, Politics." *American Journal of Semiotics* 4 (1–2): 43–51.

Larsen, Neil. 1990. *Modernism and Hegemony: A Materialist Critique of Aesthetic Agencies.* Minneapolis: University of Minnesota Press.

Lash, Scott. 1990. "Postmodernism as Humanism? Urban Space and Social Theory." In *Theories of Modernity and Postmodernity*, ed. Bryan S. Turner. Newbury Park, Calif.: Sage.

Lash, Scott, and John Urry. 1987. *The End of Organized Capitalism.* Madison: University of Wisconsin Press.

Latimer, Dan. 1984. "Jameson and Post-modernism." *New Left Review*, no. 148 (Nov./Dec.): 116–28.

Latour, Bruno. 1987. *Science in Action.* Cambridge: Harvard University Press.

———. 1988. *The Pasteurization of France.* Cambridge: Harvard University Press.

Latour, Bruno, and Stever Woolgar. 1979. *Laboratory Life.* Beverly Hills, Calif.: Sage.

Laudan, L. 1984. *Science and Values.* Berkeley: University of California Press.

Lechner, Frank. 1990. "Against Modernity: A Sociological Analysis of Forms of Anti-modernism." Paper presented to the World Congress of Sociology, Madrid, July 9–14.

Lefebvre, Henri. 1988. "Toward a Leftist Cultural Politics." In *Marxism and the Interpretation of Culture*, ed. Cary Nelson and Lawrence Grossberg. Chicago: University of Illinois Press.

Lehman, David. 1988. "Deconstructing de Man's Life." *Newsweek*, February 15, 83.

Leiss, William. 1983. "The Icons of the Marketplace." *Theory, Culture and Society* 1 (3): 10–21.

Leiss, William, S. Klilne, and S. Jhally. 1986. *Social Communication in Advertising.* New York: Methuen.

Lenin, V. I. 1905. "Two Tactics of Social-Democracy in the Democratic Revolution." In *Collected Works*, Vol. 22 [originally published in 1964]. London: Laurence and Wishart.

———. 1917. "State and Revolution." In *Collected Works*, vol. 25 [originally published in 1964]. London: Laurence and Wishart.

Lentricchia, Frank. 1980. *After the New Criticism.* London: Methuen.

Levin, Charles. 1987. *Pathologies of the Modern Self.* New York: New York University Press.

Levin, Charles, and Arthur Kroker. 1984. "Baudrillard's Challenge." *Canadian Journal of Political and Social Theory* 8 (1–2): 5–18.

Levine, George. 1987. "Literary Science—Scientific Literature." *Raritan* 6 (3): 24–41.

Levinson, Sanford. 1982. "Law as Literature." *Texas Law Review* 60 (3): 373–403.

———. 1988. *Constitutional Faith*. Princeton, N.J.: Princeton University Press.

Lévi-Strauss, Claude. 1966. *The Savage Mind*. London: Weidenfeld.

Lindblom, C. E. 1959. "The Science of Muddling Through." *Public Administration Review* 19 (Spring): 79–99.

Lipovetsky, Gilles. 1983. *L'ère du vide: Essais sur l'individualisme contemporain*. Paris: Gallimard.

Lipsitz, George. 1986–87. "Cruising Around the Historical Bloc—Postmodernism and Popular Music in East Los Angeles." *Cultural Critique*, no. 5 (Winter): 157–78.

Longley, Clifford. 1989. "Inquest on the Enlightenment." *The Times* (London), March 25, 12.

Luke, Timothy. 1989a . " 'What's Wrong with Deterrence?' Alternative Perspectives on International Conflict: Semiotic and Symbolic Interactionist Interpretations of National Security Policy." In *International/Intertextual Relations: Postmodern Readings of World Politics*, ed. James Der Derian and Michael J. Shapiro. Lexington, Mass.: Lexington Books.

———. 1989b. "Class Contradictions and Social Cleavages in Informationalizing Post-Industrial Societies: On the Rise of New Social Movements." *New Political Science* 16/17 (Fall/Winter): 125–54.

———. 1989c. *Screens of Power*. Urbana: University of Illinois Press.

Lyotard, Jean-Francois. 1982. "Presenting the Unpresentable: The Sublime." *Artform* 20 (8): 64–69.

———. 1984. *The Postmodern Condition: A Report on Knowledge*, trans. Geoff Bennington and Brian Massouri. Minneapolis: University of Minnesota Press.

———. 1986–87. "Rules and Paradoxes." *Cultural Critique*, no. 5 (Winter): 209–19.

———. 1988a. *L'inhumain, causeries sur le temps*. Paris: Galilée.

———. 1988b. *The Differend: Phrases in Dispute*. Minneapolis: University of Minnesota Press.

Lyotard, Jean-Francois, and Jean-Loup Thébaud. 1985. *Just Gaming*. Minneapolis: University of Minnesota Press.

Macedo, Stephen. 1986. *The New Right v. The Constitution*. Washington, D.C.: Cato Institute.

Macherey, P. 1978. *A Theory of Literary Production*. London: Routledge and Kegan Paul.

Macy, Joanna. 1990. "The Ecological Self: Postmodern Ground for Right Action." In *Sacred Interconnections; Postmodern Spirituality, Political Economy, and Art*, ed. David Griffin. Albany: State University of New York Press.

Madison, Gary B. 1988. *The Hermeneutics of Postmodernity: Figures and Themes*. Bloomington: Indiana University Press.

Maier, Charles. 1987. "The Politics of Time: Changing Paradigms of Collective Time and Private Time in the Modern Era." In *Changing Boundaries of the Political*, ed. Charles S. Maier. Cambridge: Cambridge University Press.

Malkan, Jeffrey. 1987. "Against Theory: Pragmatism and Deconstruction." *Telos*, no. 71 (Spring): 129–54.

Marcus, George E., and Michael Fischer. 1986. *Anthropology as Cultural Critique: An Experimental Moment in the Human Sciences*. Chicago: University of Chicago Press.

Marcuse, Herbert. 1956. *Reason and Revolution*. New York: Humanities Press.

———. 1969. *Negations: Essays in Critical Theory*. Boston: Beacon Press.

McCloskey, Donald N. 1985. *The Rhetoric of Economics*. Madison: University of Wisconsin Press.

———. 1990. *If You're So Smart: The Narrative of Economic Expertise*. Chicago: University of Chicago Press.

McHale, Brian. 1987. *Postmodernist Fiction*. New York: Methuen.

Meehan, Eugene. 1979. *Quality of Federal Policymaking*. Columbia: University of Missouri Press.

———. 1981. *Reasoned Argument in Social Science*. Westport, Conn.: Greenwood Press.

———. 1990. *Ethics for Policy Making*. Wesport, Conn.: Greenwood Press.

———. 1991. "The University and the Community: Social Science and Public Authority." Unpublished paper.

Megill, Allan. 1985. *Prophets of Extremity: Nietzsche, Heidegger, Foucault, Derrida*. Berkeley: University of California Press.

———. 1989. "Recounting the Past: 'Description,' Explanation, and Narrative in Historiography." *American Historical Review* 94 (3): 627–53.

Melucci, Alberto. 1990a. "Paradoxes of Post-Industrial Democracy: Everyday Life and Social Movements." Paper presented to the World Congress of Sociology, Madrid, July 9–14.

———. 1990b. "Frontierland: Collective Action Between Actors and Systems." Paper presented to the World Congress of Sociology, Madrid, July 9–14.

Meyrowitz, Joshua. 1985. *No Sense of Place*. New York: Oxford University Press.

Michaels, Walter Benn. 1983. "Is there a Politics of Interpretation"? In *The Politics of Interpretation*, ed. W. J. T. Mitchell. Chicago: University of Chicago Press.

Miller, J. Hillis. 1971. "The Fiction of Realism." In *Dickens Centennial Essays*, ed. Ada Nisbet and Blake Nevius. Berkeley: University of California Press.

———. 1972. "Tradition and Difference." *Diacritics* 4 (2): 6–13.

———. 1977. "The Critic as Host." *Critical Inquiry* 3 (3): 439–47.

———. 1981. "The Disarticulation of the Self in Nietzsche." *The Monist* 64 (April): 247–61.

———. 1986. *The Ethics of Reading*. New York: Columbia University Press.

———. 1988. "Two Current Debates." *Times Literary Supplement*, June 17, 676.

———. 1990. "Narrative." In *Critical Terms for Literary Study*, ed. Frank Lentricchia and Thomas McLaughlin. Chicago: University of Chicago Press.

Minow, Martha. 1987. "Law Turning Outward." *Telos*, no. 73 (Fall): 79–100.

Mitchell, W. J. T. 1990. "Representation." In *Critical Terms for Literary Study*, ed.

Frank Lentricchia and Thomas McLaughlin. Chicago: University of Chicago Press.

Mitscherling, Jeff. 1987. "Reformulation de l'alternative gadamerienne au post-modernisme." *Petite Revue de philosophie* 9 (1): 1–24.

Moi, Toril. 1986. "Introduction." In *The Kristeva Reader/Julia Kristeva*. New York: Columbia University Press.

———. 1988. "Feminism, Postmodernism and Style: Recent Feminist Criticism in the United States." *Cultural Critique*, no. 9 (Spring): 3–22.

Mokrzyski, Edmund. 1983. *Philosophy of Science and Sociology*. London: Routledge and Kegan Paul.

Montofiore, Janet. 1984. "The Rhetoric of Experience." *New Left Review*, no. 145 (May/June): 122–28.

Morgan, Edmund. 1988. *The Rise of Popular Sovereignty*. New York: W.W. Norton.

Morgan, Thais. 1985. "Is There an Intertext in this Text?" *American Journal of Semiotics* 3 (4): 1–40.

Morin, Edgar. 1986. "Ce qui a changé dans la vie intellectuelle française." *Revue Le débat*, no. 40 (été): 72–81.

Morris, M., and Paul Patton, ed. 1979. *Michel Foucault: Power, Truth, and Strategy*. Sydney, Australia: Ferral Publications.

Morris, Robert. 1988. "Words and Images in Modernism and Post Modernism." *Critical Inquiry* 15 (Winter): 337–47.

Mouffe, Chantal. 1988. "Hegemony and New Political Subjects." In *Marxism and the Interpretation of Culture*, ed. Cary Nelson and Lawrence Grossman. Chicago: University of Illinois Press.

Murphy, John. 1987a. "Deconstruction, Discourse, and Liberation." *Social Science Information* 26 (2): 417–33.

———. 1987b. "The Importance of Postmodernism for Marxist Literary Criticism." *Studies in Soviet Thought* 34: 233–53.

———. 1988. "Computerization, Postmodern Epistemology and Reading in the Postmodern Era." *Educational Theory* 38 (2): 175–82.

Nachmias, David, and Chava Nachmias. 1976. *Research Methods in the Social Sciences*. New York: St. Martin's Press.

Nelson, Cary, and Lawrence Grossberg, ed.1988. *Marxism and the Interpretation of Culture*. Chicago: University of Illinois Press.

Nelson, John. 1987. "Postmodern Meaning of Politics." Paper presented at American Political Science Association, annual meeting; Chicago, Illinois, September 3–6.

———. 1988. "Discourse, Text or Rhetoric? Postmodern Participation in Political Science." Paper presented at American Political Science Association, annual meeting, Washington, D.C., September 1–4.

Nicholson, Linda J., ed. 1990. *Feminism/Postmodernism*. New York: Routledge.

Nietzsche, Friedrich. 1954. *Thus Spoke Zarathustra*. New York: Viking Press.

———. 1967. *The Birth of Tragedy and the Case of Wagner*. New York: Vintage Books.

———. 1969. *On the Genealogy of Morals and Ecce Homo*. New York: Vintage Books.

Nietzsche, Friedrich. 1974. *The Gay Science*. New York: Vintage Books.

———. 1979. "On Truth and Lies in a Nonmoral Sense." *Philosophy and Truth, Selections from Nietzsche's Notebooks in the Early 1870's*. Atlantic City, N.J.: Humanities Press.

———. 1980. *On the Advantage and Disadvantage of History for Life*, trans. Peter Preuss. Indianapolis: Hackett Publishing.

Nodoushani, Omid. 1987. "Note on Progress: Postmodern Transformation in the Systems Age." *Systems Research* 4 (1): 59–64.

Norris, Christopher. 1982. *Deconstruction: Theory and Practice*. New York: Methuen.

———. 1985. *The Contest of Faculties*. New York: Methuen.

———. 1988. *Deconstruction and the Interests of Theory*. London: Pinter.

Norton, Anne. 1988. *Reflections on Political Identity*. Baltimore, Md.: Johns Hopkins University Press.

Oakeshott, Michael. 1933. *Experience and Its Modes*. Cambridge: Cambridge University Press.

———. 1956. "Political Education." In *Philosophy, Politics and Society*, ed. Peter Laslett. Oxford: Basil Blackwell.

Offe, Claus. 1987. "The Utopia of the Zero-Option, Modernity and Modernization as Normative Political Criteria." *Praxis International* 7 (April): 1–24.

O'Kane, John. 1984. "Marxism, Deconstruction, and Ideology: Notes Toward an Articulation." *New German Critique*, no. 33 (Fall): 219–47.

Olkowski, Dorothea. 1988. "Heidegger and the Limits of Representation." In *Postmodernism and Continental Philosophy*, ed. Hugh J. Silverman and Donn Walton. Albany: State University of New York Press.

O'Neill, John. 1988. "Religion and Postmodernism." *Theory, Culture and Society* 5 (2–3): 493–508.

Pacom, Diane. 1989. "La querelle des modernes et des postmodernes." *Possibles* 13 (1–2): 55–73.

Pangle, Thomas L. 1989. " 'Post-Modernist' Thought." *Wall Street Journal*, January 5, A9.

Parker, Ian, and John Shotter, ed. 1990. *Deconstructing Social Psychology*. London: Routledge.

Patterson, Annabel. 1990. "Intention." In *Critical Terms for Literary Study*, ed. Frank Lentricchia and Thomas McLaughlin, Chicago: University of Chicago Press.

Pavic, Milorad. 1988. *Dictionary of the Khazars*. New York: Knopf.

———. 1990. *Landscape Painted with Tea*. New York: Knopf.

Pecheux, M. 1969. *Analyse automatique du discours*. Paris: Dunod.

Pecora, Vincent P. 1988. "Simulacral Economies." *Telos*, no. 75 (Spring): 125–40.

Pfeil, Fred. 1986. "Postmodern and our Discontent." *Socialist Review* 16 (87–88): 125–34.

———. 1988. "Postmodernism as a 'Structure of Feeling.' " In *Marxism and the Interpretation of Culture*, ed. Cary Nelson and Lawrence Grossberg. Chicago: University of Illinois Press.

Pinter, Stephen. 1987. "Fading Postmodern Subjects." *Canadian Journal of Political and Social Theory* 11 (3): 140–47.

Pitkin, Hanna. 1967. *The Concept of Representation*. Berkeley: University of California Press.

Platten, David. 1986. "Postmodern Engineering." *Civil Engineering* 56 (6): 84–86.

Popper, Karl. 1959. *The Logic of Scientific Discovery*. New York: Basic Books.

———. 1962. *Conjectures and Refutations*. New York: Basic Books.

———. 1979. *Objective Knowledge*. Oxford: Clarendon Press.

Posner, Richard. 1988. "Interpreting Law: Interpreting Literature." *Raritan* 7 (4): 1–31.

Poster, Mark. 1987. "Foucault, Post-Structuralism and the Mode of Information." In *The Aims of Representation*, ed. Murray Krieger. New York: Columbia University Press.

Poster, Mark. 1990. *The Mode of Information*. Chicago: University of Chicago Press.

Potter, Jonathan, and Margaret Wetherell. 1987. *Discourse and Social Psychology: Beyond Attitudes and Behavior*. Newbury Park, Calif.: Sage.

Pratt, Mary Louise. 1986. "Fieldwork in Common Places." In *Writing Culture: The Poetics and Politics of Ethnography*, ed. James Clifford and George Marcus. Berkeley: University of California Press.

Prigogine, Ilya. 1986. "Science, Civilization and Democracy." *Futures* 18 (4): 493–510.

Prigogine, Ilya, and Isabelle Stengers. 1984. *Order Out of Chaos*. New York: Bantam Books.

Putnam, Hilary. 1981. *Reason, Truth and History*. Cambridge: Cambridge University Press.

Rabinow, Paul, ed. 1984. *The Foucault Reader*. New York: Pantheon Books.

———. 1986. "Representations Are Social Facts: Modernity and Post-Modernity in Anthropology." In *Writing Culture: The Poetics and Politics of Ethnography*, ed. James Clifford and George E. Marcus. Berkeley: University of California Press.

Rafie, Marcel. 1987. "La crise des savoirs revisitée." *Revue international d'action communitaire*, no. 57 (printemps): 153–59.

Rajchman, John, and Cornel West, ed. 1985. *Post-Analytic Philosophy*. New York: Columbia University Press.

Redner, Harry. 1987. "Representation and the Crisis of Post-Modernism." *PS: Political Science & Politics* 20 (3): 673–79.

Reid, Herbert G., and Ernest Y. Yanarella. 1974. "Towards a Post-Modern Theory of American Political Science and Culture: Perspectives from Critical Marxism and Phenomenology." *Cultural Hermeneutics* 2 (1): 286–316.

Reid, Herbert G., and Ernest Y. Yanarella. 1975. "Political Science and the Post-Modern Critique of Scientism and Domination." *Review of Politics* 37 (3): 91–166.

Renaut, Alain. 1989. *L'ère de l'individu*. Paris: Gallimard.

Ricci, David M. 1984. *The Tragedy of Political Science: Politics, Scholarship and Democracy*. New Haven: Yale University Press.

Richardson, Laurel. 1988. "The Collective Story: Postmodernism and the Writing of Sociology." *Sociological Focus* 21 (3): 199–207.

Rochlitz, Rainer. 1986. "Des Philosophes allemands face à la pensée française: alternatives à la philosophie du sujet." *Critique* 42 (464–65): 7–39.

Roochnik, David L. 1987. "Plato's Critique of Postmodernism." *Philosophy and Literature* 11 (2): 282–91.

Rorty, Richard. 1982. *Consequences of Pragmatism.* Minneapolis: University of Minnesota Press.

———. 1985. "Habermas and Lyotard on Postmodernity." In *Habermas and Modernity*, ed. Richard Bernstein. Cambridge: MIT Press.

———. 1979. *Philosophy and the Mirror of Nature.* Princeton, N.J.: Princeton University Press.

Rose, Richard. 1988. *The Postmodern President.* London: Chatham House.

Rosenau, James. 1990. "Interdependence and the Simultaneity Puzzle: Notes on the Outbreak of Peace." In *The Long Postwar Peace: The Sources of Great Power Stability*, ed. C. W. Kegley. New York: Harper Collins.

Rosenau, Pauline. 1988. "Post-structural, Post-modern Political Science: Toward Global Paradigm Change?" Paper presented at the 14th World Congress of the International Political Science Association, Washington, D.C., August.

———. 1990. "Once Again into the Fray: International Relations Confronts the Humanities." *Millennium: Journal of International Studies* 19 (1): 83–110.

———. 1992. "Modern and Post-Modern Science: Some Contrasts." *Review: A Journal of the Fernand Braudel Center for the Study of Economics, Historical Systems, and Civilization* 15 (1).

———. Forthcoming. "Post-modern Analysis and Political Interpretation: Is Deconstruction Inherently Right-Wing or Left Wing." *Type of Analysis and Interpretation*, ed. Jean Michel Berthelot and Karl Van Meter. London: Sage.

Rosenau, Pauline, and Robert Paehlke. 1990. "The Exhaustion of Left and Right: Perspectives on the Political Participation of the Disadvantaged." *International Political Science Review* 11 (1): 123–51.

Rosmarin, Adena. 1985. "On the Theory of 'Against Theory.' " In *Against Theory: Literary Studies and the New Pragmatism*, ed. W. J. T. Mitchell. Chicago: University of Chicago Press.

Roso, Stefano. 1987. "Postmodern Italy." In *Exploring Postmodernism*, ed. Matei Calinescu and Douwe Fokkema. Amsterdam: John Benjamin.

Ross, Andrew, ed. 1988. *Universal Abandon?: The Politics of Postmodernism.* Minneapolis: University of Minnesota Press.

Rushdie, Salman. 1989. *Satanic Verses.* New York: Viking Press.

Ryan, Michael. 1981. "New French Theory in New German Critique." *New German Critique* no. 22 (Winter): 145–61.

———. 1982. *Marxism and Deconstruction: A Critical Articulation.* Baltimore, Md.: Johns Hopkins University Press.

———. 1988. "Postmodern Politics." *Theory, Culture, and Society* 5 (2–3): 559–76.

Said, Edward W. 1976. "Interview." *Diacritics* 3 (6): 30–47.

———. 1979. "The Text, the World, the Critic." In *Textual Strategies: in Perspec-*

tives in Post-structuralist Criticism, ed. Josue Harari. Ithaca, N.Y.: Cornell University Press.

———. 1982. "Opponents, Audiences, Constituencies and Communities." *Critical Inquiry* 9 (September): 145–62.

Sangren, P. Steven. 1988. "Rhetoric and the Authority of Ethnography: 'Postmodernism' and the Social Reproduction of Texts." *Current Anthropology* 29 (3): 405–35.

Santos, Bonaventura. 1987. "Law: A Map of Misreading." *Journal of Law and Society* 14 (3): 279–302.

Sarup, Madan. 1989. *An Introductory Guide to Post-Structuralism and Postmodernism*. Athens: University of Georgia Press.

Sayres, Sohnya, Anders Stephanson, Stanley Aronowitz, and Frederic Jameson. 1984. *The 60s without Apology*. Minneapolis: University of Minnesota Press.

Scherpe, Klaus. 1986–87. "Dramatization and De-dramatization of 'The End': The Apocalyptic Consciousness of Modernity and Post-modernity." *Cultural Critique*, no. 5 (Winter): 95–129.

Scholes, Robert. 1989. *Protocols of Reading*. New Haven, Conn.: Yale University Press.

Schrag, Calvin. 1988. "Liberal Learning in the Postmodern World." *The Key Reporter* 54 (1): 1–4.

Schrift, Alan D. 1988a. "Genealogy and/as Deconstruction: Nietzsche, Derrida, and Foucault on Philosophy as Critique." In *Postmodernism and Continental Philosophy*, ed. Hugh J.Silverman and Donn Walton. Albany: State University of New York Press.

———. 1988b. "Foucault and Derrida on Nietzsche and the End(s) of 'Man.' " In *Exceedingly Nietzsche*, ed. David Krell and David Wood. London: Routledge.

Schutz, Alfred. 1962–66. *Collected Papers*. The Hague: Martinus Nijhoff.

Schwartz, Joel. 1990. "Antihumanism in the Humanities." *The Public Interest* 99 (Spring): 29–44.

Scott, Jean Wallach. 1989. "History in Crisis? The Others' Side of the Story." *American Historical Review* 94 (3): 680–92.

Seabrook, John. 1991. "The David Lynch of Architecture." *Vanity Fair*, January, 74–79, 125–29.

Seidel, Gill. 1985. "Political Discourse Analysis." In *Handbook of Discourse Analysis*, Vol. 4, ed. Teun Van Dijk. London: Academic Press.

Seidl, Amanda. 1988. "Property's Lord of the Manner." *Business*, March, 100–102.

Seidman, Stever. 1989. "The Tedium of General Theory." *Contemporary Sociology* 18 (3): 634–36.

———. 1990. "Against Theory as a Foundationalist Discourse." *Perspectives: The Theory Section Newsletter, the American Sociological Association* 13 (2): 1–3.

Seligman, Adam. 1990. "Toward a Reinterpretation of Modernity in an Age of Postmodernity." In *Theories of Modernity and Postmodernity*, ed. Bryan S. Turner. Newbury Park, Calif.: Sage.

Sennett, Richard. 1977. *The Fall of Public Man*. New York: Knopf.

Shapiro, Michael. 1988. *The Politics of Representing*. Madison: University of Wisconsin Press.

Shapiro, Michael. 1989a. "Textualizing Global Politics." In *International/Intertextual Relations: Postmodern Readings of World Politics*, ed. James Der Derian and Michael J. Shapiro. Lexington, Mass.: Lexington Books.

———. 1989b. "Representing World Politics: The Sport/War Intertext." In *International/Intertextual Relations: Postmodern Readings of World Politics*, ed. James Der Derian and Michael J. Shapiro. Lexington, Mass.: Lexington Books.

Shapiro, Michael, and Deane Neubauer. 1989. "Spatiality and Policy Discourse: Reading the Global City." Paper delivered at the International Studies Association Meeting, London, March 29–April 1.

Sheridan, Alan. 1980. *Michael Foucault: The Will to Truth*. New York: Tavistock Publications.

Shusterman, Richard. 1988. "Postmodernist Aestheticism: A New Moral Philosophy?" *Theory, Culture, and Society* 5 (2–3): 337–57.

Shweder, R. A. 1986. "Divergent Rationalities." In *Metatheory in Social Science*, ed. Donald W. Fiske and Richard A. Shweder. Chicago: University of Chicago Press.

Shweder, R. A., and D. W. Fiske. 1986. "Introduction: Uneasy Social Science." In *Metatheory in Social Science*, ed. Donald W. Fiske and Richard A. Shweder. Chicago: University of Chicago Press.

Silverman, Hugh, ed. 1989. *Derrida and Deconstruction*. London: Routledge.

Silverman, Hugh J., and Donn Walton, ed. 1988. *Postmodernism and Continental Philosophy*. Albany: State University of New York Press.

Skinner, Quentin. 1969. "Meaning and Understanding in the History of Ideas." *History and Theory* 8 (1): 3–53.

———. 1972. "Motives, Intentions and the Interpretations of Texts." *New Literary History* 3 (2): 393–408.

———. 1985. "Jacques Derrida." In *The Return of Grand Theory in the Human Sciences*, ed. David Hoy. Cambridge: Cambridge University Press.

Sloterdijk, Peter. 1984. "Cynicism—The Twilight of False Consciousness." *New German Critique*, no. 33 (Fall): 189–206.

———. 1987. *Critique of Cynical Reason*. Minneapolis: University of Minnesota Press.

Smart, Barry. 1990. "Modernity, Postmodernity and the Present." In *Theories of Modernity and Postmodernity*, ed. Bryan S. Turner. Newbury Park, Calif.: Sage.

Smith, Barbara Herrnstein. 1988. *Contingencies of Value*. Cambridge: Harvard University Press.

Smith, Paul. 1988. *Discerning the Subject*. Minneapolis: University of Minnesota Press.

Smith, Steven. 1984. *Reading Althusser*. Ithaca, N.Y.: Cornell University Press.

Snyder, John. 1989. "Translator's Introduction." In Gianni Vattimo's *The End of Modernity*, i–lvii. Baltimore, Md.: Johns Hopkins University Press.

Soja, E.W. 1986. "Taking Los Angeles Apart: Some Fragments of a Critical Human Geography." *Environment and Planning D: Society and Space* 4: 255–72.

———. 1987. "The Postmodernization of Geography: A Review." *Annals of the Association of American Geographers* 77 (2): 289–323.

——. 1989. *Postmodern Geographies: The Reassertion of Space in Critical Social Theory*. London: Verso.

Sontag, Susan. 1969. *Against Interpretation and Other Essays*. New York: Farrar, Strauss and Giroux.

Soper, Kate. 1986. *Humanism and Anti-humanism*. London: Hutchinson.

Sorel, Georges. 1987. *From George Sorel: Essays in Socialism and Philosophy*, ed. John Stanley. New Brunswick, N.J.: Transaction Books.

Spivak, Gayatri. 1980. "The Revolutions That as Yet Have No Model." *Diacritics* 10 (4): 47–48.

——. 1988. "Can the Subaltern Speak." In *Marxism and the Interpretation of Culture*, ed. Cary Nelson and Lawrence Grossberg. Chicago: University of Illinois Press.

Stauth, George, and Bryan S. Turner. 1988. "Nostalgia, Postmodernism and the Critique of Mass Culture." *Theory, Culture and Society* 5 (2–3): 509–27.

Stearns, Peter N. 1976. "Coming of Age." *Journal of Social History* 10 (2): 246–55.

Steinfels, Peter. 1990. "Beliefs." *New York Times*, January 20, 12.

Stephanson, Anders, and F. Jameson. 1988. "Regarding Postmodernism—A Conversation with Frederic Jameson." In *Universal Abandon?: The Politics of Postmodernism*, ed. A. Ross. Minneapolis: University of Minnesota Press.

Strathern, Marilyn. 1987. "Out of Context: The Persuasive Fiction of Anthropology." *Current Anthropology* 28 (3): 251–81.

Struever, Nancy. 1985. "Historical Discourse." In *Handbook of Discourse Analysis*, Vol. 1, ed. Teun Van Dijk. London: Academic Press.

Suleiman, Susan, and Ingre Crosman, ed. 1980. *The Reader in the Text*. Princeton, N.J.: Princeton University Press.

Susman, Warren I. 1985. *Culture as History*. New York: Pantheon Books.

Swimme, Brian. 1988. "The Cosmic Creation Story." In *The Reenchantment of Science: Postmodern Proposals*, ed. D. R. Griffin. Albany: State University of New York Press.

Swyngedouw, E. 1986. "The Socio-Spatial Implications of Innovation in Industrial Organisation." Working Paper no. 20. Lille, France: Johns Hopkins University European Center for Regional Planning and Research.

Taylor, Mark C. 1984. *Erring: a Postmodern A/theology*. Chicago: University of Chicago Press.

Thompson, John. 1984. *Studies in the Theory of Ideology*. London: Polity Press.

Todorov, Tzvetan. 1984. *Mikhail Bakhtin: The Dialogical Principle*. Special number, *Theory and History of Literature*, vol. 13. Minneapolis: University of Minnesota Press.

——. 1988. "Two Current Debates." *Times Literary Supplement*, June 17, 676, 684.

Tomkins, Calvin. 1988. *Post- to Neo-*. New York: H. Holt & Company.

Tompkins, Jane. 1980. "The Reader in History." In *Reader-Response Criticism From Formalism to Post-Structuralism*, ed. Jane Tompkins. Baltimore, Md.: Johns Hopkins University Press.

Toulmin, Stephen. 1982. *The Return to Cosmology: Postmodern Science and the Theology of Nature*. Berkeley: University of California Press.

Toulmin, Stephen. 1983. "The Construal of Reality: Criticism in Modern and Post-modern Science." In *The Politics of Interpretation*, ed. W. J. T. Mitchell. Chicago: University of Chicago Press.

————. 1985. "Pluralism and Responsibility in Post-Modern Science." *Science, Technology, Human Values* 10 (1): 28–38.

————. 1990. *Cosmopolis: The Hidden Agenda of Modernity*. New York: Free Press.

Touraine, Alain. 1988a. *Return of the Actor: A Social Theory in Postindustrial Society*. Minneapolis: University of Minnesota Press.

————. 1988b. "Retour du sujet." Public lecture presented in French, University of Montreal, Montreal, Quebec, October 25.

————. 1990. "Modernity and the Subject." Paper presented to the International Sociological Association Congress, Madrid, July 10.

Trachtenberg, Stanley. 1985. *The Postmodern Moment*. Westport, Conn: Greenwood Press.

Tucker, Aviezer. 1990. "Vaclav Havel's Heideggerianism." *Telos*, no. 85 (Spring): 63–80.

Turner, Bryan S. 1989. "From Postindustrial Society to Postmodern Politics." In *Contemporary Political Culture*, ed. John R. Gibbins. Newbury Park, Calif.: Sage.

————, ed. 1990. *Theories of Modernity and Postmodernity*. Newbury Park, Calif.: Sage.

Tyler, Stephen. 1984. "The Poetic Turn in Postmodern Anthropology—the Poetry of Paul Friedrich." *American Anthropologist* 86: 328–36.

————. 1986. "Post-modern Ethnography: From Document of the Occult to Occult Document." In *Writing Culture: The Poetics and Politics of Ethnography*, ed. James Clifford and George E. Marcus. Berkeley: University of California Press.

Ungar, Roberto. 1986. *The Critical Legal Studies Movement*. Cambridge: Harvard University Press.

Vaillancourt, Pauline M. 1986a. *When Marxists Do Research*. Westport, Conn.: Greenwood Press.

————. 1986b. "Dialectics, Marxism and Social Science Research." *Bulletin de méthodologie sociologique* (Paris) no. 11 (July): 83–100.

————. 1987. "Discourse Analysis, Post-Structuralism, Post-Modernism, Deconstruction, Semiotics: A New Paradigm for the Social Sciences?" *Polish Sociological Bulletin* 80 (4): 89–100.

Van Dijk, Teun, ed. 1985. *Handbook of Discourse Analysis*. 4 vols. London: Academic Press.

van Vucht Tijssen, Lieteke. 1990. "Women between Modernity and Postmodernity." In *Theories of Modernity and Postmodernity*, ed. Bryan S. Turner. Newbury Park, Calif.: Sage.

Vattimo, Gianni. 1982. "Bottle, Net, Truth, Revolution, Terrorism, Philosophy." *Denver Quarterly* 16 (4): 24–34.

————. 1988. *The End of Modernity: Nihilism and Hermeneutics in Post-modern Culture*. London: Polity.

Vester, Heinz-Gunter. 1990. "Collective Behavior and Social Movements Under Postmodern Conditions." Paper presented to the International Sociological Association Congress, Madrid, July 10.

Virilio, P. 1983. *Pure War*. New York: Semiotext(e).

———. 1989. "The Last Vehicle." In *Looking Back on the End of the World*, ed. D. Kamper and C. Wulf. New York: Semiotext(e).

Walker, R. B. J. 1988a. "Genealogy, Geopolitics, and Political Community: Richard K. Ashley and the Critical Social Theory of International Politics." *Alternatives* 13: 77–102.

———. 1988b. *One World, Many Worlds*. Boulder Colo.: Lynne Rienner Publishers.

Wartofsky, Marx W. 1984. "The Paradox of Painting: Pictorial Representation and the Dimensionality of Visual Space." *Social Research* 51 (4): 861–83.

Weber, Alexander. 1990. "Lyotard's Combative Theory of Discourse." *Telos*, no. 83 (Spring): 141–50.

Weber, Cynthia. 1990. "Representing Debt: Peruvian Presidents Belaunde's and Garcia's Reading/Writing of Peruvian Debt." *International Studies Quarterly* 34 (3): 353–65.

Weedon, Chris. 1987. *Feminist Practice and Poststructuralist Theory*. Oxford: Basil Blackwell.

Wellberg, David. 1985. "Appendix 1: Postmodernism in Europe: On Recent German Writing." In *The Postmodern Movement*, ed. Stanley Trachtenberg. Westport, Conn.: Greenwood Press.

Wellmer, Albrecht. 1985. "On the Dialectic of Modernism and Postmodernism." *Praxis International* 4 (4): 337–62.

———. 1990. *In Defence of Modernity*. London: Blackwell.

White, Hayden. 1978. *Tropics of Discourse: Essays in Cultural Criticism*. Baltimore Md.: Johns Hopkins University Press.

———. 1986. "Historical Pluralism." *Critical Inquiry* 12 (3): 480–93.

White, James Boyd. 1982. "Law as Language: Reading Law and Reading Literature." *Texas Law Review* 60 (March): 415–45.

White, Stephen K. 1986. "Foucault's Challenge to Critical Theory." *American Political Science Review* 80 (2): 419–32.

———. 1987. "Poststructuralism and Political Reflection." *Political Theory* 16 (2): 186–208.

Widgery, David. 1989. "Postmodern Medicine." *British Medical Journal* 298 (6677): 897.

Wiener, Jon. 1988. "Deconstructing de Man." *Nation*, January 9, 22–24.

Wikstrom, J. H. 1987a. "Moving Forestry into the Post-Modern World." *Ambio* 16 (2–3): 154–56.

———. 1987b. "Moving into the Post-Modern World." *Journal of Forestry* 85 (1): 65.

Wisdom, J. O. 1987. *Challengeability in Modern Science*. Dorset: Blackmore Press.

Wolfe, Alan. 1988. "Suicide and the Japanese Postmodern: A Postnarrative Paradigm?" *South Atlantic Quarterly* 87 (Summer): 571–90.

Wolin, Richard. 1984–85. "Modernism vs. Postmodernism." *Telos*, no. 62 (Winter): 9–31.

Wolin, Sheldon. 1985. "Postmodern Politics in the Absence of Myth." *Social Research* 52 (2): 217–40.

Wolter, Louis J., and Stephen Miles. 1983. "Toward Public Relations Theory." *Public Relations Journal* 39 (9): 12–16.

Woo, Henry K. H. 1989. "Taking Method Seriously." *Methodus: Bulletin of the International Network for Economic Method* 1 (December): 4–8.

Wood, D. C. 1979. "An Introduction to Derrida." *Radical Philosophy*, no. 21 (Spring): 18–28.

Wood, Ellen Meiksins. 1986. *The Retreat From Class*. London: Verso.

Wood, Gordon S. 1988. "The Fundamentalists and the Constitution." *The New York Review of Books*, February 18, 2.

Wood, Gordon S., and Louis A. Zurcher. 1988. *The Development of a Postmodern Self: A Computer-Assisted Comparative Analysis of Personal Documents*. Westport, Conn.: Greenwood Press.

Woodiwiss, Anthony. 1990. *Social Theory After Postmodernism: Rethinking Production, Law, and Class*. Winchester, Mass.: Unwin and Hyman.

Wortman, Marc. 1987. "Book Review of *The Post-Modern Aura*." *Telos* 71 (Spring): 171.

Wulf, Christoph. 1989. "The Temporality of World-Views and Self-Images." In *Looking Back on the End of the World*, ed. D. Kamper and C. Wulf. New York: Semiotext(e).

Zagorin, Perez. 1990. "Historiography and Posmodernism: Reconsideration." *History and Theory* 29 (3): 263–75.

Zeldin, Theodore. 1976. "Social History and Total History." *Journal of Social History* 10 (2): 237–45.

Zukin, Sharon. 1988. "The Postmodern Debate over Urban Form." *Theory, Culture and Society* 5 (2–3): 431–46.

INDEX

absence, 22, 36. *See also* presence
accountability, 32–33
action, 157n. *See also* social movements
action research, 117
activist post-modernists. *See* affirmative post-modernists
administration, 131
advocacy, 171
affirmative post-modernism: definition of, 14–17; compared to skeptical post-modernism, 174
affirmative post-modernists
—author, 31
—communication, 178
—consistency and political relevance, choice between, 175
—deconstruction: critique of, 124; interpretation and, 118
—epistemology: general views of, 23, 109; normative preferences, 23; reason, 23, 130, 132–33; on truth and social science, 86; values, 114–15; view of reality, 110–11; views of theory, 77; views of truth, 22, 77, 80–81
—geography, 69–70
—history, 66, 72; End-of-History movement, 63; New History, 66
—law: definition of, 125; post-modern forms of, 127
—methodology, views of, 23, 109, 117, 123
—politics: on democracy, 22–23, 145; political action, 145–48; political orientations, 24, 144–55, 173; political participation, 145; and post-modernism, 166; on public sphere theory, 23, 100, 102–3; and social science, 138. *See also* social movements
—reader: role of, 40; view of, 39
—representation: and democracy, 93–94, 98–100, 107–8; general views of, 22–23, 93–94, 96; in the social sciences, 105
—science: critique of modern science, 169; post-modern, 123–24
—social science: 23; compromises with, 181–82; influence on post-modern forms

of, 169–73; views of theory, 22, 80–81, 82–84
—space, 69–70, 72
—standards of evaluation, 136. *See also* evaluation
—subject: general views of, 21, 42, 44, 52–53; return of, 56–60
—text, 35–36
—time, 72
—types of: activist, 145–48; extreme forms, 4–5, 16, 19–20, 169, 180; moderate forms, 183; New Age, 148–52; Third World, 152–55
affluence, 11, 153
agency, xii, 32–33, 47, 117n, 158, 163, 168. *See also* author
agent, xi, 26, 46, 170
Agger, Ben, 16n, 57, 57n, 101, 103, 103n, 156, 161n
agnosticism, 168
AIDS, 111
alchemy, 151
Amnesty International, 147n
anarchism, 13, 144, 160n
Anglo-North America, 15
animal rights, 144
anthropology, 4, 7, 21–23, 27, 40, 51, 85, 87–88, 105, 106, 107, 119, 123, 167, 172. *See also* ethnography
anti-abortion, 145
anti-democratic perspective, 139. *See also* democracy
anti-foundational predispositions, 81
antihumanism, 12–13. *See also* humanism
anti-intellectualism, 13, 55, 132–33
anti-nuclear movements, 168
anti-positive empiricism, 83
anti-representationalism. *See* representation
anti-subject, 42. *See also* subject
apocalyptic destruction, 183
architecture, 7, 7n, 127; and laws of science, 127n
armed forces, 157
Aronowitz, Stanley, 160, 164
art, 7, 94, 142